Alexander Dana Noyes

American Finance

1865-1896

Alexander Dana Noyes

American Finance
1865-1896

ISBN/EAN: 9783742810762

Manufactured in Europe, USA, Canada, Australia, Japa

Cover: Foto ©ninafisch / pixelio.de

Manufactured and distributed by brebook publishing software
(www.brebook.com)

Alexander Dana Noyes

American Finance

THIRTY YEARS OF AMERICAN FINANCE

A SHORT FINANCIAL HISTORY OF THE
GOVERNMENT AND PEOPLE OF
THE UNITED STATES SINCE
THE CIVIL WAR
1865–1896

BY

ALEXANDER DANA NOYES

G. P. PUTNAM'S SONS
NEW YORK AND LONDON
The Knickerbocker Press
1898

COPYRIGHT, 1898
BY
G. P. PUTNAM'S SONS
Entered at Stationers' Hall London

The Knickerbocker Press, New York

PREFACE

THIS book undertakes a single task: to narrate the series of events which influenced American financial history between 1865 and 1897, and to point out clearly and concisely the relation of those events to one another. I have made no attempt at abstract economic argument; therefore the reader will not find in these pages discussion of theories such as bimetallism and protection. That the narrative should repeatedly encounter these and other theories in active operation, is of course inevitable; the purpose and results of such experiments will be fairly and fully examined; but this book is designed to do no more. It is not an economic treatise; it is a history of our own times.

I have not limited my narrative to public finance. Taken alone, a story of administrative experiments in revenue or currency could hardly be other than a dry and barren chronicle. But when surveyed along with the political history of a period, with its industrial, agricultural, and commercial history, the story of Government finance becomes a vivid panorama in the struggle of society to solve the riddle of material progress. The fourteen-year contest over resumption of specie payments, the fall in staple prices, the railway expansion, the great harvests of 1879 and 1891, the efforts to get the silver dollars into circulation, the career of the American speculators, the enormous surplus revenue of 1888, the growth of public expenditure, the tariff and silver laws of 1890, the rise of the Populist party, the expulsion of gold, the panic of 1893, the industrial revolt of 1894, the Treasury deficit, and the bond-issues from 1894 to 1896—each of these episodes, and with them many others which will find place in our discussion, bear directly, not on their own financial periods alone, but on all subsequent financial history. Understanding them, the American citizen holds the key to the present and the future. Without such knowledge, American finance must be to him a sealed book.

I have few acknowledgments to make for assistance in preparing this history; most of the facts with which it concerns itself are obtainable only from original sources. The list of public documents and other works to which reference is made will be found on another page. For directing me to sources of information on some of the more obscure events in the Government's operations I have to thank especially Mr. C. N. Jordan, now Assistant U. S. Treasurer at New York, Mr. M. L. Muhleman, Deputy Assistant U. S. Treasurer, and Mr. W. C. Ford, Chief of the U. S. Bureau of Statistics.

On some of the topics included in this volume I have hitherto written in the *Political Science Quarterly*. Nothing has, however, been repeated from those articles except the general line of discussion and the facts and authorities therein compiled.

A. D. N.

NEW YORK, *January, 1898.*

CONTENTS.

                                                                       PAGE

I.—THE INFLATION PERIOD . . . 1

Reasons for writing the history of the past thirty years—Distinctive character of the epoch—Industrial expansion of the United States after the war—Opening up of the West—Rise of the American grain trade—Origin of the nation's currency problems—The Legal-Tender Act—Purposes of its authors—Congress resolves to retire the legal tenders—The Contraction Law of 1866—Hugh McCulloch and the anti-contractionists—Congress revokes the Contraction Law—The Presidential campaign of 1868—The repudiation plan and the Public-Credit Act of 1869—Inflation at its worst—The panic of 1873—Defeat of the Administration party—Congress passes the Resumption Act.

II.—THE STRUGGLE FOR RESUMPTION . . . 23

Character of the Resumption Act—Its large grant of power to the Executive—Its vague provisions—Problems of its administration—The question of a gold reserve—John Sherman in the Treasury—His career as legislator and administrator—His skill in financial negotiation—His relations with the banks—Congress threatens the Resumption Act—It passes the Silver-coinage Law—Declares Government bonds payable in silver—Sectional breach in the Administration party—Attitude of President Hayes—The elections of 1878—Gains of the Administration—Final preparations for resumption.

III.—Resumption of Specie Payments . . 48

Doubts over the maintenance of resumption—The compulsory re-issue of redeemed notes—Secretary Sherman's equivocal attitude—Unfavorable trade conditions of the resumption year—The rise of foreign exchange—Gold taken from the Treasury for export—The grain-market situation—Harvest failure in Europe—Enormous American exports—Trade revival and import of gold—The return of prosperity—Development of the interior—The markets of 1880—Jay Gould and the railway speculation—Great activity in trade—Administration victory of 1879—The election of 1880—Hayes and Sherman on the legal tenders.

IV.—The Silver Problem 73

Change in Secretary Sherman's views—His prediction of a silver standard—The silver dollars rejected from circulation—The New York Clearing-House excludes silver from its settlements—Congress prohibits national banks from joining in such exclusion—Sherman succeeds in circulating silver certificates—The culmination of trade activity—Harvest failure of 1881—Export of gold begins—The reaction of 1882—Fall in prices—The surplus revenue—Tariff reduction urged by President Arthur—Extravagance of Congress—Veto of the River and Harbor Bill—The elections of 1882—Severe defeat of the Republican party—The Tariff Act of 1883—Reduction of internal revenue—Renewed trouble with the silver currency—The panic of 1884—Its peculiar features—Its brief duration—The low grain prices of 1884—Election of President Cleveland—Discouraging Treasury outlook.

V.—The Surplus Revenue of 1888 . . . 104

Solving the silver-coinage problem—Gold obtained from the banks—Pushing the silver into circulation—Contraction of the bank-note currency—Rise of the public revenue—Five years of heavy importations—The active markets of 1888—Large railway construction—The period of labor

disputes—The labor movement in politics—Rise of the
industrial trusts—Europe buys American securities—England's
search for an export trade—The Treasury surplus
after 1886—Difficulty in releasing the Government's accumulations—Public
deposits with the banks—Congress refuses
to reduce the revenue—Bond redemption at heavy premiums—The
Treasury and the currency.

VI.—THE TWO LAWS OF 1890 127

The Presidential campaign of 1888—Declaration of the Republican
party—Of the Democratic party—Two opposing
plans to reduce the surplus—Election of Mr. Harrison—
The party's policy—The President's Message—His advice
on appropriations—Congress raises the tariff rates—Increases
appropriations—Heavy fall in revenue—Approach
of a deficit—The Silver-Purchase Act—Its origin—Its
hasty preparation—William Windom in the Treasury—
His previous official career—His faults as an economist—
His purpose in framing the Silver-Purchase Bill—His argument
in its favor—Nature of his plan—Confusion of its details—His
views on currency contraction—On silver coinage
—On the price of silver—His mistakes of judgment—
House of Representatives modifies the bill—Senate votes
for free coinage—The compromise committee—Purpose of
their measure—Opinions of free-coinage Senators—Gold
redemption asserted—Passage of the law.

VII.—THE EXPULSION OF GOLD 153

The Silver-Purchase Act and the silver market—The law
fails of its purpose—Fall in silver bullion—Altered views
of Secretary Windom—Of President Harrison—The markets
of 1890—Violent expansion of the currency—The foreign
speculation—Deficient wheat crops and high grain
prices—London and its Argentine venture—Failure of
Baring Brothers—The panic of 1890—Recall of English
capital—Continued increase in United States currency—
Gold export begins in quantity — Various explanations
offered—The true cause—Its menace to the Treasury—

Heavy gold payments by the Government—Fall of the gold reserve—The harvest of 1891—Its remarkable influences—Situation changes for the worse—The "hundred-million reserve"—Its history—Its legislative authority—Displacement of gold with legal tenders—Gold payments stopped by the New York banks—By the Treasury—The gold exporters and the banks—They fail to get gold in New York—Presentation of legal tenders for redemption—Why it was unavoidable—The elections of 1890—Sweeping opposition victory—The Fifty-second Congress—It attempts to pass a Free-coinage Law—To change the tariff—It increases expenditures—The election of 1892—The curious political platforms—The Democrats and silver—Breach in the party—Rise of the Populist party—Mr. Cleveland re-elected President.

VIII.—THE PANIC OF 1893 182

Last days of the Harrison Treasury administration—Secretary Foster and the banks—Problems of the new Administration—Secretary Carlisle and the gold reserve—The hundred-million fund impaired—Rumors of silver redemption—Their effect on the markets—The Secretary's declaration—The President pledges gold payments—Precarious nature of the situation—Outbreak of panic—The corporation failures—The run on the country banks—Heavy strain on the New York institutions—Issue of clearing-house certificates—Cash payments suspended by numerous city banks—The premium on currency—Its good effects—Its evil effects—Heavy gold imports—Gold the sole medium of exchange—Extra session of Congress—The Repeal Bill—Attitude of the Republicans—Of the Democrats—The struggle in the Senate—The Silver-Purchase Law repealed—The effect on the silver market—On general trade—End of the panic—Record of failures in 1893—Industrial depression returns—Great increase of the money supply—The Treasury and the gold imports—Gold reserve paid out to meet the deficit—Decrease in merchandise importations—In revenue—Attitude of Secretary Carlisle.

IX.—The Government Loans and the Tariff
   of 1894 207

   Secretary Carlisle's embarrassments—His appeal to Congress—Critical condition of the Treasury—Congress refuses help—The first bond-issue announced—Attacks on the Treasury in Congress—The courts sustain the Administration—Difficulties in floating the loan—Mr. Carlisle's policy—The banks finally subscribe—Treasury gold withdrawn for subscription purposes—Questionable character of the action—Gold exports resumed—Recall of foreign capital—Discouraging commercial outlook—The railway insolvencies—The labor uprising—"Coxey's army" and the Railway Union strike—Failure of the corn crop—Fall in the price of wheat—Tariff legislation begun—Necessity for such legislation—The question of a deficit—Mistakes of the framers of the Wilson Act—Motives of the House of Representatives—Of the Senate—The breach with the President—Blunders in the revenue estimates—The income tax before the Supreme Court—Declared unconstitutional—Grounds for the decision—Probable yield of the tax overestimated—Congress votes to coin the seigniorage—The President's veto—Continued fall in the gold reserve—The second bond-issue—The "endless chain"—Heavy gold exports—Crisis in the Treasury.

X.—The Bond Syndicate Operation . . . 234

   International bankers take the loan of 1895—Their remarkable contract—Its harsh terms—Its pledge to stop gold withdrawals—Exasperation in Congress—The President defends the contract—Nature of the syndicate operation—Its magnitude—All the sterling bankers unite to protect the Treasury—Skepticism of European critics—Progress of the operation—The gold reserve restored—Change in the trade situation—Rapid advance in prices—Foreign buying of American securities—Its connection with the London mining craze—Decline in foreign exchange—Bad results of the American speculation—Balance of foreign trade reversed—The wheat market blockaded—Europe sells back its American securities—Defects in the syndicate plan come to light—The redundant money supply increased—Artificial rates for exchange—The syndicate loses control of the sterling market—Gold exports begin again—Situation at the close of 1895—The industrial outlook—The political outlook—The change in currency conditions—Plans for a new loan—The $100,000,000 bond sale—Its curious influence on the money market—Legal tenders at a premium—Success of the loan of 1896—Great change in the commercial situation—Conclusion.

INDEX 255

LIST OF AUTHORITIES REFERRED TO IN THIS BOOK

GOVERNMENT PUBLICATIONS

Annual Reports, Comptroller U. S. Currency.
Annual Reports, Director U. S. Mint.
Annual Reports, Secretary of U. S. Treasury, 1861–1896. Washington: Government Printing Office.
Annual Reports, U. S. Treasurer.
Annual Reports, U. S. Bureau of Statistics.
Annual Reports, U. S. Department of Agriculture.
Annual Reports, U. S. Commissioner of Internal Revenue.
Annual Statistical Abstract of the United Kingdom. London: Eyre & Spottiswoode.
Annual Trade Statement of the United Kingdom. Ibid.
Congressional Globe and *Congressional Record.*
Specie Resumption and Refunding of National Debt; U. S. Treasury's Official Correspondence, Aug. 24, 1876, *to Oct.* 18, 1879. Washington: Government Printing Office, 1880.

U. S. Annual Statistical Abstract.

U. S. Senate Report on Prices, Wages, and Transportation during Fifty-one Years. Washington: Government Printing Office, 1893.

PERIODICAL LITERATURE AND REPORTS

Annual Reports, New York Chamber of Commerce.
Annual Reports, New York Produce Exchange.
BEERBOHM'S *Corn-Trade List.* London.
Bradstreet's. New York.
BROOMHALL'S *Corn-Trade News.* Liverpool.
Commercial and Financial Chronicle. New York, 1873–1896.
Dun's Review. New York.
Economist. London, 1879–1895.
ELLISON & CO.'S *Annual Cotton-Trade Review.* Manchester.
Forum. New York.
Mark Lane Express. London.
Poor's Manual of Railroads. New York.
Statist. London.

BOOKS OF PRIVATE AUTHORSHIP

ADAMS, H. C. *Public Debts: An Essay in the Science of Finance.* New York, 1893.

LAUGHLIN, J. LAURENCE. *History of Bimetallism in the United States.* New York, 1892.

MCCULLOCH, HUGH. *Men and Measures of Half a Century.* New York, 1889.

MUHLEMAN, MAURICE L. *Monetary Systems of the World.* New York, 1896.

SAUERBECK, AUGUSTUS. *Annual Table of Commodity Prices in Great Britain.* London.

SHERMAN, JOHN. *Recollections of Twenty Years in the House, Senate, and Cabinet: An Autobiography.* Chicago, 1895.

SHINN, CHARLES HOWARD. *The Story of the Mine.* New York, 1896.

SŒTBEER, ADOLPH. *Comparative Tables of Hamburg Prices.*

SPAULDING, E. G. *History of the Legal-Tender Money Issued during the Great Rebellion.* Buffalo, 1869.

TAUSSIG, F. W. *Tariff History of the United States.* New York, 1888.

WHITE, HORACE. *Money and Banking.* New York, 1895.

THIRTY YEARS OF AMERICAN FINANCE

CHAPTER I

THE INFLATION PERIOD

THERE are two good reasons for writing the financial history of the United States since the Civil War. The first is, that no comprehensive history of the period has yet been written. The progress of events in American finance, from the earliest years of the community down to the resumption of specie payments, has been thoroughly examined and reviewed; the financial movement since resumption is for the most part unwritten history. Yet it is during this later period that nearly all the pressing financial problems of to-day had both their origin and their development. They who are not familiar with the phenomena of 1873, of 1879, and of 1886 cannot possibly understand the remarkable incidents in private trade and Government finance between 1893 and 1898.

The second reason for writing such a history is the distinctive character of the past thirty years. The nation's change from a depreciated and fluctuating money standard to the basis of the world's commercial values was of itself a factor of profound importance; yet this was only one of the influences which shaped and altered the financial future. War which has ravaged a continent during a series of years cannot be suddenly abandoned without immense effect on industrial conditions, and the new conditions will never duplicate those which existed before the war began. This was the lesson which Europe learned in 1815. Such was the singular combination of events after the peace of 1865, however, that almost at the moment when a million citizens were turned from organized destruction to pursuit of peaceful industry, the avenues of American employment and production were widened in a degree unprecedented in the history of trade. Within eight years after Lee's surrender, the railway mileage of the United States was literally doubled. Only a fraction of this increase belonged to the transcontinental lines which linked the two oceans in 1869. Quite aside from the 1800 miles of the Pacific Railways, upwards of 30,000 miles of track were laid in the United States between 1865 and 1873. Four noteworthy economic developments accompanied this extension of the transportation system. A fertile interior domain, hitherto untouched, was opened up to industry. With the rush of population to these Western districts, not only did the disbanded army resume production without industrial overcrowding such as followed the Napoleonic wars, but provision was made for three or four hundred thousand immigrants annually. European capital in enormous volume was drawn upon to provide the means for this development. Finally, the United States rose from the position of a second- or third-class commercial state to the first rank among agricultural producers and exporters. Each of these several phenomena had its special influence on the period. The new West, the contented or discontented farmer, the foreign investor, and the export trade in grain, will come into very frequent view during the progress of this history.

Not less immediately connected with this opening up and settlement of our agricultural West was still another phenomenon, of peculiar interest to the study of the ensuing period. The average price of grain had advanced with great rapidity during the Civil War. In 1867, the price of wheat, even on the Chicago market, reached the remarkable level of $2.85 per bushel; nor was this price very greatly above the annual maximum of the period. In a large degree, this advance resulted from inflation of the American currency. But the upward movement was world-wide; in 1867 and 1868 the average price, even in England, was close to the equivalent of two dollars a bushel.[1] That any such abnormal market could be maintained in the face of the new American supplies was at least improbable. The area of wheat, corn, oats, rye, and barley in the United States rose from 64,418,518 acres in 1867 to 86,287,-

[1] Sauerbeck's tables of English prices.

648 in 1875, and to 100,283,160 in 1878.¹ The yield of these five crops increased from 1,320,236,000 bushels in 1866 to 2,290,008,000 in 1878, the annual wheat crop more than doubling in magnitude.² The increase in cereal production was twice as rapid as the country's increase in population; the United States became therefore the leading figure in the world's export markets; and this was certain to have important influence on prices.

But prices did not yield at once. A series of deficient harvests, after 1870, accompanied by the suspended production of the Franco-Prussian war, abruptly checked the downward movement. After 1872, however, the new supplies made their influence positively felt. For in this increase of agricultural production, the United States was now not alone. Precisely as 1865 marked the end of war on the North American continent, so the Treaty of Paris in 1871 brought to a close the seventeen years of almost uninterrupted warfare among European states. As in America, so in Europe, production received immediate stimulus. While American capital was opening up the Mississippi Valley, European capital was similarly busy along the fertile river-basins of the Dnieper and the Danube. The Russian railway system grew during this period from something like 2000 miles to upwards of 13,000.³ In Austro-Hungary, the percentage of increase was almost equally large. All of these new transportation lines, like our

¹ *Annual Reports*, U. S. Bureau of Agriculture.
² *Ibid.*
³ *Official Russian Report on Railways*, 1878.

own new Granger railways, were at once engaged in carrying to the seaboard supplies of grain which never before had reached an export market. Commercial estimates placed the total wheat crop of 1875, in the world's ten chief producing states, at 1,501,000,000 bushels. In 1878, the same ten states produced 1,763,000,000, and another increase, equally large, was made within the next four years.[1] The problem of an earlier generation had been how to feed the constantly increasing population; a wholly new problem was presently to arise, based on the question how to find a ready and profitable market for the year's output of breadstuffs. Prices, in short, which rose almost continuously throughout the world during the period of slack production from 1858 to 1873, receded almost as continuously in the ensuing generation. Nowhere was this phenomenon destined to have more immediate importance, economically, socially, and politically, than in the United States.

In my examination of the thirty years after 1865, I shall endeavor to give due attention to the influence of these grain markets on national politics and finance. The opinion is more or less widely held that the decline in prices, notably of grain, has resulted from legislation on the currency. Without for the present arguing that proposition, it may be affirmed with entire safety that a good share of the period's currency legislation has resulted from the decline in the price of grain. The fall in wheat has been the typical argument for arbitrary increase of the silver or paper currency in almost every Con-

[1] Liverpool *Corn Trade News* estimates.

gressional debate since 1872. What is perhaps even more significant, the division in almost every Congressional vote upon these subjects has been, not political but geographical — the commercial East against the agricultural West.

The questions of silver coinage and of Government issues of paper currency have had as profound an influence on public finances, during the last thirty years, as the question of agricultural prices and production has had on private trade. Both of these currency problems, in their present form, have arisen since the Civil War. There had indeed been silver coinage and suspension of silver coinage long before 1865; but there had been neither a " silver question " nor a " silver party." The legal-tender notes had been introduced and brought to their maximum issue before the return of peace, but there had never been a " greenback party," or a demand in any responsible quarter for a permanent currency of Government paper.

During the eighty-four years after Washington's inauguration, only a trifle over eight million silver dollars in all had been coined at the mints of the United States;[1] when, therefore, in the statute revision of 1873 the silver dollar was dropped from the nation's coinage list, the action was received with indifference by the entire community. The question of " free coinage " was not so much as named in any Presidential platform, even as late as 1876. The sudden appearance of the " silver problem," only one year after the 1876 election, resulted very

[1] *U. S. Mint Report*, 1893, p. 282.

largely from the decline in agricultural prices. It resulted also, beyond any reasonable question, from the fact that silver production in the United States, reckoned prior to 1861 at less than a million dollars annually, and in 1869 at only twelve million dollars, had risen by 1878 to no less an annual sum than $45,200,000. It will be found that even in 1880 a conservative President was reciting, not without approval, the maxim that the United States, producing "more silver than any other country," was "directly interested in maintaining it as one of the two precious metals."[1]

If silver coinage was not a political issue at the close of the Civil War, the policy of a permanent currency of Government legal-tender paper was equally unknown. Upwards of four hundred million notes of the United States were, it is true, in circulation at the return of peace. There were doubtless many individuals who approved the continuance of exactly this form of currency. But no such proposition had been advanced by any public man of influence or by any political organization. The "greenback party," like the "silver party," was distinctly a product of hard times. The Specie-Resumption Act was a compromise with the extremists of the fiat-money school, as the compulsory Silver-Coinage Act of 1878 was a compromise with the extreme bimetallists. Each created a currency system never imagined by the statesmen of the war. The theory of the authors of the Legal-Tender Act was clearly understood. They held the issue of

[1] President Hayes, Annual Message, Dec. 6, 1880.

these notes to be simply creation of a Government floating debt, the notes being endowed with special privileges only in order that they might be floated.[1] That the resort to legal-tender powers was an evil justified only by extreme emergency, and that the circulation of Government notes in any form was a purely temporary measure, were the unanimous convictions of the statesmen who contrived the system.[2] The logical inference that these Government notes would be paid off and cancelled, as soon as the war deficiency had ended, was publicly accepted. This fact is clearly proved by the record. The statesmen of the day built up the national banking system on the express theory that the bank notes would provide the requisite currency of the future, whereas the Government notes would not.[3] No better witness could be had than the Legal-Tender Act itself, which provided, in its terms as first submitted to the Ways and Means Committee, that the notes should be issued "for temporary purposes," and should moreover be convertible at the holder's option into interest-bearing bonds.

Such was the theory and purpose of the public

[1] Secretary Chase, letter to Ways and Means Committee, January 29, 1862; Justice Bradley, opinion in Legal-Tender cases, 1871, 12 Wallace, 560.

[2] Spaulding, p. 5. W. P. Fessenden, Senate speech, February 12, 1862; Charles Sumner, Senate speech, February 12, 1862; Samuel Hooper, House of Representatives speech, February 21, 1866; John Sherman, Senate speech, March 6, 1876.

[3] President Lincoln, Annual Message, December 1, 1862; Secretary Chase, *Treas. Rep.*, 1863, p. 20; Secretary Fessenden, *Treas. Rep.*, 1864, p. 24; Spaulding, Appendix, p. 16.

men through whom the Legal-Tender Act was constructed and applied. Nor is the general position of our statesmen, at the close of the Civil War, any more obscure than their original position. The first financial resolution adopted by Congress, in December, 1865, was an explicit promise to retire the legal tenders. The first legislation of that Congress gave discretionary powers to the Secretary of the Treasury for continuous contraction. Very few legislative victories are won without at least a temporary popular endorsement, and the votes of December, 1865, and of March, 1866, were no exceptions. But the popular approval of contraction in that year, exception as it was to all our subsequent legislation, is readily enough explained. Public opinion, when the war had ended, was governed by impatience with inflated prices; inflation far beyond the European level, and properly ascribed to the condition of the currency.[1] The cost of living reached during 1865 the highest point recorded in this country's history. From 1860 to 1865, inclusive, the average of European prices rose only 4 to 6 per cent.; average prices in the United States advanced, in the same period, no less than 116 per cent.[2] Even in 1866, a full year after Appomatox, the general average of our staple prices was more than 30 per cent. above the average of 1863. The erratic gold market of 1865, moreover, forced as a necessary measure of

[1] Speeches of Morrill and Hurlburd, House of Representatives, February 21 and March 15, 1866.
[2] *U. S. Senate Report* of 1892, Part I., p. 91; Sauerbeck's London tables; Soetbeer's Hamburg tables.

precaution a large margin of safety in the retail price of goods, and this bore heavily on ordinary purchasers. With flour at $16 a barrel, butter at 55 cents a pound, coal at $10 a ton, and wages and salaries advanced since 1860 hardly one third as far as prices, the demand for currency reform obtained ready endorsement from the people.

This popular sentiment was further strengthened by the Administration's attitude at the opening of Lincoln's second term. Hugh McCulloch, then Comptroller of the Currency, and a well-known advocate of retirement of legal-tender notes, was appointed Secretary of the Treasury. He held this office up to the end of President Johnson's term. Mr. McCulloch's first official Treasury report, dated December 4, 1865, took positive ground for the reduction of the legal-tender debt. Although conceding that contraction ought to be and must be slow, he declared that " there is more danger to be apprehended from the inability of the Government to reduce its circulation rapidly enough, than from a too rapid reduction of it." He asked, therefore, authority to issue bonds in his discretion, at six per cent. or less, " for the purpose of retiring not only the compound interest notes, but the United States notes." [1]

The report containing this outline of policy was, like all Mr. McCulloch's public documents, a state paper of exceptional ability; it may be profitably read to-day for its broad and lucid treatment of the problem. Together with the Secretary's public

[1] *Treas. Rep.*, 1865, pp. 12, 13, 14.

speeches, it had decided influence. Two weeks after the publication of this report, on December 18, 1865, the House of Representatives resolved, by a vote of 144 to 6,

" that this house cordially concurs in the view of the Secretary of the Treasury in relation to the necessity of a contraction of the currency, with a view to as early a resumption of specie payments as the business interests of this country will permit; and we hereby pledge co-operative action to this end as speedily as practicable."

This resolution of 1865, however, marked the climax of the movement. Never thereafter did the policy of retiring the legal-tender notes even approach success. The truth is, that the inflated prices had begun already, during the three months after the resolution of December, to recede. This was inevitable, from the very nature of the previous expansion; and it was a welcome movement to consumers. But it necessarily caused some derangement in the plans of trade, and politicians began to ask, when they had to face the fulfilment of their pledge through a formal act of Congress, how the contraction policy would be greeted by producers. The bill, as originally introduced, granted full powers to the Secretary of the Treasury to issue new bonds for the retirement both of interest-bearing and of non-interest-bearing debt. In the spring of 1866 this measure was defeated in the House of Representatives by a vote of 70 to 64. Reconsidered and amended so as to restrict contraction of the legal tenders to $10,000,000 in the first six months and to $4,000,000 per month thereafter, the compromise measure did indeed pass the House by 83 to 53, and the Senate by 32 to 7. But a victory thus won was ominous. Mr. McCulloch himself declared the amended act to be awkward and ineffective.[1] Still more significant was the character of opposition developed in the course of the debate. It had a dozen varying grounds of argument, most of them pretty certain to appeal to popular prejudice later on. Some Congressmen objected to the discretionary powers as revolutionary, and, while conceding Mr. McCulloch's ability and conservatism, pointed out that a very different Treasury Secretary might succeed him.[2] Some denounced the contraction policy in itself as a " double-quick march to bankruptcy "[3]; others, less extreme in view, nevertheless pronounced the notion of immediate resumption of specie payments to be " Utopian in the extreme."[4] Much was heard of the comfortable theory that if Congress would " allow things to go on without active interference," the " natural development of events " would automatically bring about resumption.[5] It was promised, indeed, by one eminent Congressman, destined later to take up McCulloch's uncompleted work, that if the Secretary would do nothing else but meet current obligations, " no power could prevent" resumption within twelve or eighteen months.[6] More than one legislator could not understand, " when we have $450,000,000 [debt] bearing no in-

[1] *Treas. Rep.*, 1866, pp. 8, 9; *Men and Measures*, p. 211.
[2] Thaddeus Stevens, House of Representatives, March 16, 1866.
[3] W. D. Kelley, House of Representatives, February 21.
[4] Hiram Price, House of Representatives, March 16.
[5] G. S. Boutwell, House of Representatives, March 16.
[6] John Sherman, Senate, April 9.

terest, and which need bear no interest, why it is to be taken up and put into bonds."[1] The excellence of a circulating medium " that rests on the property of the whole country, and has for its security the faith and patriotism of the greatest and freest country on the face of the globe,"[2] played its usual part in the discussion; so did the argument that " the amount of legal tenders now outstanding is not too much for the present condition of the country."[3] In short, all the arguments which have been made familiar by the twenty subsequent years of controversy, cut a figure in this opening discussion. Even the peculiar virtues of a high protective tariff, through which the country might by a short cut reach a situation where resumption would be easy, were recited in this debate of 1866.[4]

As a matter of fact, even the restricted powers of note retirement granted under the law of March, 1866, were revoked within two years. Little or no progress had meantime been made towards resumption of specie payments. The Secretary himself had officially pointed out that two commercial influences must be removed before resumption would be possible; the excessively high prices in the United States and the heavy balance of foreign trade against us.[5] But prices continued above the European level, and, as a consequence, export of mer-

[1] Thaddeus Stevens, House of Representatives, March 16.
[2] W. A. Darling, House of Representatives, March 16.
[3] John Sherman, Senate, April 9.
[4] W. D. Kelley, House of Representatives, February 21; W. A. Darling, House of Representatives, March 16.
[5] *Treas. Rep.*, 1865, p. 13; 1866, p. 11.

chandise was checked and imports greatly stimulated. The entire gold product of each year in the United States was sent abroad. Some effort had indeed been made to accumulate a specie reserve in the Treasury, obtained through the required payment of customs dues in gold. But part of this fund was disbursed again for interest on the public debt; the mercantile community protested urgently against the hoarding of any excess, with gold selling at 150[1]; and in the end, the Treasury was forced repeatedly to throw its own coin surplus on the market, simply in order to check the disastrous operations of the speculators.[2] Resumption, in short, which Mr. Sherman had predicted as a certainty within eighteen months of March, 1866, was, if anything, further off than ever.

Contraction of the inflated currency, even if pursued under the limitations of the Act of 1866, would in time have brought about conditions under which resumption might have been planned. But events outside of the United States now moved in such a way as to turn the entire financial community against the Secretary's policy. Hardly two months after the vote of March came a wholly unexpected crisis in the foreign money markets. The London collapse, precipitated by the Overend-Gurney failure of May, 1866, was in some respects as complete as any in the history of England. It affected every nation with which Great Britain had commercial

[1] Memorial of New York bankers and shipping merchants to Secretary McCulloch, July, 1866.
[2] *Treas. Rep.*, 1866, p. 9.

dealings; not least of all the United States, of whose securities it was estimated that European investors even then held $600,000,000.[1] During three months the Bank of England kept its minimum discount rate at the panic figure of ten per cent.; the consequent sudden recall of foreign capital put a heavy strain on the American markets.

With the familiar disposition of the trade community to lay the blame for disordered markets on some move of public policy, the Treasury's operations to reduce outstanding notes were made the scapegoat.[2] Politicians with an eye to popularity were quick to catch this drift of public sentiment. Some of them honestly believed that McCulloch's action in the currency was the cause of the trade distress; others, better informed but equally politic, avoided personal declaration of opinion, but characteristically announced that whether the theory was correct or not, the public believed it, and that in deference to the public, currency contraction ought to cease.[3] The usual result ensued. Under the previous question, and without debate, a measure revoking absolutely the Secretary's power of contraction passed the House of Representatives in December, 1867, by a vote of 127 to 32. In the Senate there was an able show of opposition, but it was plainly put on the defensive. Even its very mild amendment hinting at future return to the contrac-

[1] McCulloch, *Treas. Rep.*, 1866, p. 12.
[2] O. P. Morton, Senate speech, January 9, 1868; A. G. Cattell, Senate speech, January 10, 1868.
[3] John Sherman, Senate speech, January 9, 1868.

tion policy was promptly rejected by the House, and on January 22, 1868, the resolution passed both chambers in its original and final shape.

This was the end of the McCulloch plan. It was the end of all serious debate upon resumption, for at least six years. It was also, and very logically, the beginning of the fiat-money party and of the plan to pay the Government's bonded debt, wherever practicable, in notes. This second proposition was thrown into the arena of a Presidential canvass within six months of the vote of January, 1868, being formally proposed in the platform of the Democratic party. Governor Seymour, it is true, rejected this financial plank of the convention which nominated him, and rejected it as plainly as General McClellan had rejected the " peace plank " of the same party four years before. But the repudiation issue was fought out, in the canvass, nevertheless. The Republicans were forced into open defence of sound financial principles by the very recklessness of their opponents. As happened under very similar conditions twenty-eight years later, the compromisers and waverers, who had cut so prominent a figure in the debates of 1866 and 1868, were compelled to show their colors, and the result, for the time at any rate, was salutary. Helped by the great personal prestige of its candidate, General Grant, the Republican party won a sweeping victory. Having won, the party's representatives hastened, while still under the excitement of the canvass, to make their public pledge for the future. President Johnson, who was then at open odds with his party, had produced in his Annual Message of December 7, 1868, the extraordinary suggestion that " the six per cent. interest now paid by the Government " on its debt " should be applied to the reduction of the principal in semi-annual instalments "; in other words, that the plan of repudiating interest obligations—since adopted, with no agreeable results, by Turkey and Greece—should be formally approved by the United States. This remarkable utterance was first condemned by an overwhelming vote in both House and Senate; next, by an almost equally decisive vote, on March 3, 1869, Congress adopted the Public Credit Act, promising coin redemption of both notes and bonds, and concluding with the declaration that the United States " solemnly pledges its faith to make provision, at the earliest practicable period, for the redemption of the United States notes in coin."

The promise was as easily made as the similar pledge of December, 1865; it was still more easily broken. No such arrangement was made, nor any serious attempt in that direction, until the matter was forced on the party by the exigency of politics. Not only was no effort made to reduce outstanding legal tenders, but the supply in circulation was heavily increased; rising from $314,704,000 in the middle of 1869 to $346,168,000 in 1872, and two years later, as a result of the Treasury's weak experiments in the panic, to $371,421,000.

The period was congenial to such juggling with public credit and legislative pledges. Socially, financially, and politically, it stands out quite apart from any other decade of the century. It comprised, in the United States, such a succession of episodes as the plundering reign of the Tweed cabal in New York City; the impeachment of President Johnson for purposes of political revenge; the infamous gold-market conspiracy of 1869, into which the ringleaders very nearly dragged the Federal Administration; the rise of vulgar and dishonest railway speculators to public eminence; the notorious corruption of the courts by such adventurers; scandal fixed upon Congress by the *Crédit Mobilier* disclosures and on the Administration by the Belknap impeachment trial. Moral sense seemed for a time to have deteriorated in the whole community; it was a sorry audience, at Washington or elsewhere, to which to address appeals for economy, retrenchment, and rigid preservation of the public faith. The Government's financial recklessness was readily imitated by the community at large; debt was the order of the day in the affairs of both. As the period approached its culmination, foreign trade reflected the nature of the situation. Merchandise imports in the fiscal year 1871 rose $84,000,000 over 1870; in 1872 they increased $106,000,000 over 1871. This movement was the familiar warning of an approaching crash; but the warning fell on deaf ears, as it usually does. In 1873 the house of cards collapsed.

The panic of 1873 left the country's financial and commercial structure almost a ruin. It had, however, several ulterior results so valuable that it is not wholly unreasonable to describe the wreck of credit as a blessing in disguise. American prices, long out of joint with the markets of the world, and thoroughly artificial in themselves, were certain to be eventually brought down. They would have been lowered, necessarily, under the McCulloch contraction plan, but the fall would have been gradual. This means of readjustment Congress and the people rejected; there was left, therefore, only the severe alternative of sudden and violent liquidation. But this very liquidating process served a useful double purpose; it disclosed the nation's true resources, and it placed the United States on equal footing with the commercial world at large. With the bursting of the bubble of inflated debt and inflated prices, the excessive importations ceased. Simultaneously the export trade, which had halted during 1872, in spite of the continued agricultural expansion, rose to proportions never before approached in our commercial history. In 1874, the balance of foreign trade, which during the twenty-five preceding years, with only four exceptions, had been running heavily against the United States, turned permanently in our favor. In the fiscal year 1872, imported merchandise exceeded exports by $182,417,000; in 1878, the export excess reached the unprecedented sum of $257,814,000. By 1876, even the continuous outflow of gold was checked. In short, the two conditions fixed by Hugh McCulloch, ten years before, as indispensable to resumption of specie payments, had now been realized.

Congress was not by any means disposed, however, to seize the opportunity. The first result of the money market crisis in 1873, as in all similar years, was urgent public clamor for more currency. The

Supreme Court had decided finally, in 1871, for the constitutionality of the legal tenders; the Secretary of the Treasury, in 1873, had so far yielded to the prevalent excitement as to reissue legal-tender notes already formally retired.[1] The first response of Congress, therefore, was an inflation measure. By a vote of 140 to 102 in the House of Representatives, and of 29 to 24 in the Senate, a law was passed for the permanent increase of the legal-tender currency by $18,000,000. The Republican party controlled Congress by unusually large majorities; but sixty per cent. of the party's vote in each chamber was cast in favor of the bill. Only the interposition of Grant's Presidential veto prevented this first positive backward step in the direction of fiat money.

It is reasonable to suppose that this curious vote of the Administration party, which occurred in April, 1874, measured the party's political desperation. They were about to receive, in the Congressional elections, the usual chastisement experienced by a dominant party when the people vote in a period of hard times; the inflation act was an anchor thrown desperately to windward. The experiment was in all respects a failure. Even the party's own State conventions failed to say a good word for the inflation bill, and it gained no mitigation of sentence in the November vote. In the Forty-third Congress, the House of Representatives had been Republican by the unusual plurality of 110; in the Forty-fourth, chosen in 1874, the Democrats controlled the House by 74 plurality.

[1] *N. Y. Financial Chronicle*, Dec. 6, 1873.

The Forty-third Congress had three months of existence left to it after the vote of November, 1874. Already defeated overwhelmingly at the polls, it had nothing to risk by a move in sound-money legislation, and possibly much to gain. It used this three-months' period to enact a law of the first importance, not only to the nation, but to the Republican party's future history—a law which must fairly be described, however, under the circumstances of the time, as an expression of death-bed repentance. This was the Specie-Resumption Act, drawn up, in its most important clauses, by Senator John Sherman and Senator George F. Edmunds.[1] It fixed the date for resumption of specie payments at January 1, 1879, provided for the reduction of legal-tender notes from $382,000,000 to $300,000,000, but made no provision for any further retirement of the notes. It conferred, for redemption purposes, the discretionary bond-issue power, afterwards employed by Secretary Sherman in 1878 and 1879, and by Secretary Carlisle in 1894 and 1895. It went through Congress on January 7, 1875, and with its enactment this chapter may properly be closed. Unlike most subsequent financial measures, the Resumption Act won its majorities in both Houses by the strictest kind of party vote. Not one Democratic Congressman supported it in either chamber; but the large Republican majorities of the 1872 election were still available. The bill passed the Senate by a vote of 32 to 14, and the House by 136 to 98. When it passed, it was generally declared by financial critics

[1] *Recollections*, i., p. 510.

that specie resumption under the measure was impossible, and it was openly promised by the opposition party, about to come into control of Congress by a large majority, that they would make short work of the Act of 1875 on their return to power.

CHAPTER II

THE STRUGGLE FOR RESUMPTION

THE Resumption Act is one of the most curious laws in financial history. It was plain in its requirement that on and after January 1, 1879, the Treasury should " redeem in coin the United States legal-tender notes then outstanding, on their presentation for redemption "; but it left the Treasury to make whatever arrangements it might choose. The law, it is true, conferred ample powers. In order " to prepare and provide for the redemption in this Act authorized or required," it empowered the Secretary of the Treasury " to use any surplus revenues, from time to time, in the Treasury not otherwise appropriated, and to issue, sell, and dispose of, at not less than par in coin, either of the descriptions of bonds of the United States described in the Act of Congress approved July 14, 1870." [1] This power was not only enormous in its immediate possibilities, but it was perpetual. The notes redeemed were not, as in 1866, to be cancelled or retired, but to be reissued. When reissued, they

[1] U. S. Statutes, 43d Congress, 2d session, chap. xv.

must necessarily become again redeemable in coin, with all the provisions of the Resumption Act again applying. This fact was recognized even in the debate upon the bill. Since the discretionary power of bond-issue was granted " not only to prepare for but to maintain resumption," [1] it followed that the power might legally be exercised by any future Administration.[2]

Now laws which make such extraordinary grants to the Executive commonly specify with the minutest care how the powers granted shall be employed. The Resumption Act does nothing of the kind. It places in the Secretary's hands, as the author of the law correctly pointed out, " the whole credit and money of the United States," [3] but it does not give the slightest hint as to what use he shall make of it. Resumption of specie payments is associated, in the average mind, with the accumulation of a coin reserve, out of which, when necessary, notes may be redeemed. But the Resumption Act makes no mention of a coin reserve. This omission left it wholly to the discretion of the administrator of the law how much gold he should accumulate for the purpose. He might, in strict accordance with the law, use his powers so as to throw the money market into convulsion. He might, on the other hand, either through choice or necessity, make such inadequate provision, that after January 1, 1879, his entire

[1] John Sherman, Senate speech, December 22, 1874.
[2] *Treas. Rep.*, 1879, p. xi.; 1880, p. xi. ; *Report H. R. Judiciary Committee*, July 6, 1892.
[3] John Sherman, Senate speech, December 22, 1874.

stock of gold would be withdrawn for hoarding or export purposes. There was involved, therefore, a double problem of great delicacy: could a large gold reserve be acquired and kept in the Treasury before 1879, and could it be protected afterwards?

At first glance, it would appear that the Treasury's discretionary power in the loan market, under the Act of 1875, made it an easy matter to obtain a sufficient coin reserve. But there was no such certainty when the law was passed. On the basis solely of domestic loans, the operation was impossible. As late as 1877, it was officially estimated that the total stock of gold in the United States, outside the Treasury, was less than $100,000,000,[1] and of that sum the two thousand national banks, on which the Treasury must mainly depend for a domestic gold loan, held only $22,658,820.[2] This was a wholly inadequate supply, and, what made the matter worse, the country had been losing annually, through export, more gold than it produced from its mines. In 1875 and the four preceding years, the United States produced $182,000,000 gold, and exported, net, $204,000,000.[3] So far as could be judged in 1875, an attempt to hoard in the Treasury even a moderate sum of domestic gold would revive the commercial dissatisfaction of 1866. In fact, the Treasury was more than once compelled, even after

[1] Director of the Mint, *Annual Report*, 1877.
[2] Comptroller Knox, *Treas. Rep.*, 1877, p. 163.
[3] *Annual U. S. Mint Reports;* U. S. Bureau of Statistics, *Annual Reports.*

the passage of the Resumption Law, to throw part of its gold fund on the market.[1]

There remained the foreign markets from which to obtain a gold supply. It was possible to buy gold abroad, even with foreign exchange against the United States. But Secretary Bristow expressed, in 1875, the very general doubt as to whether such an operation would not be deliberately obstructed by foreign institutions.[2] Nor was this apprehension groundless. France and Germany were already accumulating specie for exactly the purpose contemplated by the United States,[3] and it was common belief, even three years later, that the Bank of England would resort to extreme measures for the protection of its own reserve.[4]

I have said that the Law of 1875 involved the double problem of providing for resumption at the stipulated date, and of maintaining it afterward. It is the first of these undertakings which we shall survey in the present chapter. There were, as we have seen already, two influences at work in 1875, which made possible the achievement as it would not have been in 1866. These influences—the shifting of the foreign trade balance in favor of the United States and the subsequent check to gold exports—were factors on which no finance minister could have reckoned. Both in fact developed after the passage of the Resumption Law. But even after allowing for these accidental commercial ad-

[1] *Treas. Rep.*, 1875, p. xxii. [2] *Ibid.*, p. xxi.
[3] Letters of Treasury's London agent, August 11 and 15, 1877.
[4] *Ibid.*, August 10, 1878.

vantages, the credit for the return to specie payments on January 1, 1879, belongs individually and without dispute to John Sherman.

Mr. Sherman was the author of the Resumption Act; he was responsible both for its virtues and its vices. His appointment to the Treasury, therefore, in the Administration under which resumption must by law be carried out, was entirely logical. It is true, the Presidential canvass of 1876 was not conducted on the issue of resumption. The Act of 1875, a Republican party measure, and passed without one Democratic vote in either House of Congress, was not so much as named in the Republican national platform of 1876. But in politics, the candidate often counts for quite as much as the platform, and Mr. Hayes had won the Ohio Governorship, only a year before, after a contest pivoting wholly on the specie-payment issue. The choice of Mr. Sherman for finance minister in his national Administration was a normal sequel. Yet the practical efficiency of Mr. Sherman, in an administrative office, could not then have been foretold. The Secretary's previous career, though useful and industrious, had been marred by weaknesses which did not promise well. As a legislator, he belonged to the school of compromisers who have indirectly been responsible, in a score of critical emergencies, for the gravest mischief in our history. If his concessions had been proposed only after aggressive contest, when deadlock or defeat was the only alternative in sight, the criticism might be qualified. But it was Mr. Sherman's unfortunate policy as a legislator that he either opened the contest with a plan of compromise—thereby surrendering most of his legitimate vantage-ground—or else abandoned his position long before the battle was fought out. So eager was he, in the initial currency debate of 1866, to fix upon this middle ground, that he played directly and effectually into the hands of the opponents of resumption. He openly confessed his deference to public clamor in the vote of 1868.[1] In the Resumption Act of 1875 he suppressed, with deliberate evasion which was close to insincerity, any provision for or against reissue of the legal tenders.[2] It is impossible to harmonize with one another his public utterances and his public votes. He acknowledged freely, on various occasions, that extinction of the legal-tender notes was the simplest road to specie payments[3]; he declared with equal frankness that inflated prices must come down in the movement towards resumption, and that the shrinkage would be positive advantage to our industries.[4] Yet he made these very incidents of the McCulloch contraction movement the basis of a determined opposition. From the floor of Congress he attacked this plan, the only alternative to the fiat-money carnival of the next five years, with arguments which were effectively used in behalf of every future movement of inflation.[5]

[1] Senate speech, January 9, 1868.
[2] Senate speeches, December 22, 1874; March 16, 1876; *Recollections*, i., 510.
[3] Senate speech, December 22, 1874.
[4] Senate speech, January 15, 1868.
[5] Senate speech, April 9, 1866.

For a Secretary of the Treasury, at a peculiar crisis in the Government's finance, these were unpromising antecedents. But Mr. Sherman was not the first of public men to show that the faults or weakness of a legislator, whose purpose is to obtain enactment of a policy, will sometimes disappear in the administrator, who presses settled policies into execution. As Secretary, he was unwavering in pursuit of the resumption goal; practical, resolute, and adroit in the means employed. His official correspondence gives consistently the picture of a public officer of foresight and decision. It was in the face of the repudiation clamor that he declared officially for payment of the Government bonds in gold.[1] This action fixed a precedent of the highest value. Equally distinct was the Secretary's public declaration that the Act of 1875 conferred the power to issue bonds after, as well as before, resumption[2]; another precedent which did invaluable service sixteen years afterward. Only on one conspicuous occasion, hereafter to be noticed, did he revert to his old-time juggling with a public question, and then the strong good sense of the President overruled him.

What was perhaps still more essential, at this juncture in the Government finances, was the faculty displayed by Mr. Sherman, of keeping the mastery of outside negotiation. This was no small achieve-

---

[1] Letter to Colgate & Co., December 1, 1877; *Specie Resumption*, pp. 22, 23, 24, 80, 81, 201, 709; *Treas. Rep.*, 1877, p. ix.; 1878, p. xiv.

[2] *Treas. Rep.*, 1878, p. x.; 1879, p. x.; 1880, p. xiv.

ment; for, in addition to the doubts surrounding the resumption operation at the start, angry and bitter opposition from Congress confronted the Secretary at every step. The banking community was not enthusiastic in its offers; even the domestic institutions believed that the risk was great enough to call for large concessions from the Treasury. Mr. Sherman made no such concessions, and the banking interests were presently aware that a cool head and an experienced hand were in control of the Government's side of the bargain. He sounded all parties before committing himself to any, forced reluctant interests to bid through fear of losing entirely the prestige of the operation, and held his own position by compelling them to bid against each other. The manner in which the Secretary, in his loans of 1878 and 1879 particularly, played off the London syndicate against the hesitating New York banks, and the city banks against the syndicate, gave him, from first to last, the advantage of the situation.[1] This advantage he retained in the face of adverse movements of international exchange,[2] stringency in the London discounts,[3] and distinctly hostile operations on the gold market.[4] Results, in cases of this kind, speak for themselves. To say, therefore, that Secretary Sherman's management of the Treasury achieved

---

[1] *Recollections*, ii., 638; *Specie Resumption*, 291, 665; letter of August Belmont, February 13, 1879.

[2] *Specie Resumption*, pp. 280, 358.

[3] London *Economist*, October 19, 1878; Treasury's London correspondence, August 3, 10, and 17, 1878.

[4] Letter of August Belmont to Sherman, April 26, 1878.

during his time precisely the results proposed, and achieved them promptly, is to concede his administration's practical success. Nor were these results attained through extravagance or waste. In his refunding and resumption operations, Mr. Sherman placed the bonds of the United States on better terms than any of his predecessors.[1] On one noteworthy occasion, he sold to a foreign syndicate a considerable block of bonds at a figure virtually above the price of the same bonds on the open market, and he did this after banking acquaintances had warned him that the achievement was impossible.[2] It was through Secretary Sherman that the plan of sales direct to the investor, without the intervention of a syndicate, was afterwards introduced.[3]

Some mistakes in detail policy usually occur in any complex banking operation, and criticism has by no means spared Mr. Sherman. But even in these disputed questions, the Treasury had a good defence. The blunder of fixing a thirty-year term to the $741,000,000 4 per cents., frequently laid at his administration's door, was in fact decreed arbitrarily by the Funding Act of 1870, and was inserted in that statute against Mr. Sherman's own advice.[4] Conceivably, the extension of maturing 6

---

[1] *Treas. Rep.*, 1877, p. viii; *Recollections*, i., 570, 571.
[2] Letter of H. C. Fahnestock, March 23, 1878; *Specie Resumption*, pp. 279, 281, 283, 284, 285, 294.
[3] *Recollections*, i., 574; letter to the Senate, March 26, 1879; H. C. Adams, *Public Debts*, 236.
[4] *Recollections*, i., 454.

per cents. at 3½ subject to call, arranged a few months after Secretary Sherman's term expired, might have been feasible in 1877 and 1878. Yet it must be remembered that the credit of the United States, after two years of specie payments, was a very different thing from its credit in the earlier period. Congress, moreover, true to its record of the whole Administration, used the 3½ per cent. proviso as a means of deliberate embarrassment to the Secretary's operations. It loaded down its new refunding bill, in which that rate was authorized, with stipulations of a character so wild as to necessitate a Presidential veto.[1]

Of all the criticism on the Secretary's policy, that which clung longest was the charge that in the use of Government deposit funds, he granted undue favors to the banks. That Mr. Sherman was at times politically indiscreet, in permitting concentration of the bulk of his deposits with a single bank, cannot be doubted. But it by no means follows that the action was unwise financially. The syndicate of foreign bankers, through whom the large resumption loan was placed, were allowed to name their own depository, and the institution named by them had been the most efficient agent of the Government.[2] Politically, the Secretary would have played a wiser part had he distributed this deposit; from any other point of view, it was a matter of complete indifference. If the example of foreign

---

[1] *Recollections*, ii., 758, 796.
[2] *Recollections*, ii., 798 ; letter to a New York banker, January 13, 1879 ; *Specie Resumption*, p. 459.

governments had any bearing on the matter, the
selection of a single bank was preferable. As for
the general policy of bank deposits, that was not
only sustained by precedent in this and other countries,[1] but it was indispensable. When any block of
new refunding bonds had been sold and paid for,
ninety days had to elapse, under the formal notice,
before the old bonds could be taken up. In the
British Government, all such surplus of the exchequer goes, as a matter of course, on deposit with
the Bank of England. Common prudence required
that the purchase money in our Government's possession, during these three-months intervals, should
be similarly kept on the open market.[2] In extend-
ing these deposits, always abundantly secured, Mr.
Sherman not only followed common-sense and
precedent, but had the best advice, legal and financial, to sustain him.[3]

I have spoken of the obstacles thrown in the Administration's way by Congress. The circumstances
under which the Hayes Administration entered office
were in all respects discouraging. Administrative
plans and policies have frequently enough been obstructed by opposition majorities in one or the other
branch of Congress, by dissension in the Administration party, or by the popular discontent arising from
hard times. The Hayes Administration had to meet
all these obstacles at once, and at a time when its

[1] Report of Treasurer Spinner, *Annual Treas. Rep.*, 1866, p. 171.
[2] Letter to the Senate, March 26, 1879.
[3] Opinions of Attorney-General Devens, of Comptroller Knox, of Geo. S. Coe ; *Specie Resumption*, pp. 117, 135, 136.

own official prestige was marred by its disputed title. Whether Mr. Hayes was entitled to the two doubtful States whose votes were eventually awarded to him, and without which he could not have been elected, is a question regarding which opinion will probably always differ. The elaborately constructed Electoral Commission, to whom the question was referred, divided almost exactly on the lines of party affiliation. But that the actual majority of the voters was against Mr. Hayes in 1876, and in favor of Mr. Tilden, there is no doubt whatever. The Republican count itself awarded to Mr. Tilden a popular plurality, in the whole United States, of 252,224. The tangible result of this popular minority was a House of Representatives containing an opposition plurality of twenty votes.

Nor was this opposition content with a mere blockade of Administration measures. It undertook to wreck the entire policy of the President. The Senate was Republican by a plurality of three, but on questions of finance, this slender plurality could not be trusted. The first year of the new Administration was a period of stagnant trade and popular unrest; its second year was a period of falling prices. The Pittsburg railway riots, which rose for a time to the proportions of industrial insurrection, broke out hardly four months after the inauguration of President Hayes. Business failures were more numerous and serious in 1877 than in 1874, the increase being particularly rapid in the younger Western States; and in 1878 the record of insolvencies far exceeded even that of the panic year

1873.[1] Four years of prostrated enterprise had utterly discouraged the people; when, therefore, politicians laid the blame on the Treasury's operations, they had no trouble in getting a hearing. The opposition to Mr. Sherman's plans, which in fact included many well-known Republican Congressmen, believed itself to be backed by an overwhelming popular sentiment. It therefore laid its plans deliberately to upset the pending negotiations.

The attack began with a bill revoking all power of bond-issues for resumption purposes, and in effect repealing the Resumption Act. This measure went through the House in November, 1877, by a majority of thirteen votes. Before its fate in the Senate was at all certain, the House had challenged public attention with another bill to open the mints of the United States to the free coinage of silver. This measure was not entirely new. In the summer session of 1876, several bills had been introduced, providing for increased silver coinage and for remonetization of the silver dollar. None of these propositions came to anything; they were chiefly remarkable from the fact that they first gave vogue to the theory of the " crime of 1873 "—a theory which assumed that the dropping of the silver dollar from the list of coins in the statutes of that year was the outcome of a conspiracy which carried its legislation through in secret. The entire baselessness of this assertion has been demonstrated often enough and in convincing detail; this very provision regarding the silver dollar was a subject of public discussion

[1] *Dun's Review*, annual tables,

in the House, and met with no serious opposition.¹
The assertion in itself is so patently absurd that I
shall not pause to discuss it. The truth is that silver
in 1873, and during a generation before that date,
was worth more to its owner in the form of bullion
than in the form of coin. In 1872 the silver requisite to coin a dollar at the established ratio was worth
$1.02.² For years, therefore, nobody thought of
bringing his silver to the mint for coinage; he sold
it in the commercial markets. As we have seen, the
total silver-dollar coinage of the United States, between 1789 and 1873, was barely eight million dollars,
and when, in 1873, the law provided that except for
the so-called trade dollar coined for export, " no
deposit of silver for other coinage shall be received,"
no one had interest enough in the matter to offer
criticism.³

But in 1874 and 1875 came one of those curious
coincidences which render possible for all time conflicting theories of an economic event. Germany,
having adopted the gold standard of currency in July,
1873, began to sell its old silver coin as bullion. At
exactly the same time, Mackay and Fair, in the
heart of the Nevada Mountains, were opening up
the Great Bonanza. The Pacific Coast was in fact
going wild over the rise in mining shares while the
East was financially and industrially paralyzed. For
one instance, the famous Consolidated Virginia mine,

[1] White, *Money and Banking*, p. 213; Laughlin, *Bimetallism*, p. 98; *Congressional Globe*, April 9, 1872.
[2] *U. S. Mint Reports*, annual tables.
[3] *Treas. Rep.*, 1878, p. xxiii.

which produced in 1873 only $645,000 of silver ore, turned out $16,000,000 in 1875.[1] In the three years following 1874, the two mines of the "Comstock lode" yielded $42,000,000 silver.[2] The statute dropping the silver dollar from this country's coinage list was enacted February 12, 1873; the German law for retirement of silver coinage was adopted July 9, 1873; and a year later the news of the rich Nevada "ore-finds" became public property. Between the German sales and the sales at Nevada City, the price of silver yielded. In 1874, for the first time in a generation, $412\tfrac{1}{2}$ grains of standard silver would have been worth more when coined into a legal-tender dollar than when sold in the bullion market.[3] The motive of the mining interest in the free-silver coinage agitation of 1876 and 1877 was not mysterious.

The motive of the anti-Administration party in Congress was somewhat different. There is not the slightest question that the silver-coinage movement, in the agricultural West particularly, had the same origin and the same following as the paper inflation movement of a few years before. Mr. Bland himself, the author of the silver bill, declared that the question was presented as between what he called "honest resumption" with silver coinage, "or on the other hand a forced unlimited inflation of paper money."[4] In the heat of debate on the silver bill, the same statesman declared in Congress that if his

[1] Shinn, *The Story of the Mine*, p. 191.
[2] Lindermann, *U. S. Mint Report*, 1877.
[3] *Annual Reports, U. S. Mint.*
[4] *Congressional Record*, Aug. 5, 1876.

coinage plan could not be passed, he was " in favor of issuing paper money enough to stuff down the bond-holders until they are sick."¹ The point of these remarks lies in their frank assumption that the free-silver sentiment and the fiat-money sentiment were interchangeable.

So much, then, for the origin and nature of the silver movement. The Bland Bill passed the House on November 5, 1877, under the previous question and without debate, by a vote of 164 to 34, and the resumption operations of the Government came to an instant halt. The market price of silver then was such that the legal-tender dollar of the Act would have been worth intrinsically less than ninety cents. Foreign subscribers to our resumption bonds suspected instantly that payment of the Government debt in a depreciated coin was planned by Congress; their suspicions were confirmed by a resolution introduced December 6th by Stanley Matthews, Mr. Sherman's own successor in the Senate, and passed by both Houses. The resolution explicitly declared that in the opinion of Congress, all the bonds of the United States, " issued or authorized to be issued," were payable in the silver dollars of the Bland Law. The extraordinary character of this resolution may be judged from the fact that it was proposed and passed in both Houses while the Coinage Act was still pending, and while, therefore, there was not in existence the coin which was duly declared a legal tender for settlement with public creditors.² To the

¹ *Congressional Record*, February 21, 1878.
² Benjamin H. Hill, Senate speech, January 25, 1878.

conservative portion of the public, the resolution seemed a piece of financial lunacy; to the Treasury, it was not only embarrassing but humiliating. Hardly a month before, in his annual report to Congress, the Secretary had repeated his official statement, previously made to bond subscribers, that payment of the bonds in gold might safely be anticipated.[1] The publication of this statement in New York and London had been followed by greatly increased subscriptions to the bonds, in payment of which gold was required by the Government.[2] The Matthews resolution amounted, so far as Congress was concerned, to repudiation of a formal bargain of which the Government had already obtained the fruits. The debate was such as might have been expected on a measure of the sort. It centred repeatedly on denunciation of Government bond investors.[3] Foreign subscribers were treated with especial scorn; indeed, our foreign customers in general were not spared. It was this debate which drew forth Senator Matthews's somewhat celebrated query: " What have we got to do with abroad ?"— a remark which was perhaps as typical of the session's deliberations as any utterance made from the floor of Congress.[4]

In each of these three controversies the Adminis-

[1] *Treas. Rep.*, 1877, p. iv.
[2] Sherman to F. O. French, June 19, 1877; *Specie Resumption*, pp. 80, 81, 84, 91.
[3] Speech of D. W. Voorhees, Senate, January 15, 1878; of F. M. Cockrell, Senate, January 23, 1878; of W. H. Felton, Senate, November 14, 1877.
[4] Senate speech, December 10, 1877.

tration was deserted by a good part of its natural supporters. Twenty-seven Republicans voted in the House for the virtual repeal of the Resumption Act. Sixty-seven out of the 164 votes for the free-silver coinage bill were Republican. The Matthews resolution was not only proposed by a Republican, but Senators and Representatives of the Administration party took the floor to advocate it. Indeed, the party chaos during the session of 1877 and 1878, on all financial questions, can find no parallel short of the stormy legislative days of 1894 and 1895. The personality of debate and vote, during this earlier upheaval, is extremely curious. The vote in the House of Representatives, for instance, on the original free-coinage bill of 1877, was non-partisan and almost wholly sectional. From districts west or south of Pennsylvania, only six votes were cast against the bill, two of these votes being cast by Democrats; from Pennsylvania and the districts east or north of it, the bill received only nine supporting votes, and three of the nine votes were Republican. The representatives from Ohio, Indiana, Illinois, Wisconsin, Iowa, Kansas, California, and Minnesota, so far as they answered to the roll-call, voted solidly for the free-coinage bill; the New England States voted solidly against it. Not least remarkable, in the alignment of our public men during the session, was a coincidence which made the proposed repeal of the Resumption Act an example in the irony of history. The Treasury Secretary whose authority the bill assailed had in 1868 led a similar movement to break down the Administration's resumption plans. The future Secretary of 1894, destined to issue under the Resumption Act more bonds than even Secretary Sherman, sat in the House in 1877 and voted to revoke the power of issue.

The situation, during the early months of 1878, was in fact extremely critical. For the time the three direct assaults on the public credit were warded off. The Matthews resolution was "concurrent," and hence a mere expression of opinion without binding force. The bill repealing the Resumption Act of 1875 was killed by disagreement in the Senate. Meantime the Silver-Coinage Act was modified by the Senate into a compromise requiring purchase and coinage by the Government of two to four million silver dollars monthly. Even thus modified, it encountered the veto of the President, but was passed over his veto, without a day's delay, by the requisite two-thirds majority. Executive conservatism seemed to be fruitless; nevertheless, there is no doubt whatever that the steadfast policy of Mr. Hayes did much to stem the current of reaction. Although his veto did not prevent enactment of the silver-coinage policy, his Annual Message of December 3, 1877, submitted when Congressional majorities were not yet defined, so plainly intimated veto that it obstructed efforts to force the absolute free-coinage measure through the Senate. The President's services certainly do not merit less of recognition, from the fact that his Secretary of the Treasury gave him at this point only nominal support. For once at least in his executive career, Mr.

Sherman's comment on the reactionary policy, even before the Allison substitute bill had been framed, was as faltering in its tone, and as thoroughly imbued with timid compromise, as if its author was again the Sherman of the Senate.[1] A personal letter of the Secretary, in September, 1877, to the author of the Matthews resolution, contains the most extraordinary quibbling with the question.[2] Mr. Sherman himself confessed, seventeen years after the struggle of 1878, that the veto message did not meet with his approval.[3]

Congress adjourned on June 19th. Even before Congressional adjournment, the canvass for the November State elections had begun. The State Convention platforms, in the summer of 1878, were not in all respects such as the session's work in Congress would have suggested. It is true, the Democrats throughout the West and South went to extremes in denouncing the Administration's policy. The Ohio Democrats, for instance, demanded "absolute repeal of the Resumption Act," "removal of all restrictions to the coinage of silver," and "substitution of United States legal-tender money for national bank notes,"[4] and Democratic Conventions in Indiana, in Iowa, and in most other Western and Southern States, made exactly similar declarations. The policy set forth by the Ohio Democrats was

[1] *Treas. Rep.*, 1877, p. xxi.
[2] Letter to Stanley Matthews, September 11, 1877; *Recollections*, i., 593.
[3] *Recollections*, ii.. 623.
[4] Ohio Democratic Convention of June 26.

certainly no more reactionary than what had been proclaimed that very season on the floor of Congress, and by eminent Republicans.[1] It was the policy which the majority of public men, in both parties, had indicated, two or three months before, as certain of popular endorsement. But the Republican Convention leaders, in Ohio and in other Western States, were shrewder. Signs of protest against the anti-Administration Republicans in Congress, more ominous because they came from staunch and life-long supporters of the party, were visible even before Congress adjourned. The great business communities were speaking out with considerable emphasis, and this indication was not lost on the Republican managers. With much political adroitness, the Western Conventions of the party based their chief appeal on "opposition to further financial agitation," as " injurious to business and devoid of other than evil results."[2] Republican platforms in the Eastern States were even more distinct in declaring for the Administration's policy; endorsement of the specie-resumption plan, for instance, as carried out by Secretary Sherman, was voted without a qualifying word.

The trend of public sentiment, in fact, very soon showed itself to be unmistakably in that direction, and this was shown by the altered tone of the oppo-

[1] W. D. Kelley, House of Representatives, November 3, 1877; J. J. Ingalls, Senate, December 6, 1877; W. A. Wallace, Senate, January 29, 1878; T. O. Howe, Senate, February 5, 1878.

[2] Platforms of the Indiana and Ohio Republican Conventions, June 5 and 12, 1878.

sition Convention platforms, in the fall. Some of
these platforms made obvious attempts to square
their party with the voters. The financial plank of
the New York Democratic Convention, for instance,
on September 25th, reads like actual endorsement
of the Republican Administration. It was too late,
however, for such manœuvres to be of any value.
The opposition had gone too far in Congress, and
popular opinion to that effect was expressed with
sufficient emphasis in November, 1878. The Administration party gained what amounted to a decided victory. New York, Connecticut, and Ohio,
which had been carried by the Democrats in 1877,
now swung back to the Republicans, New York
leading with a majority of 34,661. In 1877, the
Democratic party had captured Pennsylvania by
nearly 10,000; it lost the State now by upwards of
22,000. The opposition still retained control of the
House of Representatives, but by a reduced plurality. There were but four States, East or West,
where opposition majorities were increased in 1878
or Administration majorities diminished, and these
were agricultural States, where the season's sharp
decline in wheat had stirred up discontent.

There was not much danger from the closing
session of a Congress whose earlier ventures had received this response from the people. Without interruption or annoyance from the legislative body,
the Secretary of the Treasury now put the final
touches on his arrangements for resumption. Partly
by accident and partly through stress of circumstances, the Treasury gold reserve was defined, in

later years, at a fixed and arbitrary minimum. The theory adopted by Mr. Sherman, however, in his early operations, was different and undoubtedly better. Following probably the practice of the Bank of England, he fixed his reserve at forty per cent. of outstanding notes—"the smallest reserve," he wrote to Congress, "upon which resumption could be prudently commenced and successfully maintained."[1] On this basis he held in the Treasury, on December 31, 1878, $114,193,000 gold in excess of outstanding gold certificates, which was a trifle over forty per cent. of the Government notes then circulating outside the Treasury.[2] Of this gold reserve, $95,500,000 had been obtained through sale of bonds,[3] part of the coin being procured in Europe.

There remained now to be settled only the formal machinery of exchange between the Treasury and outside institutions. The city banks were naturally willing to lend all possible aid to the achievement. But the mere good-will of the banks has proved largely useless to the Treasury on two not at all dissimilar occasions—in 1861 and in 1894—and at both those junctures the fault distinctly lay in lack of timely business management by the Treasury. It is conceivable that with the vacillating policy of those two years applied in 1878, the Government's financial schemes might even now have broken down.

[1] Letter to President of the Senate, May 17, 1879; interview with H. R. Banking and Currency Committee, April 18, 1878; *Recollections* ii., p. 631.
[2] *Treasurer's Annual Report*, comparative tables.
[3] *Treas. Rep.*, 1878, p. ix.

If, for example, the Treasury had left the banks to pursue unchanged their policy of keeping special gold deposits, the Government reserve would have been at once imperilled. If the banks had continued to present their individual drafts for redemption across the counter of the Sub-Treasury, any timid or blundering banker might have started a general drain of gold. Against these possibilities Mr. Sherman now took measures. He applied for the admission of the New York Sub-Treasury as a member of the clearing-house. Nowadays, when the Government's participation in this privilege has become a matter of every-day routine, it is easy to underrate the work of the Administration which effected it. In 1878, however, the project was both new and startling. This occasion, it is true, was not the first on which the clearing-house proposition had been mooted. But the previous Administration which considered the suggestion had abandoned it.[1] Even in 1878, the judgment of the Secretary's own associates was against the plan[2]; nevertheless, he brought the matter to a head with business-like directness, and within two weeks after the project was officially submitted, arrangements had been made. At New York and Boston, the clearing-houses modified their rules, agreed to abolish " gold deposits " after January 1st, to accept the legal tenders freely in discharge of balances against one

[1] Letter of Assistant-Treasurer Hillhouse; *Specie Resumption*, p. 398.
[2] Letter of Assistant-Secretary French, November 5, 1878; *Specie Resumption*, p. 396.

another and against the Government, and to admit the New York Sub-Treasury into regular membership.¹ At the same time, the requirement of coin payment of customs duties was revoked, and public officers were directed to receive coin or legal tenders at the payer's option—a move of obvious propriety, since refusal to take notes in payment would merely send the importer to the Treasury's redemption office to convert them into coin.² All these preliminaries had been formally and positively settled before the close of 1878. On December 17th, the premium on gold disappeared, for the first time since 1861; on January 1st, specie payments were quietly resumed. Whether resumption could be maintained without fresh purchases of gold, without new bond issues, and without recurrent strain on financial confidence, depended on influences no longer subject to the Government's control.

¹ Resolution of the clearing-house at New York, November 12, 1878, *Specie Resumption*, p. 401; at Boston, November 15, *Specie Resumption*, p. 408.

² *Treas. Rep.*, 1878, pp. xii., xiii.; Treasury circular to disbursing and receiving officers, December 14, 1878.

CHAPTER III

RESUMPTION OF SPECIE PAYMENTS

THE danger to the Treasury's redemption fund lay, as every one understood, in possible gold exports. As it happened, there was no gold movement in progress at the time of specie resumption; but foreign exchange was only a trifle below the normal gold-exporting point, and no spring season for eighteen years had passed without gold shipments. In the first half of 1877, nearly twenty millions gold had been exported from New York, chiefly obtained from the city banks. On January 1, 1879, these New York banks held in specie only $19,781,400, but they held twice as much in legal-tender notes redeemable at the Treasury in gold. Supposing, then, a further rise in exchange and a heavy export of gold, there was not the least doubt over what would happen to the Treasury reserve.

Now it is true that every bank of issue is confronted continually with this possibility. In 1878 and 1879, while gold exports from London were in progress, the exporters carried their Bank of England notes to the Bank as a matter of course for redemption in gold, and shipped the gold. What was true

of the London gold operations then is true to-day.
But the Bank of England, like all properly managed
banks of issue, exercises the power of holding back
from circulation the notes redeemed, whenever its
reserve has been drawn down too far. This practice, in the case of the Bank of England, automatically checks a large gold export movement, through
the resultant contraction of the money market. So
far was the United States Treasury, in 1879, from
enjoying any such precautionary power, that it was
expressly forbidden to hold back notes after redemption. As originally passed, the Resumption Act
was ambiguous on this question. It did provide for
redemption of notes, prior to 1879, "until there
shall be outstanding the sum of three hundred
million dollars of such legal-tender United States
notes, and no more." This provision obviously
meant cancellation of $82,000,000 out of the $382,-
000,000 existing legal tenders, and it was so applied.
But the question of retirement was purposely left in
doubt as regarded notes redeemed in gold after resumption.[1] Before even the notes in excess of $300,-
000,000 had been retired, moreover, Congress took
the matter in hand, and as it made its move in the
midst of the legislative hurly-burly of 1878, its purpose was likely to be plain enough. The law of May
31, 1878, declared that cancellation of the notes should
cease at once. The amount outstanding was then
$346,681,000, instead of the $300,000,000 maximum
fixed by the Resumption Act; and to this extent

[1] *Recollections of John Sherman*, i., 510; John Sherman, Senate speech, December 22, 1874.

the Resumption Law was positively revoked. It
was further provided, in this Act of 1878, that
" when any of said notes may be redeemed or received into the Treasury under any law, from any
source whatever, and shall belong to the United
States, they shall not be retired, cancelled, or destroyed, but they shall be re-issued and paid out
again and kept in circulation."

It is impossible to mistake the meaning of this
provision. It not only fixed the minimum of legal-
tender notes, but expressly forbade the Treasury to
exercise any power of even temporary contraction.
Mr. Sherman's attitude as regards this measure is
difficult to understand. He openly approved the
compulsory re-issue clause of the Act of 1878,[1] and
in fact admitted that he had himself entertained
some purpose of the kind. He was, however, too
intelligent a financier not to foresee its dangers, and
as we shall presently see, these dangers were seriously impressed upon him by certain incidents of the
resumption year. In his annual report of December, 1879, he therefore set up a theory of his own
that notes redeemed out of the gold reserve could
not be used for ordinary purposes, and therefore,
with the reserve impaired, were not subject to re-
issue.[2] There is, unfortunately, not the slightest
ground for such a contention. The reader must
have perceived that the compulsory re-issue clause,
cited above from the Act of 1878, is framed with
particular care to exclude any such interpretation.

[1] *Recollections*, ii., p. 659.
[2] *Treas. Rep.*, 1879, p. x. ; 1880, p. xiii.

Mr. Sherman's assumption in his report of 1879 was as unwarranted as his criticism of a later Secretary of the Treasury for not claiming precisely the same discretionary privilege.[1]

The ordinary banking safeguard, then, was wholly withdrawn from the Treasury. Under such circumstances, the resumption experiment was necessarily hazardous, and its success, even in its first year of operation, was bound to depend very largely on the commercial situation. In this regard, the resumption year did not begin auspiciously. In 1878, the merchandise trade balance in favor of the United States had been very large; in the first five months of 1879, it decreased steadily. " These figures," wrote a commercial firm of which an ex-Secretary of the Treasury was the head, " indicate the beginning of a change in the relative volume of imports and exports."[2] Domestic markets were unfavorable. In the cotton-goods industry, demand had slackened so far that wage reductions were impending.[3] The iron trade, a traditional barometer of industrial situations, opened the year with so little activity that prices fell below the actual average cost of production.[4] With hardly an exception, the country's staple industries sank, during the early months of 1879, into complete stagnation. Three months after resumption, the leading financial weekly of New York remarked: " ' Where is the prosperity

[1] *Forum* for April, 1896.
[2] Circular of McCulloch & Co., New York, May, 1879.
[3] Ellison & Co.'s cotton circular, January, 1879.
[4] *Annual Report*, New York Chamber of Commerce, 1879, p. 104.

promised with that event?' is the question frequently coming to us. 'Wheat is no higher. Corn is no higher. There is no money in any of the earth's products. Where is the promised prosperity?'"[1]

It is true, formal resumption of specie payments was reflected, in the home security markets, by a recovery in prices. This recovery, though extremely irregular, was permanent. But foreign capital gave no assistance to the movement; on the contrary, the higher range of domestic prices served to stimulate sales for European account, and there was abundant opportunity for such sales because of the very large amounts of United States Government bonds floated abroad during 1877 and 1878. In February, 1879, the London agent of the Treasury reported that, since the opening of the year, $43,000,000 of these bonds, and $7,000,000 of a single American railway stock, had been re-sold by London to the United States.[2] These sales were reflected in a rise of foreign exchange almost to the normal gold-export level.[3] In London, the most experienced international bankers, including the Rothschilds, who had placed the bulk of the recent American loans, predicted that gold was about to move in quantity from the United States to Europe.[4] By the middle of March, the Secretary was disturbed enough to set

[1] New York *Financial Chronicle*, March 8, 1879.
[2] London correspondence of Treasury, February 22, 1879; *Specie Resumption*, p. 525.
[3] Fry to Sherman, January 13, 1879; *Specie Resumption*, p. 461.
[4] Treasury's London correspondence, February 22; *Specie Resumption*, pp. 525, 536, 723.

on foot inquiry into the possibility of controlling specie exports through sales of Government exchange. Such recourse, Mr. Sherman plainly intimated, might become necessary " in preventing popular alarm."[1] Not even this expedient was feasible; sterling continued to advance, and finally, in the second week of June, a million and a quarter gold was shipped. This gold was obtained from the Treasury in exchange for notes; it reduced to precisely that extent the Government reserve.[2] London financial judgment of the time was thus expressed: " The effect of resumption has passed off, and we may expect to find gold steadily drifting from that side to this."[3]

The wheat harvest of 1878, in England and on the European continent, had been, as we have seen, one of the largest on record. When 1879 was well advanced, wheat from the English farms was still moving in quantity to storage-points. At the close of March, the stock of wheat at Liverpool was larger than at any time within five years; the same was true of every cereal product.[4] Frosty weather and heavy rains in England had indeed advanced the price of wheat sixpence a bushel, and it was then admitted that the English crop of 1878 would not be duplicated. But meantime the reserved supply was ample, demand from consumers was only

[1] Sherman to Conant, March 15; Conant to Sherman, April 3; *Specie Resumption*, pp. 569, 602.
[2] *Treas. Rep.*, 1879, p. 338.
[3] London *Statist*, June 7, 1879.
[4] *Annual Report*, New York Produce Exchange, 1879, p. 447.

moderate, and early in March observers of the market predicted that prices had reached their high level for the year.[1] This forecast seemed for some time to be correct. Wheat had advanced nine cents per bushel on the New York market since the opening of January; the price now fell from $1.17½ in March to $1.10 in the second week of April.

Little by little the foreign situation changed. As is usual with highly speculative markets, the news was contradictory, and the truth developed slowly. But it was evident in May, while the outlook for this country's harvest was steadily improving, that the European grain markets were beginning to stir with apprehension. In France, snow fell heavily late in the spring; in England, after a late and destructive frost, rain set in and continued almost incessantly through the summer. It was literally a sunless season. At the opening of July, people were wearing heavy overcoats in London, and in the country all the crops were moulding.[2] By this time the impending harvest failure had begun to assume the dimensions of a national calamity. On Sunday, July 6th, by the Archbishop of Canterbury's direction, prayers for fair weather were offered in the English churches.[3] In another month the time was past when even favorable weather would help, and by August it was made clear to all the markets that, while the United States would yield the largest

---

[1] London correspondence, New York *Financial Chronicle*, March 7, 1879.   [2] *Ibid.*, July 11, 1879.

[3] Treasury's London correspondence, July 12; *Specie Resumption*, p. 739.

harvest in its history, every growing crop in the British Islands was practically ruined. No such disaster had befallen English agriculture within the memory of living men.¹ The actual decrease in the wheat crop especially, as compared with 1878, was fifty-four per cent.; the total yield was smaller by thirty million bushels than in the leanest recorded year since the middle of the century.² Nor was this Europe's only agricultural catastrophe. Until midsummer, there had been favorable news from the continental crops. But the blight which fell on England's harvest—the sunless July with its succession of soaking rain-storms—did equal damage beyond the Channel. France, Austria, Germany, and Russia yielded, in 1879, the smallest and poorest wheat crops in ten years; the whole continental harvest fell off fifteen per cent. from the average of the three preceding years.³ European states, which usually exported wheat, had not raised enough to feed their own people. "It is the American supply alone," one contemporary critic wrote, "which has saved Europe from a great famine."⁴

To the United States, the huge American grain crop of 1879 was a double stroke of fortune. In England, it stopped the mouths of Mr. Chaplin and the protectionist reactionaries, who had begun to clamor against the free right of entry to American export grain. In the United States, it settled the question of resumption. All circumstances seemed to con-

¹ *Mark Lane Express*, London, January 5, 1880.
² *Gazette* tables. ³ *Bulletin des Halles*, Paris, January, 1880,
⁴ London *Economist*, November 22, 1879.

spire in favor of this country. Sunny and favorable
" farmer's weather," with the due proportion of
rains, prevailed throughout the season. The wheat
fields under cultivation had increased over 1878 by
half a million acres, the average yield per acre has
never but twice been surpassed in this country, and
the total crop exceeded by 28,000,000 bushels the
crop of any previous year.[1] Until midsummer, as
we have seen, prices for wheat had moved irregu-
larly; even in July and August, the market broke
no less than twenty cents a bushel, wholly because
of the certainty of an exceptionally large American
harvest. But the positive news of Great Britain's
crop failure carried the price up no less than forty
cents a bushel within six weeks.[2] Along with this
advance in prices, exports of wheat rose to wholly
unprecedented volume. The foreign buying was so
urgent that the country's wheat shipments, which
even in 1878 did not run beyond two million bushels
weekly, averaged, in September, 1879, a million
bushels daily,[3] a volume of grain exports equalled
only twice in the country's subsequent history. The
crop of Indian corn was the largest on record; this,
too, found a ready and profitable export market.
Cattle raised on the interior farms were sent abroad
in such numbers that the foreign trade complained
that British graziers were being forced out of the
British market.[4] By a rather remarkable coinci-

[1] *Annual Reports*, U. S. Department of Agriculture.
[2] New York Produce Exchange, *Annual Report*, 1879, p. 395.
[3] *Financial Chronicle*, October 4, 1879.
[4] Glasgow *Herald*, November, 1879.

dence, the famous tide-water pipe-line from the Pennsylvania oil-wells was completed in 1879, and the year's export of this product rose nearly two million barrels over the highest previous record.[1] By another coincidence, equally independent of any events already noticed, the cotton crop of India in 1879 was a partial failure[2]; Europe's supply on hand fell off thirty per cent. from the autumn stock of 1878 and fifty per cent. from 1877, and with the consequent heavy purchases by foreign spinners, the season's export of American cotton was the largest ever yet recorded.

The first result of this sudden change in the situation was a fall in the foreign exchanges, and consequent dissipation of all fears that the resumption fund would be impaired. With this menace removed from the financial outlook, the country's torpid enterprise awoke. The trade revival which ensued was without question the most remarkable in this country's commercial history. In the entire range of American industries, there was practically no exception to the movement. In the iron trade, consumption, which had been cramped and paralyzed for half a dozen years, and which at the opening of 1879 was not large enough to move the surplus stocks, had by December run so far beyond capacity for immediate production as to yield a profit of one hundred per cent. on current rates of cost.[3]

In spite of the rise in raw cotton, the spinning in-

[1] *Annual Report*, New York Chamber of Commerce, 1879, p. 50.
[2] New York *Financial Chronicle*, September 27, 1879.
[3] *Annual Report*, New York Chamber of Commerce, 1879, p. 104.

dustry, whose depressed condition at the opening of
the year has been noticed already, enjoyed its full
share of the trade revival. Print cloths, the staple
of the dry-goods trade, not only advanced fifty per
cent. over their price of January 1st, but closed the
year with stocks depleted, mills running at full
pressure, and large orders booked ahead.[1] This was
the story in almost every trade. By August, the
money market rose sharply under the heavy demand
for this expanding trade, and import of gold began
in quantities vastly beyond what had ever been witnessed in the previous trade history of the United
States. Within three months, $20,000,000 had
come from Great Britain, $30,000,000 from France,
and $10,000,000 from Germany; and as the special
need of the American bankers was currency suitable
for use in interior trade, a large part of this specie
went directly into the Treasury in exchange for
legal-tender notes—another wholly new phenomenon, impossible except under resumption.

On January 1st, as we have seen, only one third
of the cash reserves of New York banks was specie,
and the aggregate thus held was only $19,494,700.
On December 12th, they held $53,157,700 specie,
and this was nearly eighty per cent. of the total cash
reserve.[2] In the early months of 1879, almost the
whole of the customs payments at New York were
made in legal tenders; in November and December,
upwards of sixty-six per cent. were made in gold.[3]

[1] *Annual Report*, New York Chamber of Commerce, 1879, p. 100.
[2] New York Clearing-House statements.
[3] Records of the Treasury.

The Government's gold reserve accordingly rose from $119,956,655 at the close of June to $157,140,-114 at the opening of November. As early as September, Secretary Sherman notified agents of the Treasury that " gold coin, beyond the needs of the Government, having accumulated in the Treasury," they were thenceforward to pay out gold freely on ordinary disbursements.[1]

The industrial, social, and political results of this extraordinary year were permanent and far-reaching. The series of commercial windfalls which gave the United States the upper hand in half the foreign markets came, as we have seen, on top of a five-year period of economy and liquidation; there was, therefore, a firm substratum on which to build. Enough of an impulse was given to industry to have carried forward the movement of prosperity beyond 1879, even if succeeding years had not been equally favorable to our producing markets. But the good fortune of the American farmers did not end with 1879. Conforming to a principle old as the days of Pharaoh, Europe passed through a series of lean years, of which 1879 was only the first. The disastrous foreign shortage of that year was not indeed repeated, but the European harvests did not soon duplicate the yield of 1878 again. In 1880 the output of the world's chief wheat-producers rose some 30,000,000 bushels over that of 1878[2]; but this was solely because of a seventy-million bushel increase in the American harvest; so that this country still

[1] Circular to disbursing officers; *Specie Resumption*, p. 780.
[2] Liverpool *Corn Trade News* estimates.

had the advantage in the foreign trade. Even in 1881, when a good part of the American crop was destroyed by drought, the foreign harvest too ran short, and what our farmers could spare for export was sold at the highest prices in nine years.

The prosperity enjoyed by the United States was real, and its foundation solid; a fact which nothing proved more clearly than the manner in which the markets sustained reactions from excessive speculation. With all the increase in real capital and in commercial demand, the speculators forced prices repeatedly beyond the ability of capital to sustain or of demand to meet. Had it not been for the solid foundation underlying the trade revival of 1879, they would have wrecked the movement. They began with an attempt, in the winter months, to make their own price for wheat, and did succeed in forcing the market up to such a figure that for a time exports were actually blocked, and a fleet of grain vessels, sent to New York for charters, lay idle for weeks at the city wharves.[1] The result of this experiment was a demoralized wheat market, and eventually, in the early part of 1880, a break of thirty-four cents a bushel. In the iron market a similar attempt was made. The price at the close of 1879, after a rise of nearly one hundred per cent. in eight months, was $35 per ton; the speculators put it up to $42 by February, 1880, and by so doing attracted from every iron-producing foreign state not only huge supplies of new material, but of old scrap-

---

[1] New York Chamber of Commerce, *Annual Report*, 1880-81, p. 85.

iron.¹ Of course this bubble too collapsed; by June, the price had fallen to $23.

But after each of these speculative collapses, with the individual disasters which attended them, the underlying strength and healthfulness of the markets was asserted. The spectacular market for corporation shares was in a high degree typical of the general situation. This market broke sharply in November, 1879; in May and June of 1880, what seemed to be a sudden and wholesale wreck of values swept over the Stock Exchange. But from each of these reactions, which measured the previous excesses of the speculators, values recovered and moved up again under the stimulus of real investment, reaching eventually a much higher level. The movement of the railway shares responded normally to the immense increase in opportunities and profits for these enterprises, as the interior lands were opened up. Not even during the development of the Western States after the war did population of these districts in particular, and of the country as a whole, increase as rapidly as it did after resumption. Annual immigration doubled in 1880 as compared with 1879, and quadrupled in the next two years. The highest annual record in the country's previous history was 459,803, in the twelve months before the panic of 1873. In 1882, the immigration was 788,-992, a total which has never since been equalled, and nearly one third of that year's immigrants were Germans, the most useful of all our foreign population.

¹ New York Chamber of Commerce, *Annual Report*, 1880–81, p. 99.

This rapid interior development gave legitimate opportunity for extension of the transportation industry, and prompt use was made of it. Unfortunately, the spirit of speculation which pervaded all other markets governed the railway market also, and though it served at the time only to emphasize the seemingly irresistible movement of prosperity, its permanent results were mischievous in the extreme, and will be found playing an important part in episodes which we shall review later. The seeds of so many future disasters to this important industry were sown in the resumption period that it will be advisable to notice here exactly what happened at this epoch of its history. The performances of 1868 in the railway market were not, to be sure, repeated. The open robbery, the fraudulent stock issues, and the judicial corruption which marked the earlier history of the Erie, for instance, had disappeared with the other appurtenances of the vulgar inflation period. They were replaced, however, by another form of plunder on a larger scale. The combination of scattered railways, covering half a dozen interior States, into systems under single managements, was a normal and necessary outgrowth of the new expansion of the West. In many instances it was wisely and prudently managed. But with the prevalent spirit of speculation, it gave almost boundless opportunities to shrewd and unscrupulous capitalists with one hand on the Western railway coalitions and the other in the stock market.

Most unfortunately for the transportation industry, the leader in the movement was Jay Gould, whose disreputable record in the railway and gold markets of the inflation period made his appearance in the field after resumption sufficiently ominous. Few properties on which this man laid his hand escaped ruin in the end. He mastered more completely than any other promoter in our history the art of buying worthless railways for a song, selling them at fancy figures to a solvent corporation under his own control, and then so straining the credit and manipulating the books of the amalgamated company as to secure his own safe retreat through the stock market. He was not a builder, he was a destroyer, and the truth of this statement may be easily demonstrated by tracing out the subsequent history of the corporations which he got into his clutches. That Gould had a genius for making combinations is unquestionable; but in almost every instance—the Wabash Railway, the Union Pacific, the Missouri Pacific, and the elevated railways of New York City are notable examples—he obtained this power by tempting other men to join him in a speculation for personal profit acquired through methods which sapped the financial resources of the properties concerned. In some properties, as with the Western Union Telegraph, he forced a reputable concern to admit him to partnership through the shrewd and daring use of a species of corporation blackmail, in which he was always an adept. His favorite method of operation was exemplified in the purchase of the Kansas Pacific in 1880 by the Union Pacific on the basis of new Union Pacific stock exchanged on equal terms for shares of the smaller company, notwithstanding the fact that Kansas Pacific stock was earning nothing while Union Pacific was earning and paying six per cent. per annum. Gould and his confederates of course played this particular game through the stock market, where it was easily possible for any one aware of the purposes of the two companies to buy Kansas Pacific stock at nominal figures and sell it out in the advance accompanying the announcement of the combination. At the close of 1880, it was possible to say that Jay Gould controlled every important through railway route west and southwest of St. Louis, except the Atchison, Topeka, and Santa Fé and the Atlantic and Pacific.[1] The opportunities for mischief of this kind, with such power in the hands of such a man, were almost unlimited.

The reckoning for all this chapter of railway plunder came in 1893, when the extraordinary list of railway bankruptcies cannot easily be explained without tracing the history of the companies back to 1880. For other companies were bound to imitate the methods of this arch-plotter; going so far, in one notorious instance, as to sell to shareholders a new issue of six-per-cent. thirty-year bonds at twenty cents on the dollar, when the shares themselves were selling between 80 and par. Yet the extent to which all these companies continued to prosper and profit under this load of improperly incurred liabilities was perhaps the strongest of all testimony to the soundness of the trade revival. The Chicago, Rock Island, and Pacific company, for instance, doubled its stock in 1880 through a " scrip

[1] New York *Financial Chronicle*, January 8, 1881.

dividend" of one hundred per cent., and continued to pay seven per cent. per annum on its doubled stock; the Louisville and Nashville paid six, after a similar increase ; the Chicago, Burlington, and Quincy, after a twenty-per-cent. "stock dividend," paid eight per cent. Actual increase in the total stock and bonds of railways in the United States, during 1880, was $524,411,843 ; but net earnings increased no less than $39,000,000.[1]

What was true of railway profits was true also in other lines of trade, and 1880 was undoubtedly the most prosperous year of the generation. This may be fairly judged by that faithful index, the record of business failures. In 1878, there were 10,478 such commercial deaths; in 1880, there were only 4735. The liabilities involved fell from $234,383,-000 in 1878 to $65,752,000 in 1880.[2] The people were contented, employment was abundant, and the industrial agitation of the preceding years had apparently disappeared.

No one who has followed thoughtfully the influence of trade conditions on the sentiment of voters, as already reviewed in our study of 1866, of 1874, and of 1878, will doubt what was the reasonable political expectation after the trade revival of 1879 and 1880. If the elections of 1879 had been held in June, it is doubtful what the verdict would have been. Resumption was then denounced in many quarters as a failure. The best financial plea that the Ohio Republicans could put forward, in their

[1] Poor's *Manual of Railroads*, 1880.
[2] *Dun's Review*, annual tables.

convention platform of May 28th, was the saving of interest charges through the Administration's refunding operations. On June 4th, the Democrats of that State retorted by demanding " the full restoration of silver . . . as a money metal," and " the gradual substitution of Treasury notes for national bank currency," and by nominating for Governor Thomas Ewing, the author of the bill of 1877 to repeal the Resumption Act. This attitude was imitated, to a greater or less extent, by the opposition party in other Western States. It affected even the East. On July 1st, the Democrats of Maine declared for " the free and unlimited coinage of silver"; as late as July 16th, the Pennsylvania Democrats adopted a platform framed to suit anybody and mean anything on the currency.

But the situation, long before election day, was wholly reversed. By the early autumn months, the Administration could point out results following specie resumption even larger than what had been promised in advance,—a very unusual advantage. In 1878, the party had lost heavily in many Western constituencies; mainly, as we have seen, because of the low price of grain. In 1879, election day came at the very climax of a violent rise in agricultural prices, paid for the largest crops ever produced in the United States. Naturally, the autumn party declarations changed their tone along with the rapidly changing business outlook. The proclamations of Republican conventions began to strike a note of triumph. " We congratulate our fellow-citizens upon the restoration of confidence and the revival of business," were the words in which the Massachusetts convention of September 16th introduced its eulogy of the Administration. "The successful resumption of specie payments . . . followed by returning national prosperity," was the theme of the New York Republican declaration on September 2d. As in the preceding year, so in 1879, the autumn Democratic conventions in the East were forced to a sullen echo of this rejoicing.[1] There was an occasional effort, such as that of the New York State Democratic convention of September 11th, to divert the issue into condemnation of the Secretary's "speculative methods," "questionable favoritism" to particular institutions, and "extravagance" in refunding. In the West, the opposition, engaged in the same losing fight against the odds of a great harvest and a profitable grain market, declared that the Treasury's achievement was a stroke of luck. "Now that resumption is a success," Secretary Sherman himself remarked in a campaign speech, "Democrats say the Republican party did not bring it about, but that Providence has done it; that bountiful crops here and bad crops in Europe have been the cause of all the prosperity that has come since resumption."[2]

As we have seen, there was more or less truth in this allegation. But the public mind does not trouble itself with such subtleties; it rewards or punishes, usually, on a strict basis of *post-hoc* reasoning, and in the vote of 1879 it recognized properly enough the

[1] Massachusetts Democratic convention, October 7, 1879.
[2] Speech at Cooper Union, New York, October 27, 1879.

really great achievement of the Administration. The three political battle-grounds of the year were Maine, Ohio, and New York, in each of which States a Governor was to be elected. Maine led off in September with a Republican plurality 6000 greater than in 1878. Ewing was beaten in Ohio by a plurality of 17,129, the Republican plurality of the year before having been only 3154. In New York State the opposition party had already split up into factions, and Cornell was elected by the sweeping plurality of 42,777, the largest Republican majority in the State since 1872. Meantime the Western States, which had gone quite uniformly against the Administration in 1878, made a similar response. In Michigan, one of the largest winter-wheat-producing States, a fusion of Democrats and Greenbackers, whose votes combined would in the previous year have carried the State by 25,000, was squarely beaten in November, 1879, by a Republican majority of 6043. In Iowa, the corn-growing State, the Administration majority increased over 1878 by 14,221 votes.

The Administration's victory was complete. After five years of almost uninterrupted contest over the standard of value, the battle was ended. This fact was tacitly conceded in the Presidential platforms of both parties during the summer of 1880. On the 6th of June the Republican National Convention at Chicago endorsed in the most unqualified language the financial achievement of the Hayes Administration. Both the Stanley Matthews wing of Republicanism and the timid jugglers with the issue in the

Western Republican conventions of 1878 and 1879 were repudiated; there was not inserted in the party's Chicago platform of 1880 a single word to favor even silver coinage. Instead, appeal was made in behalf of a party which had " raised the value of our paper currency," " restored upon a solid basis payment in coin for all national obligations," and " lifted the credit of the nation." No protest was made against these declarations, even by those unlucky Republicans who had sustained the Congressional resolution, two years before, to pay the Government bonds in silver, and who had urged repeal of the Resumption Act. Still more significant was the platform of the Democratic party at Cincinnati, three weeks later: whose only declaration on the currency was a plank for " honest money, consisting of gold and silver, and paper convertible into coin on demand; the strict maintenance of the public faith." In short, what the Hayes Administration had achieved, the Administration party, reasonably enough, appropriated to its own advantage, and the opposition could not contest its right to do so.

Except for the disputed claim involved in the 1876 election, the party had small reason to apprehend the national vote of November, 1880. The event proved even this misgiving to have been exaggerated. But for this same clouded title, President Hayes would logically have sought renomination, and would have deserved it. When Mr. Hayes refused to submit his name, there seemed to be some probability that Secretary Sherman's services would be recognized by the nomination. But there was an instinctive distrust of Mr. Sherman in his own party, which can only be explained by his record as a political opportunist in the years before his Cabinet career. Those who did not question his sincerity doubted his stability—a doubt not wholly unwarranted by his repeated change of front before what seemed to be the ruling popular sentiment. There was, moreover, an equally instinctive feeling that the nominee of the Chicago convention would certainly be the winner at the polls in November. This conviction always leads to a sharp convention struggle. Into the details of the very singular preliminary contest at Chicago it is needless to enter here. Only on the thirty-sixth convention ballot was the deadlock between the adherents of Secretary Sherman, of ex-President Grant, and of Mr. James G. Blaine broken by concentration upon General Garfield of nearly all delegates, except the Grant contingent.

At Cincinnati, three weeks later, the National Democratic convention was a gathering as tame as the Chicago convention had been exciting. The rank and file were full enough of confidence, but the party's experienced leaders were well aware that with industrial contentment on all sides their case was hopeless. The manner in which a candidate manœuvres for the nomination, or his friends in his behalf, is governed wholly by the prospect of success. For nomination and defeat, especially if the defeat be overwhelming, commonly lead in the United States to political oblivion. In the party's National Convention of 1868, with a somewhat parallel situation, nearly all of the shrewdest Democratic leaders avoided nomination, and Horatio Seymour was eventually forced to take it against his will. The case of 1880 was similar. The party's strongest candidates were named to the Convention in a perfunctory way, there was little or no contest, and on the second ballot General Hancock, who with his purely military record had nothing to lose through a political defeat, was readily placed in nomination. The result of the November ballots amply justified such misgivings. Against the 185 electoral votes awarded to Hayes in 1876, Garfield in 1880 captured 214. Tilden, in 1876, obtained on popular vote a plurality over Hayes, even by the Republican count, of 252,224; Garfield's plurality over Hancock, in 1880, was 9464.

The party whose most sagacious leaders had fought and won the resumption battle seemed, in brief, to be surely seated in the control of public matters, from which the panic of 1873 and the resultant trade stagnation had so nearly banished it. But the problem of the currency remained. The silver question was not the only cloud on the party's horizon. The problem of resumption had been solved for 1880, and for many subsequent years, by a happy accident of nature. Far-sighted public men recognized, however, even at the climax of the party triumph of 1880, that the system on which resumption had been founded still left the national finances at the mercy of future commercial accidents. In almost the last official papers of the Hayes Administration occur two declarations very remarkable for their positive contradiction of one another. In his annual Treasury report of December 6, 1880, Secretary Sherman remarked: " United States notes are now, in form, security, and convenience, the best circulating medium known."[1] In his message to Congress on the same day, President Hayes declared : " The retirement from circulation of United States notes is a step to be taken in our progress towards a safe and stable currency, which should be accepted as the policy and duty of the Government and the interest and security of the people." The President, in short, condemned as unsafe and mischievous a currency which his financial minister, enjoying the full personal confidence of the President,[2] declared to be safe, satisfactory, and worthy of perpetuation. The incident was sufficiently singular; one of the two responsible leaders in the financial reform of 1879 must have been mistaken. We shall discover, before our study of the ensuing period is completed, which of the two was right.

[1] *Annual Treas. Rep.*, 1880, p. xiv.
[2] *Recollections*, ii., p. 808.

CHAPTER IV

THE SILVER PROBLEM

ALTHOUGH President Hayes and his Secretary of the Treasury differed radically in their opinion of the legal tenders, they were agreed, at the close of the Administration, in their judgment regarding compulsory coinage of silver dollars. This was the more noteworthy, in view of Mr. Sherman's expressed disapproval of the President's veto message of 1878. But the Secretary had begun to change his own mind, even before the year was over. When the Act of 1878 was passed, Mr. Sherman held that the Senate amendments " seemed to remove all serious objections to the measure."[1] A few months later, he took a very different view. He began by suggesting compromises, recommending, first, " the addition of one tenth or one eighth to the thickness of the silver dollar,"[2]—a singular proposition to make on a steadily declining silver market, and one for which, curiously enough, he obtained the President's approval.[3] Congress having paid no attention to this proposition, the Secretary made a still more

[1] *Recollections*, ii., p. 623. [2] *Treas. Rep.*, 1878, p. xvi.
[3] President Hayes, Annual Message, December 6, 1880.

definite appeal for the "importance of further limiting the coinage of the silver dollar."[1] But the Law of 1878 was left in force, and so rapidly now did the Secretary's misgivings deepen, that in the summer of 1880 he privately declared that "the silver law threatens to produce within a year or so a single silver standard. . . . I could at any moment, by issuing silver freely, bring a crisis."[2]

Let us see what was the reason for this remarkably pessimistic judgment, at the very time when outside trade was moving towards the high tide of prosperity. When President Hayes vetoed the Silver Act of 1878, he expressed his judgment that circulation of a dollar worth intrinsically less than the gold dollar would sooner or later " put an end to the receipt of the revenue in gold," and thus deprive the Government of the means of paying its gold obligations.[3] It was this objection to the law which presently turned out to be the matter of serious concern. The Silver Coinage Act had been only a very short time in operation before the President's prediction was confirmed by the movement of events.

The legal-tender notes were redeemable in coin, and since the Resumption Act was passed when the only authorized United States coin, except the trade dollar, was gold, it was quite universally conceded that gold redemption was peremptory. Even the Congressional resolution of January, 1878, which declared for silver payment on the bonds, had made

[1] *Treas. Rep.*, 1879, p. xiv.; 1878, p. xv.
[2] Letter to James A. Garfield, July 19, 1880.
[3] Veto Message, February 28, 1878.

no such suggestion regarding the legal-tender notes. Being redeemable in gold, the notes could not depreciate so long as the Treasury had the power and means of providing gold for such redemption. They therefore circulated freely, and were not only used for banking purposes in the cities, but were absorbed in the every-day interior exchanges, being easily portable and issued in convenient denominations.

But the silver dollars established by the Law of 1878 stood on a different basis. To begin with, it developed almost immediately that the people did not want this heavy coin for their every-day change. If any kind of currency is needed constantly by the customers of a bank, it is the business of the bank to keep that currency on hand. But if its customers do not want a given kind of currency, and ask for something different, the bank will necessarily try to pass over to other institutions the currency not in request among its depositors. This is exactly what occurred with the silver dollars throughout the United States. City and country trade alike objected to settlements in the silver dollars. At the time, the legal tenders forwarded from the East were sufficient as a basis for trade exchanges; the silver dollars were not necessary, as they might have been with materially larger trade. Every bank of deposit, therefore, passed them along at the earliest opportunity to its neighbor. Eventually, as President Hayes had predicted in his veto message, silver began to fill the channels of public revenue, which are the final outlet for a superfluous or unpopular currency. As early as 1880, it had proved to be impossible to keep in circulation more than thirty-five per cent. of the dollars coined.¹

Now it is true that what the Treasury receives in revenue—whether paper, gold, or silver—it can pay out again for public expenses. If the silver dollars would not circulate in the interior, they could be forced into circulation at the large Eastern disbursing centres, especially at New York, where the National Government's monthly expenditure at the time ran as high as twenty to thirty millions. But for a very interesting reason, this outlet was virtually blocked. The New York Sub-Treasury, it will be recalled, was a member of the Clearing-House of the New York Associated Banks. On November 12, 1878, when the Clearing-House admitted the Sub-Treasury to membership, and arranged for the free exchange of United States notes and gold, it formally resolved to " prohibit payment of balances at the Clearing-House in silver certificates, or in silver dollars, except as subsidiary coin, in small sums." ² To this condition the Treasury authorities had raised no objection.³

So long as the silver circulation was small, and the return of the silver coin from interior circulation had not yet become active, the New York Clearing-House rule was regarded as a mere routine banking arrangement. When, however, silver dollars began to crowd the channels of public

---

[1] Secretary Sherman, *Treas. Rep.*, 1880, p. xviii.
[2] *Specie Resumption*, p. 401.
[3] Sherman to George S. Coe, November 13, 1878; *Specie Resumption*, p. 402.

revenue, the Treasury's inability to get rid of its silver through the Clearing-House became a matter of considerable moment. Its stock of legal tenders was already very low, and except for the legal-tender notes, gold was the only medium for these New York payments. As a result, the silver surplus in the Treasury increased during the early months of 1880 with great rapidity, while its surplus gold fund, which had been materially enlarged during the harvest movement of the previous autumn, decreased even faster. With the Treasury's mass of gold obligations, this was a serious sign of danger.

This policy of the New York Clearing-House came in for a round of angry denunciation on the floor of Congress. It was declared to be a conspiracy of Eastern bankers, designed, first, to discredit the silver currency, and second, to get the advantage of the Treasury. It was formally proscribed in July, 1882, when the twenty-year charters of the national banks, about to expire under the banking law, were renewed by Congress. In granting extension of these charters, Congress added the positive stipulation that " no national banking association shall be a member of any clearing-house in which such [silver] certificates shall not be received in settlement of clearing-house balances."

In all this controversy, the New York banks seemed to be on the defensive. Let us see, however, what was their actual motive. The New York banks perform for the United States the office which the London banks perform for England; they manage the country's settlements on foreign exchange and they act both as depositories and remitters of funds for the interior. We have seen that the interior banks and their customers did not wish the silver currency; silver dollars were therefore superfluous in New York reserves for their inland business. But, on the other hand, silver dollars were useless, except at a heavy discount, for settlements in foreign exchange. Had the silver dollars, like the legal tenders, being convertible at the Treasury into gold, the problem would have been somewhat altered; but they were not thus convertible.[1] If the silver dollar's bullion value had advanced to equality with the gold dollar, either coin might possibly have been used for remittance against bankers' exchange. But there was no such advance. The purchase of silver bullion enough to coin two million dollars monthly did indeed temporarily raise the price of silver. The rise, however, was only slight. There was an instant increase in the output of the silver mines, production in 1878 rising four million ounces over the previous year in the United States and eleven million in the world at large. India and China, which had absorbed £17,000,000 silver from the London export market in 1877, took in the next year only £5,842,000.[2] Even without allowing for the sales of old coin by the German Government, the new demand for coinage purposes by the United States Treasury was more than offset by these plain commercial factors.

[1] Secretary Sherman, letter to President of New Orleans Clearing-House, December 10, 1878 ; *Specie Resumption*, p. 420.
[2] Pixley & Abell, annual London tables.

These influences, it may be observed, were continuous; export of silver to the East never again reached the total of 1877, and within twelve years the world's annual product had exactly doubled.[1] Even in 1878, the average intrinsic value of the silver dollar on the bullion market was barely eighty-nine cents; in 1879, it was less than eighty-seven.[2] The silver coin was unavailable, therefore, for settlements in foreign exchange, except at a discount of twelve per cent. or more. It was rejected from interior circulation. In the event of a year of dull interior trade, it was reasonably certain, first that the surplus silver currency of the interior would heap up at New York City, and second, that gold shipments to Europe would grow heavy. If to this double movement were to be added Government disbursements wholly or chiefly in silver dollars, the time must eventually come when all the bank exchanges at New York would be conducted in silver coin. That this was no idle fear, but a correct view of the situation, the experience with another form of redundant currency proved conclusively in 1892.

But the inevitable result of such conversion of the New York banking reserve into silver coin worth intrinsically less than gold would be that gold for purposes of foreign settlements could be had only at a premium. In other words, the entire currency would depreciate. It was to avert this possibility that the Clearing-House framed its rule of 1878. It was a most unusual move, and it could hardly in the

[1] U. S. Mint, *Annual Reports*.   [2] *Ibid*.

end have prevented a fall to the silver standard, if the country had remained unable to absorb the two millions' monthly coinage. At New York, nevertheless, it was regarded as a measure of self-preservation, and this was what Secretary Sherman meant when he said in 1880 that by issuing silver freely he could at any time bring on a crisis. Both the banks and the Treasury recognized the nature of the situation, even in 1882. When the New York Clearing-House, after the passage of the law forbidding national banks to co-operate in a clearing-house which excluded silver, resolved that the institution's rules " be amended so far as they conflict with section 12 of the Act of July 12, 1882," not only did no bank take advantage of the opportunity to tender silver for its balances, but the Treasury itself, in its transactions with the Clearing-House, pursued exactly the same policy.[1] It pursued it, notwithstanding the fact that the return of silver currency from circulation, in the nine months after the harvest season of 1879, increased the Government's silver surplus eleven million dollars, while its gold reserve, which had to be drawn upon for Eastern settlements, declined from $157,-000,000 to $115,000,000.

But the crisis predicted by Mr. Sherman did not come, and we shall readily discover why. The trouble in the summer of 1880 arose partly from the fact that the new silver issues were in excess of the needs of interior trade. But a money supply which is sufficient, or even superfluous, for the trade ex-

[1] Treasurer Wyman, *Treas. Rep.*, 1884, p. 414.

changes of one season, may be only large enough in another, when the volume of trade has greatly expanded. Something like this happened in the autumn of 1880, when interior trade, as we have seen, rose to unprecedented volume. Not only did the West and South retain in permanent circulation a large part of the legal-tender notes shipped to them in the harvest movement of 1879, but they now drew heavily on the East for fresh remittances. Again, as is usual under such conditions, the Eastern banks drew gold from Europe and shipped their own legal tenders inland. But the absorption of Government notes in the two preceding active seasons had largely drained the East of this form of currency. During the autumn of 1880, the legal-tender reserve of the New York banks fell to the very low aggregate of $11,989,000, only half as much as they had held a year before.[1] Their gold holdings, on the other hand, were very large, and they now applied to the Treasury, as they had done in 1879, to exchange its own surplus of legal-tender notes for gold.

Meantime, however, the very causes which had drained off the legal tenders from the Eastern banks had also reduced the Treasury's supply to small proportions. At the close of 1880 the Government held less of the legal tenders even than the New York banks. This was the opportunity for relieving the Treasury's stock of idle silver, and it was promptly utilized. In September, 1880, Secretary Sherman offered, in return for deposit of gold at seaboard

[1] Weekly statement, New York Associated Banks, November 6, 1880.

cities, to supply exchange on interior sub-treasuries, payable at those points in silver coin. The offer, under the circumstances, was very generally accepted. The silver shipments, it is true, were expensive to the Government, and the coin, even when delivered, would not stay in circulation, but was promptly tendered again for silver certificates.[1] This was interesting evidence, at the height of the interior demand for currency, that silver dollars were unpopular, even in quarters where the silver advocates had pictured the trade as eager for that form of currency. The silver certificates, under the Law of 1878, could not be issued in denominations smaller than ten dollars ; nevertheless, these bills were obviously preferred to the coin itself by the interior trade. But even in this form, the operation served the Treasury's purposes. During the twelve months following the issue of the circular, this arrangement with the Eastern banks put $23,560,000 of the Government's silver surplus into circulation from the sub-treasuries of New Orleans, St. Louis, Cincinnati, and Chicago, and replaced it with imported gold.[2] In the five last months of 1880—almost immediately after Mr. Sherman's despondent prophecy,—the silver surplus in the Treasury fell from $46,256,000 to $18,246,000, and its surplus gold fund rose from $115,000,000 to $150,000,000. The danger of a silver standard had apparently disappeared.

I have gone thus fully into this introductory silver-coinage episode, at the risk of wearying the reader

---
[1] Treasurer Gilfillan, *Annual Treas. Rep.*, 1881, p. 429.
[2] *Ibid.*, p. 436.

with particulars, because no chapter of our financial history is so widely misunderstood. The fact that the Eastern banks in 1878 and 1879 virtually refused to accept silver dollars from the Treasury, whereas in 1880 they paid gold for them, is often cited as proof that the Clearing-House rule against silver payments was unwarranted. From the fact that the interior trade absorbed the silver currency in the autumn of 1880, it has been inferred that only the opposition of the banks prevented its ready interior circulation a year before. The reader will now, I think, be able to understand the reason for both these seeming discrepancies. The silver currency was superfluous in the spring of 1880; therefore it was thrown back upon the Treasury and the East. It was not superfluous in the winter of 1880, because the volume of trade had expanded even more rapidly than the increase in the currency. Obviously, the question of the future was, whether interior trade would continue to expand with sufficient uniformity to absorb the $25,000,000 annual silver coinage of the future, as it had apparently absorbed the coinage of 1880.

There were some signs of a change in the movement of prosperity, as early as 1881. Most people, in succeeding years, were accustomed to date back the " turn of the tide " to the assassination of President Garfield on July 2, 1881. Undoubtedly this event was a shock to the financial markets; particularly to markets in which excited speculation for the rise had cut so large a figure as it did in those of 1880 and 1881. But Garfield's death was not a decisive influence on the situation; it was in fact a coincidence rather than a cause. A far more permanent influence was exerted by the destructive drought of 1881 in the entire harvest district of the United States. The country's wheat crop of that year turned out only three fourths as large as the crop of 1880; its corn crop was the smallest since 1874.[1]

To the farmers, there was an unexpected compensation for this shortage; a wet harvest season in England and on the European continent cut down the wheat yield of the foreign producers also. Foreign and home demand for grain was very heavy, and what could be spared for export was sold at high prices. According to the Agricultural Bureau's estimate, the total market value of the year's American grain harvest, small as its volume was, exceeded the value even of the great crop of 1880. But in two other directions, the harvest shortage of 1881 had more unpleasant results. The railways suffered severely from the decrease of grain supplies on which they relied for traffic. Their freight earnings, in the ensuing year, decreased no less than $45,600,000.[2] At the same time, the scarcity of grain for export cut down the country's export trade. This happened at a time when imports of foreign merchandise had been excessively stimulated by the protracted speculation for the rise in almost every market, and, as a consequence, the excess of exports over imports, which in the twelve

[1] *Annual Reports*, U. S. Bureau of Agriculture.
[2] Poor's *Manual of Railroads*, 1882.

months ending with June, 1881, had reached the
enormous sum of $259,700,000, fell in the next
twelve months to less than $26,000,000. By the
close of 1881, the foreign exchanges, so long held
down in favor of the United States, began to move
against us. By March, 1882, heavy export of gold
began; before the close of the fiscal year, in June,
$32,500,000 had been shipped,—the largest export
of gold since 1876.

This decided change in foreign trade meant, of
course, that the country's command over foreign
capital was lessened. But the impetus to industrial
prosperity, in the two preceding years, had been so
great that the reaction was slow in developing.
What was lost in foreign capital seemed to be made
up in home support, and the earlier markets of 1882
appeared to reflect actually increased prosperity.
So far as prices were an index to the situation, the
average level of 1882, on all the American commodity markets, was the highest in half a dozen years.[1]
Unfortunately, these very commodity prices were
fixed and sustained by the use of credit on a highly
speculative basis. "It could not be regarded as a
favorable circumstance," one contemporary critic
wrote, in reviewing 1882, "that so many parties in
various kinds of business, and even professional men,
were engaged in carrying stocks, produce, cotton,
petroleum, and so forth, on margin."[2] Before the
year was half over a movement of liquidation was apparent. It was disguised, as such operations always

[1] *U. S. Senate Report on Prices and Wages*, p. 9.
[2] New York *Financial Chronicle*, January 6, 1883.

are, but the facts might easily be inferred from actual results. The investment markets were then, as usual, typical of the general situation. During a good part of the year, the strongest capitalists and speculators were kept busy denying reports that they had been selling securities. Most of them, like Mr. William H. Vanderbilt, answered the accusation by liberal predictions of prices still higher than the inflated values lately prevalent. Mr. Jay Gould evolved the characteristic expedient of exhibiting to a select committee the contents of his safe, comprising $53,000,000 railway and telegraph share certificates made out in his own name. This, too, was designed to prove that the owner of the shares was not a seller. Nothing, however, to an experienced eye, could better have proved the existence of liquidation than these careful efforts to disprove it. As a matter of fact, all of the markets were moving downward by the middle of 1882. In the produce markets, the movement was emphatic, and it reflected the very patent fact that the United States was now losing the singular advantage which it had for three years enjoyed in the foreign trade. The American grain harvest of 1882 was only a trifle smaller than the great harvest of 1880. But in 1880 the European crops ran short, whereas in 1882 the foreign states produced the largest total wheat crop in their history.[1] For the first time since 1878, the American farmer met urgent competition in the export market, and the price of wheat, which in May, 1882, had touched $1.40 per bushel in Chicago, fell in December to 91½ cents.

[1] Liverpool *Corn-Trade News* estimates.

The cotton crop met with an exactly similar experience, the American yield of 1882 being by far the largest on record, in the face of flagging demand from the foreign cotton-spinners.[1] In almost every staple market, the course of events was identical; notably in the iron and steel trade, where production and speculation had been forced to the highest pitch at the moment when, as a result of 1881's unsatisfactory earnings, orders for new railway construction slackened.[2] In short, production in the majority of industries had outrun consumption; a readjustment of prices was inevitable, and producers who were slowest to reduce their prices had to make in the end the largest sacrifice. Meantime the wind was rushing out of the balloon of American speculation.

The bearing of this altered trade situation on the silver-currency problem we shall presently notice. For the time, the currency problem was in a considerable measure obscured by the question of the surplus revenue. The enormous importations of foreign merchandise, which in 1882 were larger by sixty per cent. than those of 1879, and the consequent increase of the customs, had now introduced that unique problem of American finance, a revenue too large to be conveniently disposed of. The surplus of public revenue over expenditure was $6,879,300 in the fiscal year 1879; in 1882 it was $145,543,810. Now it is true that the funded debt

[1] Ellison's *Annual Cotton Review*, January, 1883.
[2] *Annual Reports*, American Iron and Steel Association, 1882, 1883.

of the United States, even after the large redemption of bonds in the ten preceding years, remained at a billion and a half of dollars, and that nearly one third of these outstanding bonds were redeemable at par at the pleasure of the Government.[1] But the surplus revenue, if continued at the annual rate of 1882, would extinguish all this redeemable debt within three years, leaving no outlet for the surplus except purchase of unmatured bonds at whatever price they commanded in the market, or enormous increase in expenditure.[2]

The Administration reasoned that such an outlook pointed distinctly to reduction of the taxes, and to that end the President and the Secretary of the Treasury earnestly urged on Congress a revision of the customs tariff.[3] President Arthur went beyond the mere question of the surplus, and submitted a strong plea for the relief of " industry and enterprise from the pressure of unnecessary taxation." Unfortunately for this apparently reasonable advice, the customs taxes were protective, and the Republican party, then in power in all branches of the Government, was committed to protection. Rather than reduce the surplus revenue, therefore, Congress began to spend it. Out of the forty-four millions increase in the annual Government expenditure, between 1879 and 1883, only a trifling part arose from

---

[1] Secretary Folger, *Treas. Rep.*, 1882, pp. xxx., xxxi.
[2] *Ibid.*
[3] President Arthur, Annual Messages, December 6, 1881, December 4, 1882 ; Secretary Folger, *Annual Treas. Rep.*, 1882, pp. xxvii., xxix.

larger outlay for the Civil List, the Federal armament, or the Indians. In 1872, when reporting the session's appropriation bill, General Garfield had declared in the House of Representatives: " We may reasonably expect that the expenditures for pensions will hereafter steadily decrease, unless our legislation should be unwarrantably extravagant."[1] And in fact, between 1872 and 1878 the annual expenditure of the Pension Bureau did decrease some seven millions.

Now, however, the annual disbursement on that account increased from $27,137,019 in 1878 to $61,345,193 in 1882, and the new Congress, in its session during the spring of 1882, appropriated for pensions in the ensuing fiscal year no less a sum than $100,000,000. In similar spirit, these legislators had applied themselves to Federal outlay for river and harbor work. During previous administrations, such appropriations had ranged from $3,975,000 in the session of 1870 to $8,201,700 in 1878. The budget began to rise, even before the Forty-seventh Congress, elected in 1880, came into power; but this body, once assembled, broke all records. In its first session, river and harbor appropriations reached the wholly unprecedented sum of $18,743,875. Angry criticism at this extravagance was already spreading in the press and in popular discussion, and the nature of the policy now pursued by Congress was powerfully illustrated by the veto episode of 1882. In August of that year, President Arthur refused his signature to the River

[1] *Congressional Globe*, January 23, 1872.

and Harbor Bill, on the grounds of its unconstitutionality and unwarranted diversion of public funds.¹ Within twenty-four hours the bill was passed over this Presidential veto, and the majority of votes to override the veto came from Administration Congressmen.

This incident happened at an unfortunate moment for the ruling party. Up to this time the annual elections had been influenced by the remarkable prosperity of the country, which served, as such conditions usually do, to sustain the popular approval of the party in power. Severe reactions of public sentiment are not unusual in the year after a Presidential victory; but the vote of November, 1881, had been decidedly favorable to the Republican party. Even in such States as Ohio, New Jersey, Iowa, Wisconsin, and Michigan, the dominant party had retained its advantage of 1880. We have seen, however, that the trade advantage was largely lost before the autumn of 1882. The fall in wheat and cotton, however inevitable, had aroused a feeling of discontent in the West and South. In the East, the large gold exports and the irregular money market had embarrassed trade sufficiently to make the people willing to listen to criticism of public policy. When the action of Congress was as vulnerable to criticism as was that of the spring session of 1882, it is not surprising that the opposition party made the recent legislative extravagance the text of its campaign declarations. Partisan use of the " spoils " of 1880, and the very rash attempt of the Executive to control

¹ Veto Message, August 1, 1882.

the nomination for Governor of New York, were also called into public question; but since Congressional elections were impending, the record of Congress itself naturally played the leading part. The Republicans themselves could not fail to recognize the importance of this issue. So peculiarly embarrassing was the veto episode to the Administration party, that even the New York Republican State convention formally applauded the President's " courage in resisting the enactment of the River and Harbor Bill, which violated the accepted rules of constitutional power." [1]

This was hardly a serviceable " plank " for a Congressional campaign. Meantime the opposition not only assailed the extravagant expenditures, but demanded that the excessive revenue which made them possible should be cut down by remission of taxation. In short, the Administration party, no longer helped by seemingly unlimited prosperity, was clearly on the defensive, and the result was an overwhelming Republican defeat. A Republican plurality of twelve in the Forty-seventh Congress was turned in the Forty-eighth into a Democratic plurality of seventy-seven. Congressional delegations from States such as New York and Ohio, in which a large majority of the successful candidates in 1880 had been Republicans, were returned in 1882 with an almost equally large majority of Democrats. Alonzo B. Cornell had been elected Governor in New York State in 1879 by a Republican plurality of 42,777; in 1882, Grover Cleveland was chosen Governor on the

[1] September 21, 1882.

Democratic ticket by a plurality of 192,854. Robert E. Pattison, running for Governor of Pennsylvania on the Democratic ticket, carried that Republican stronghold by 40,202 plurality. In States as widely separated as Connecticut, Michigan, Kansas, Colorado, and California, the Democrats reversed majorities from the previous elections and carried their candidates for Governor into office. The tide of political reaction ran so high in Massachusetts that General B. F. Butler, who had captured the Democratic nomination despite his inflationist record, was chosen Governor by a plurality of 13,949.

This sweeping opposition victory was at once accepted as a verdict for revision of the revenue. It was publicly admitted, even by recognized friends of the protective system, that a " substantial reduction of tariff duties " was " demanded, not by a mere indiscriminate popular clamor, but by the best conservative opinion of the country."[1] In Congress, however, there was a strong minority, determined to resist, by whatever means, any concession from the protective-tariff theory. This faction had so far anticipated the situation as to secure in May, 1882, the appointment of nine commissioners from civil life to investigate the entire question of the tariff, and to report its findings to Congress in December. The move was clever; for the President named a protectionist commission, with the president of the Wool Manufacturers' Association at its head,[2] and when Congress assembled in December, the com-

[1] *Report of Tariff Commission*, 1882, i., p. 5.
[2] Taussig, *Tariff History of the United States*, pp. 230–233.

mission's voluminous report and recommended bill were ready.

The commission's recommendations were not, however, altogether what its creators had expected. According to its own statement to Congress, the commission's bill aimed at an average reduction in tariff rates of not less than twenty per cent.[1] This proposed reduction, as the president of the commission afterwards declared, was an unwilling "concession to public sentiment,"[2] and the uncompromising faction did some singular work with it in Congress. The commission bill was either blockaded or radically altered, first in one house and then, on a different basis, in the other. Eventually the House and Senate disagreed, whereupon a conference committee, after a plan which later gained even more celebrity, settled a compromise by raising duties higher than those proposed by either branch of Congress.[3] In the end, while numerous duties—those on cloths especially—were reduced, other and equally important tariffs, such as those on metal manufactures, were materially increased. Since it was doubtful if these conflicting changes in the import duties would reduce the revenue, Congress applied itself to the internal taxes. Under the Revenue Act of 1872, with its later amendments, manufactured cigars had been assessed six dollars per thousand, and had

---

[1] *Report of Tariff Commission*, 1882, i., p. 6.

[2] John L. Hayes in *Bulletin of Wool Manufacturers*, quoted in Taussig, p. 254.

[3] W. R. Morrison, House of Representatives speech, March 3, 1883; J. B. Beck, U. S. Senate speech, March 2, 1883.

yielded $18,000,000 annually; the tax was now reduced to three. On tobacco, the impost, which produced in 1882 $25,000,000, was cut down from sixteen cents a pound to eight.

There has been a curious fatality in the coincidence of tariff revision, in this country, with trade reaction. The Tariff Acts of 1872, of 1883, of 1890, and of 1894, in every case accompanied or shortly preceded a period of serious commercial distress, and the coincidence has been plausibly used by opponents of revenue revision. Now it cannot well be questioned that the American practice of ripping up by wholesale a complicated import tariff runs two very serious risks. It is pretty sure to derange at least one season's plans in the industries affected, and it is apt to make a bad miscalculation as to future public revenue. Of this second possibility, we shall find some very forcible examples in our review of 1890 and 1894. How far, if at all, these later measures were a factor in the subsequent trade reactions, we shall then inquire. It has been very commonly asserted that the change of import duties during 1883 had such unfavorable influence. The Tariff Act became a law in March, 1883; public revenue decreased $50,000,000 in the twelve months ending with June, 1884, and something like $25,000,000 in the fiscal year 1885; and in 1884 the financial situation reached a crisis. To those who opposed any change in the protective-tariff system, the inference was accordingly drawn, that the tariff changes caused the trade reaction.

Yet the argument as applied to 1883 has absolutely

no foundation. The reduction in revenue, to begin with, was no larger than the advocates of an altered tariff, including the Secretary of the Treasury, had originally recommended.¹ Under the Act of 1883, the revenue reached its lowest point in the fiscal year 1885; yet there was a surplus revenue, even in that year, of $63,463,771—larger by thirty per cent. than the requirements of the Sinking Fund. The bulk of such reductions as were actually made by Congress came, as the framers of the Law of 1883 intended, in the excise schedules. The Administration had opposed reduction of these taxes, which were a charge, not on necessities but on luxuries, and the change was nowhere seriously advocated in the electoral campaign of 1882.² But Congress, under the influences already noticed, wholly ignored such well-known facts.

Nothing can better prove the purpose of the legislators than the original title of the Law of 1883: " a bill to reduce internal taxation." We have seen already that taxes on tobacco manufactures were reduced forty to fifty per cent.; in the preceding fiscal year they had yielded $47,000,000 revenue. Taxes on bank deposits, capital, and checks, and on other miscellaneous objects, had hitherto yielded annually upwards of $10,000,000; these taxes were abolished. Here, then, was $31,-000,000 struck off deliberately,³ without considering

---

[1] Secretary Folger, *Treas. Rep.*, 1882, p. xxix.

[2] President Arthur, Annual Message, December 4, 1882; Secretary Folger, *Treas. Rep.*, 1882, p. xxxi.

[3] Commissioner of Internal Revenue, *Treas. Rep.*, 1882, p. 73; 1884, p. 79.

the movement of the customs revenue. But the conclusive proof that changes in the import duties did not affect the fall in revenue is shown by the average rate imposed and collected before and after the Act of 1883. By the official record, average rate of duty actually collected during the fiscal year 1883 (less than four months of which came under the new tariff) was 42.45 per cent., whereas in 1885 the average rate had risen to 45.86.[1]

The financial troubles of 1884, then, did not in any respect arise from changes in the tariff. What did occasion the misgivings with which that year began is not at all difficult to discover. For the time had now arrived to test the question whether it was possible, with the existing supply of other forms of currency, to circulate twenty-five million new silver dollars annually. Even in 1882, the Treasury authorities warned Congress that the seeming demand for silver in the interior was artificial and temporary, and that, despite this demand, a slow but ominous displacement of the Treasury's gold with silver was already in progress.[2] Congress had replied only by its attempt to break down the prohibitory rule of the New York Clearing-House, and thus force the dollars into Eastern circulation.

After the very general reactions in the markets of 1882, the volume of interior trade decreased continuously; a logical outcome, certainly, of the dis-

[1] U. S. Bureau of Statistics, *Annual Rep.*, 1892, p. lxxvii.
[2] Secretary Folger, *Treas. Rep.*, 1882, pp. xii., xiii; Treasurer Gilfillan, *ibid.*, pp. 365, 369.

covery that production had far outrun the immediate home and foreign demand. Genuine trade demand for money, in any country, is accurately measured by the bank exchanges of a season at the commercial centres. Now in 1881, these exchanges in the leading American cities were larger by nearly sixty per cent. than those of 1879, and the decrease in 1882 was only slight. But total exchanges at the same points in 1883 decreased fourteen per cent. from 1882; in 1884, they fell off eighteen per cent. further.[1] While, therefore, the silver currency was increasing with unaltered regularity, opportunity for its employment was decreasing even more rapidly. The question as to the movement of silver coin, in default of continuous commercial expansion, was now answered very emphatically. In 1883, as in the spring of 1880, a silver surplus again began to pile up in the Treasury. Foreign exchange moved heavily against us. Europe not only bought from the United States the smallest amount of merchandise in five years, but it sold on the American markets as large a supply of foreign goods as that of 1880, and sold in addition a heavy instalment of its American securities. In March, 1884, $12,200,-000 gold was shipped to Europe; in April, $21,000,-000. Payment of gold in public revenue decreased rapidly; payment in silver as rapidly increased. The crisis foreshadowed in 1880 by Secretary Sherman seemed to be imminent.

The so-called panic of 1884, an immediate consequence of these disquieting developments, chiefly

[1] New York *Financial Chronicle*, January 17, 1885.

affected the security markets. It was provoked, first, by the heavy liquidation of securities, already noticed, and by the embarrassment of several over-capitalized railway companies; second, by uneasiness over the currency situation, which was decidedly emphasized, in February, by the ill-judged hint of the local Treasury authorities that it might be deemed advisable to force out silver through the Treasury payments at New York.[1] This rumor had an influence much like that of a similar Treasury rumor in the financial uneasiness nine years later. But the range of the resultant panic was not much wider than New York City, nor was the financial crisis similar in gravity to those of 1873 and 1893. Symptoms such as the hoarding of currency, causing a public premium on every form of money; the complete blockade of foreign and domestic exchange, the general run upon the savings-banks, the failure of sound depository institutions, and the temporary suspension of American industry, were witnessed in both the earlier and the later panic year; but there was nothing of the kind in 1884. Business in all departments of production was indeed seriously depressed, and results unsatisfactory, as regards both volume of trade and prices.[2] But the manner in which the producing and mercantile communities endured the money-market strain proved pretty conclusively two facts: first, that the liquidating process, during the two preceding years, had been thorough; and second, that underneath the crumbling structure of specula-

[1] New York *Financial Chronicle*, March 1, 1884.
[2] New York Chamber of Commerce, *Annual Rep.*, 1884.

tion was a firm foundation of genuine and increased wealth.¹

The stock markets, however, passed in May, 1884, through an acute and very alarming convulsion; led up to by the commercial depression, the flight of foreign capital, and the disordered Treasury finances, and immediately precipitated by the discovery of several vast financial frauds. Looking at 1884 in retrospect, it would seem that the financial community for a day or two lost faith entirely in the honesty and credit of its members. It is no unusual incident for a group of swindlers and defaulters, who have escaped detection while their speculative "margins" could be sustained, to be exposed with merciless publicity when the markets break suddenly away from them, and the falling markets of the season found plenty of such ventures ripe for destruction. But the 1884 disclosures were of a peculiar order. The theft of $3,185,000 of a New York City bank's securities by its president, without the least misgiving on the part of its officers or directors; the failure of a second-rate Wall Street firm for $16,000,000, with assets of $67,000; the ruin of a strong national bank through its president's connection with this firm, despite his knowledge of its fraudulent representations²; the suspension of another well-known institution through the notorious speculations of its president,³—these were disquieting developments enough, had they come separately

¹ New York *Financial Chronicle*, January 3, 1885, p. 8.
² Comptroller Cannon, *Annual Treas. Rep.*, 1884, p. 157.
³ *Ibid.*, p. 158.

and singly. But when it is considered that the performances of John C. Eno, Grant & Ward, the Marine Bank, and the Metropolitan Bank, all came to public knowledge within a single week and in the same community, the shock to financial confidence is not hard to understand.

It resulted on the Stock Exchange, during a day or two, in what can only be described as a delirium of panic; prices of standard dividend-paying shares collapsing, from a level already very low, fifteen to twenty per cent. in as many hours, while the rate for loans on call ran up as high as three per cent. a day. But the spasm was not continuous; the low level of security prices was touched within a very few weeks of the acute collapse. Even the sudden and very serious strain upon the money market was relieved by a contrivance virtually introduced during the panic of 1873, whereby the Clearing-House issued to any bank in its membership loan certificates, secured by the deposit of that bank's securities to a value greater by twenty-five per cent. than the certificates allotted, and receivable in lieu of cash in settlement of balances at the Clearing-House. Through this emergency device, banks whose cash reserves were impaired during the panic avoided actual suspension. Against deposit with the Clearing-House of sound commercial paper not at the moment marketable, they took out $24,915,000 of such loan certificates, thus tiding over the worst of the money-market crisis.[1] We shall encounter this noteworthy banking makeshift again,

[1] Comptroller Cannon, *Annual Treas. Rep.*, 1884, pp. 139, 153.

under still more interesting circumstances, in our review of 1893.

This New York panic in the spring was followed by a heavy fall in agricultural prices; partly occasioned, perhaps, by the disordered money markets, but chiefly by the immense increase of home and foreign production. The American grain crop of 1884 was larger even than that of 1882; the whole world's wheat production was twelve per cent. larger than the crop of 1878, under which, it will be remembered, prices had broken continuously.[1] In 1884, the price of wheat fell lower than in 1878; in other staple products, prices fell nearly to the level of the earlier year of depression. If, as had been argued in the debates of 1878, the fall in prices was caused by an insufficient currency, no such result ought to have been expected in 1884; for notwithstanding the gold shipments of the year, the total money supply in circulation in the United States had increased $425,000,000, or fifty per cent., since the resumption of specie payments.[2]

The debaters of 1878 were not familiar, however, with the statistics of foreign grain production. Necessities of life can never, strictly speaking, be "over-produced," but they may be produced in such quantity that, in order to sell them all, new customers must be brought in by fixing a lower range of prices. The world's product of wheat, in 1884, was not only the largest in history, but it was not equalled again during the next half-dozen years.[3] The average price of

[1] Liverpool *Corn-Trade News* estimates.
[2] *Treas. Rep.*, 1884. [3] Liverpool *Corn-Trade News* estimates.

wheat in 1884, accordingly, was not only the lowest ever touched up to that time in American history, but it was also lower than any yearly average thereafter until 1892.[1] Public authorities on agriculture flatly declared that there was no profit in raising wheat at the prices of 1884.[2] This was undoubtedly an exaggeration; but when a National Bureau of Agriculture published such a statement, it is not difficult to guess what must have been the feeling of the farmer.

The Republican party went into the Presidential campaign of 1884 under this double handicap of acute financial depression in the East and unfavorable agricultural markets in the West. It was burdened, in addition, with its failure to modify the tariff in the direction of lower duties—a failure which drove into renewed opposition the element which won the election of 1882. The fact that, even against these odds, the Republican party actually came within 23,000 votes of a plurality on the whole country's popular vote of November, 1884, proves how powerful was the prestige gained through the achievement of resumption. As it turned out, however, the party was defeated, the vote of New York State against Mr. Blaine turning the scales.

The Democratic party thus obtained control of the National Administration, for the first time in twenty-four years. It inherited from its predecessor a very serious financial situation, the outcome of which, when President Cleveland took office in 1885,

[1] *U. S. Statistical Abstract*, 1896, p. 293.
[2] U. S. Department of Agriculture, *Annual Rep.*, 1885, p. 348.

was extremely doubtful. The pessimism prevalent even in the Administration which relinquished office was frankly voiced in its final Treasury report. Through a curious irony of fortune, Hugh McCulloch, whose own plan of resumption had been repudiated eighteen years before, was called again to the Treasury, in his old age and in the closing months of the Arthur Administration, to witness what seemed to be the undermining of the Sherman resumption plan. His view of the situation was wholly discouraging. "Silver certificates," he wrote in his report of December, 1884, "are taking the place of gold"; "a panic or an adverse current of exchange might compel the use in ordinary payments by the Treasury of the gold held for the redemption of the United States notes, or the use of silver or silver certificates in the payment of its gold obligations."[1] On one occcasion, the Treasury began to force out silver through the Clearing-House.[2] Mr. McCulloch's gloomy forecast was confirmed by the new Executive. "Silver and silver certificates have displaced and are now displacing gold," wrote the President-elect, early in 1885; adding that the part of the Treasury's gold reserve pledged for redemption of the legal tenders, "if not already encroached upon, is perilously near such encroachment."[3]

[1] *Treas. Rep.*, 1884, p. xxxi.
[2] Assistant-Treasurer Graves's reply to H. R. resolution, Feb. 10, 1885.
[3] Grover Cleveland, letter to A. J. Warner and others, February 24, 1885.

CHAPTER V

THE SURPLUS REVENUE

ALMOST the first act of the Cleveland Administration, in its management of the Treasury, suggested that Government finances were in immediate and serious straits. Its surplus gold reserve, by midsummer, 1885, was down to $115,000,000—hardly more than was held at the resumption of specie payments; this reserve was falling three or four millions every month, and the July interest-payments drew on it heavily. The Treasury's surplus of silver dollars meantime had risen by July to the unprecedented sum of $71,500,000, and was increasing two to three million dollars monthly. The recourse first adopted by the Treasury was an appeal to the New York banks for help. These institutions responded by turning over to the Treasury in July of 1885 some $5,915,000 gold from their own reserves, taking in place of it fractional silver coin, of which the Treasury happened then to have on hand an exceptionally large supply.[1] As a precedent, this action was important; as a permanent solution

---

[1] New York *Financial Chronicle*, July 8 and July 25, 1885.

of the Treasury's difficulties, it was quite as fruitless then as the similar recourse was in 1893 and 1894. The silver, after being held by the New York Clearing-House for three or four months, as security for certificates issued to its owners and used in bank exchanges, was returned to the Treasury for legal tenders.[1]

Fortunately, the new Administration did not base its subsequent operations on makeshifts such as this. What it did undertake was very interesting. It had been observed, in connection with the outflow of legal-tender currency to the interior during and after 1879, that bills in small denominations were most apt to stay in circulation. In the two years 1880 and 1881, for instance, the Treasury paid out some $70,000,000 Government notes in one-, two-, and five-dollar bills. Against this outflow of small notes, only $46,000,000 was paid back to the Treasury, during the period, in notes of the same denominations. On the other hand, the Treasury received in revenue during the same two years, in notes for one hundred dollars and upwards, four times as large a sum as it paid out.[2] I have already called attention to the automatic law under which a bank keeps on hand for permanent circulation the currency needed by its depositors for daily uses; passing along, therefore, in settlements with other banks or with the Treasury, such forms of currency as its depositors do not need. The failure of the small notes to return from circulation had proved, therefore, that

[1] New York *Financial Chronicle*, November 7, 1885.
[2] *Treas. Rep.*, 1881, p. 426.

such denominations could be kept in constant use. Nor is this preference hard to understand. Wages are paid in bills for five dollars or less; retail purchases rarely require exchange of anything larger than a ten-dollar bill. Very few people carry about with them currency in bills of one hundred or five hundred dollars, but every citizen is apt to have in his pocket-book a handful of paper money in the smaller denominations. The pocket-books of sixty million citizens, with business active, are capable of absorbing permanently, in this way, enormous sums.

Now the framers of the Silver Act of 1878 had an idea that silver dollars would serve exactly such a purpose. In this they were mistaken. The people would not take these heavy coins in any quantities from their depositories; they insisted on being supplied with other forms of currency; so much so that in 1885 a million more than the whole year's silver-dollar coinage came back to the Treasury.[1] The people had not the same objection to the silver certificates. As we saw in studying the results of the silver shipments south and west after 1880, the recipients of these dollars turned them back to the nearest sub-treasury in exchange for silver certificates, but they took the certificates readily enough. But the provision of the Law of 1878 that silver certificates should not be issued in denominations of less than ten dollars prevented their use for ordinary retail purposes. Such a provision virtually declared that there should be no pocket-money, the permanent circulating medium, in that form of currency.

[1] Treasurer Jordan, *Annual Treas. Rep.*, 1886, p. 78.

The Treasury now undertook to reverse this situation. The people had the legal-tender notes which the Treasury needed to facilitate its own New York exchanges, and they would not take the silver currency which was embarrassing the Treasury. Might it not, then, be possible to issue silver certificates in one-, two-, and five-dollar denominations, and meantime to hold back in the Treasury reserve such small legal-tender notes as should from time to time be received in revenue? The project would, of course, involve the establishment of store-houses for the idle silver dollars held against the certificates outstanding. Even in 1885, one hundred million of the coins were thus stored away. But the plan would serve at any rate, if successful, to transfer ownership of these dollars from the Treasury to outsiders; it would substitute another form of money in the Treasury's own balances, and, what was more important, it would prevent the silver currency from coming back in the revenue in such quantities as to embarrass the Treasury's operations. If the people were to keep the silver certificates for their daily uses, heavy payments to the Government must be made in gold or legal tenders, and either currency could be freely used again in all Clearing-House exchanges.

The new Administration began by keeping in the Treasury all of the one- and two-dollar legal tenders paid to it, and by using in its own disbursements only notes in large denominations. This policy had prompt results. Within a year, complaint of the scarcity of small notes came in from various sections of the country; and in 1886 Congress was asked to permit the issue of silver certificates in small denominations. Congress consented grudgingly, and in August, 1886, it authorized the issue of such silver currency in one-, two-, and five-dollar bills, and the exchange of large silver certificates for an equal amount in small denominations. With this authority, the Treasury tried at once the experiment of dislodging the legal tenders from the people's pocketbooks and replacing them with small silver certificates, and the plan succeeded. By 1888, there were $34,000,000 less in legal-tender notes for one, two, and five dollars in the country's circulation than in 1886, and all this void was filled by newly issued silver currency in the same denominations.

Meantime another influence was at work, which was much more useful to the Treasury's plans. I have mentioned the Government legal-tender currency as a permanent medium of retail circulation; I have not yet noticed the circulating national-bank notes. These notes were a very important factor in the operation just described. In 1884, there were more of the bank notes outstanding than there were of the legal tenders, and more than half of such outstanding bank notes were in denominations of ten dollars or less.[1] The demand for currency in the rapid trade expansion after 1879 had not only attracted foreign gold, and absorbed into interior circulation legal tenders and even silver, but it had stimulated the national banks to add some thirty millions to their circulating notes. It will be

[1] Comptroller Cannon, *Treas. Rep.*, 1884, p. 186.

recalled that the check to trade activity, after the summer of 1882, sent gold back to Europe and silver and Government notes back to the Eastern banks and the Treasury. The same business motive, therefore, which had inspired the banks, in the three preceding years, to increase their note circulation, now encouraged reduction of such issues.

Nor was the state of trade the only motive for such reduction. Under the National Banking Law, a bank wishing to issue notes was required to deposit Government bonds with the Treasury, against which it would receive in its own notes ninety per cent. of the par value of the bonds deposited. This is an admirable contrivance to ensure soundness in a banknote circulation, but a very doubtful expedient to ensure its permanency. The Bank of England is not allowed to sell the public securities on which its circulation rests; the banks of the United States have a perfect right to do so, provided they retire the circulation issued against such bonds. Not only did the banks possess the right of sale, but in the case of bonds, like the three per cents, redeemable on call, banks were forced to surrender both bonds and circulation when the Government was paying out its surplus. In 1883, upwards of $353,000,000 Government bonds were on deposit as a basis of bank-note circulation. Out of this total, more than $200,000,000 were in the three per cents,[1] and it was naturally these very three per cents which the Treasury selected in its public-debt redemptions. Whenever such bonds were called for redemption, the

[1] *Treas. Rep.*, 1883, p. 218.

bank possessing them was compelled either to replace them with other Government issues bought on the open market, or else to retire its circulating notes. Under the circumstances, it is not surprising that the circulation was surrendered. Fully three fourths of the bank notes thus retired from circulation were in small denominations; and this, of course, signified growing scarcity in money available for small exchanges.

Secretary Manning and his associates in the Treasury were too sagacious observers of the undercurrents of finance to have failed to reckon this banknote movement into their plans for disposing of the surplus silver.[1] But even the public men who discerned this curious phenomenon, and correctly pointed out its meaning, could hardly have imagined how far the contraction of the currency, thus automatically begun, was destined to be carried. In 1886, at the very time when the issue of small silver certificates was authorized, began the second enormous rise in public revenue since resumption. In 1885, excess of Government income over expenditure was $63,463,771; it increased thirty millions in the next twelve months; by 1888 it had reached the sum of $119,612,115.

The particular causes of this surplus revenue, whose consequences in many different directions were destined to be of the utmost importance, we shall presently examine. Its influence on the currency was immediate. To avoid direct contraction through heaping up a constantly increasing sum of

[1] Treasurer Jordan, *Treas. Rep.*, 1886, p. 100.

money in the Treasury, the Government again enlarged its purchases of outstanding bonds. In the fiscal year 1886 it had bought only $50,000,000; in 1887 it purchased $125,000,000; in 1888, $130,-000,000. When, later on, the three per cents, redeemable at the Government's will, had all been retired through such purchases, the Treasury began to bid in the open market for its unmatured bonds. Banks which had paid 102 in 1879 for the four per cents, for instance, and had since employed the bonds as a basis of circulation, were now offered a steady market for them at 125 or higher. The temptation to accept such profit was strong, and the banks accordingly began to retire the circulation based on the four per cents. Between 1886 and 1890, national bank-note circulation decreased $126,-000,000, nearly one half this decrease being in notes of five or ten dollars each.

Such a reduction in the retail currency, coming along with the Treasury's policy of keeping in its own reserve the smaller legal tenders, opened the gate wide for the silver certificates. Even in 1886, the Treasurer was able to report that the average proportion of silver currency in payments at the New York Custom-House was barely twelve per cent., against thirty-six per cent. in 1885, while the percentage paid in legal tenders, which the Treasury could freely disburse again through the Clearing-House, increased from twenty-seven per cent. to fifty-nine.[1] In the eight years between the passage of the Silver-Coinage Law and the middle of 1886,

---

[1] Treasurer Jordan, *Annual Treas. Rep.*, 1886, pp. 77, 142.

$150,000,000 silver coin and certificates had been put into general circulation; in the four years after 1886, the country absorbed $200,000,000 more, and this four-year increase happened coincidently, as we have already seen, with a shrinkage of $126,000,000 in the bank-note circulation.

The Treasury's silver surplus, meantime, was reduced with such rapidity that it fell from $97,745,750 at the opening of August, 1886, to $79,641,424 exactly one year afterwards, and to barely $19,000,000 before the close of the Cleveland Administration. Most people will remember how suddenly, in those years, they lost sight of the once familiar bank-notes and small legal-tender pocket-money, and found instead, in their daily exchanges of petty cash, the new silver certificates. Whoever noticed this was unconsciously observing the working-out of one of the most curious economic experiments of the century.

For the second time, therefore, the anticipated crisis in the currency was averted, and on this occasion, so far as the silver certificates were concerned, it was permanently set at rest. What will occur in relation to this and other forms of United States currency in the future is a matter of simple guesswork. But with the subsequent halt in compulsory silver-coinage, under the law which will be noticed in the next chapter, the silver certificates took the place of the cancelled bank-notes in the retail circulation. In 1891 the bank currency reached its lowest point since 1865, but even at the close of the fiscal year 1896, the country's national bank-note circulation was $137,000,000 less than its maximum of 1882, and the silver currency made up one fourth of the total money supply outside the Treasury.

But the solution of the silver problem, temporary or otherwise, had not solved the problem of the surplus, which now became more awkward even than in 1882. It will be necessary, before this singular episode can be properly studied, to observe the character of the period which gave rise to it. No phenomenon in our financial history has had more immediate bearing on the strange chapter in American finance from 1891 to 1897. The United States is even now affected, in its public finances, by the traditions surrounding the period of the surplus revenue. The legislation of 1890 and the financial phenomena of 1893 were distinct results, in very large measure, of the four-year period after 1886. Neither 1890, nor 1893, nor indeed the succeeding years of American finance, can be understood except in the light of the epoch which we are now to examine.

The excessive rise in surplus revenue, after 1886, happened in spite of a further considerable increase in public expenditure. It was partly caused by a general increase in the product of internal taxes, but of the total gain in annual income, sixty per cent. was made at the custom-house. In 1885, the import duties made the lowest yield of any year under the tariff of 1883; in 1890, under the same law, they had risen forty-eight million dollars, reaching the highest record in the history of the Government, before or since.

No such increase would have been possible without an equally remarkable increase in the import of foreign merchandise, and no such expansion could occur in the import trade without some notable changes in the industrial situation. Such a change had in fact occurred. As compared with the resumption period, these years did not reach the high range of prosperity. They were, however, a period of great activity in trade. We saw that recovery from the 1884 collapse was rapid. Prices did not move up as in 1879 and 1880, for the reason that foreign competition, in all branches of production, including agriculture, was continuous. But profits, though irregular, averaged fairly well on a largely increased volume of business. Of 1886 itself, contemporary critics wrote that it was " the best business year since 1880 "[1]; of 1889, that it " surpassed all predecessors in the volume of trade movements."[2] In the dry-goods industry, " an unusually large and prosperous trade was done in 1888,"[3] and in 1889, " distributors were in such good spirits that their operations for the spring were exceptionally liberal."[4]

The active markets during 1887 and 1888 induced some repetition of the experiments of 1880; wheat and coffee were " cornered " on more than one occasion in the speculative markets. In the first of these two years the experiment broke down

[1] New York *Financial Chronicle*, Review of 1886.
[2] *Ibid.*, Review of 1889.
[3] New York Chamber of Commerce, *Annual Rep.*, p. 86.
[4] *Ibid., Annual Rep.*, 1889, p. 83.

disastrously, but in September, 1888, wheat was put up to two dollars a bushel. The iron business was prosperous. Between 1885 and 1889, annual consumption of iron in the United States considerably more than doubled.¹ In 1887, came a decided rise in iron prices; a result, as usual, of sudden demand for railway purposes. There were laid down in that year 12,878 new miles of road, four times the total of 1885, and the largest year's construction in the country's history.² This increase in railway mileage, which was located almost wholly in the West and South, partly caused and was partly caused by another symptomatic movement—the active " town-lot " speculation in the newly developed regions West and South. During September and October, 1887, interior speculation reached to such a height as actually to embarrass Eastern money markets by the heavy drain of capital to the centres of excitement. During 1887 and 1888, upwards of forty-nine million acres out of the public lands were sold to settlers, an annual increase of nearly five million acres over the years immediately preceding.³ Not unconnected with this new extension of the improved interior domain, annual immigration, which in 1886 had fallen to 334,203, increased again by 1888 to 546,889.

It cannot readily be doubted, then, if the usual tests are to be trusted, that these were years of prosperity. There were, on the other hand, several

¹ *Annual Reports*, American Iron and Steel Association.
² Poor's *Manual of Railroads*.
³ *Returns of the General Land Office*, 1888.

qualifying features in the period which must be noticed before its character can be fully summed up. Labor troubles were intermittent, and in very formidable shape. These years witnessed the establishment and spread of those remarkable organizations which for half a dozen years held at bay the corporations which employed them. In the spring of 1886, the Knights of Labor strike was declared on the Missouri Pacific Railway, the switchmen's strike at Chicago and Milwaukee, and the strike of street-car employees in New York City. All of these demonstrations failed. They were followed, during May, by the memorable anarchist riot at Chicago, brought about by a concerted effort to demand an " eight-hour day " for laborers throughout the country. Checked for some months as a result of the Chicago episode, trouble began again in 1888. The Philadelphia and Reading miners' strike of January, and the strike of the Chicago, Burlington, and Quincy's locomotive engineers in March, involving 2500 of the railway's employees, were movements of even larger scope than their predecessors, and they certainly reflected industrial discontent.

For a time, signs of equally angry discontent came from the farming districts. The American wheat crop of 1885 was the smallest since 1881, and, unlike the deficient crop four years before, it came at a time when supplies left over from the crop of the preceding year were double the average,[1] and when Europe's wheat yield as a whole nearly equalled[2]

[1] Bradstreet's tables of U. S. Visible Supply, June, 1885.
[2] Liverpool *Corn-Trade Year-Book*.

that of 1884. The result in 1885 was that the American wheat-producer had to face, for the first time in a generation, the double misfortune of a short crop and low prices. When farmers are discontented, currency agitation is certain to begin, and so it turned out on this occasion. In April, 1886, a free-coinage bill came to a vote in the House of Representatives after warm debate, and was defeated by a majority of only thirty-seven votes. Better harvests in the two following years, with decrease in competitive foreign production, somewhat relieved the pressure from this particular source, and as a consequence the currency agitation waned; but the dissatisfied laborer in the East continued much longer a conspicuous factor in politics. It was in November, 1886, that Henry George, running for Mayor of New York City on a platform of discontented labor, polled 68,110 votes out of a total of 219,679. Hardly less significant was the fact that the third party in the Presidential campaign of 1888 abandoned most of its traditional watchwords, styled itself the "Union Labor party," and in its platform made the question of strikes and arbitration the central plank.

These combinations of laborers were not the only reflection of a considerably altered situation. A very singular parallel, at the opposite end of the industrial scale, was provided by combinations of corporations. This phenomenon came to public view with even greater suddenness. Political platforms may be counted on, ordinarily, to notice current events susceptible of use as " issues." But in

1884, the so-called "trust question" was not once named in any Presidential platform. The State conventions of 1886 made no reference to it; only one or two platforms of minority organizations mentioned the movement, even in 1887. In 1888, on the other hand, denunciation of the trusts was made a separate and conspicuous plank in the platform of every political party submitting nominations. As a matter of fact, the majority of the sugar refineries in the United States, and a large part of its lead, rope, oil, and spirits manufactories, had before 1889 been combined into associations under single managements. The magnitude of these undertakings may be judged from the fact that in 1890, four trusts, organized within three years, reported aggregate capital stock of $188,000,000. This enormous capital was used not only to extend the actual plant and trade of the allied manufacturers, but at times to buy off aggressive competitors simply for the purpose of shutting down competing mills.

The limits of this book will not permit me to go at any length into this question of the trusts. It may, however, be noticed that in one respect the movement was an instructive symptom of the period. The trusts were organized to restrict a competition which their organizers declared to be ruinous if left unchecked. That there was some basis for this allegation may be judged from the course of many other markets, which pretty uniformly told a story of keen, close, and sometimes destructive competition. The over-capitalized and in some quarters unwisely projected railway systems naturally felt the full force of this movement. A series of "rate wars" so far cut down profits that, although, with the heavy annual increase in the mileage, total gross earnings rose with great rapidity after 1887, net earnings and dividends actually decreased.[1] With the opening of 1889, was introduced that extraordinary plan known as a "gentlemen's agreement," whereby the presidents of the important railway systems, not at all with a sense of humor, met and pledged their personal word of honor to see that rates were conscientiously maintained.[2] Undoubtedly as a consequence of the same ruling conditions, the record of commercial failures, which stood in 1886 at 9834 individual suspensions, with total liabilities of $114,644,119, rose by 1889 to 10,882, with liabilities of $148,784,357.[3]

With home competition thus aggressive, the enormous merchandise import movement becomes a matter of curious historical interest. It might have been supposed that home competition would have shut out these imports. But the period which we are noticing was as peculiar in Europe as in the United States. Production by foreign manufacturers, during this period, reached a volume quite unprecedented; in Great Britain especially, the search for outside markets was urgent and aggressive. Merchandise exports from that country reached in 1890 by far the highest total in its history, having increased, since 1886, some $287,000,000, or very nearly twenty-five per

[1] Poor's *Manual of Railroads*.
[2] January 10, 1889.
[3] Dun's *Review*, Annual Tables.

cent.¹ In England, this was not a symptom of distress, although competition was aggressive; for 1889 was declared by English commercial authorities to be a year when labor was abundantly employed, and when trade compared very favorably, even in the matter of profits, with previous years.² But the unprecedented stimulation of production drove manufacturers to an urgent quest after new fields of export trade. In return for these heavy foreign sales of the English surplus product, securities issued by the countries to which the goods were sold were taken by English capital in enormous quantities.³

The investment phase of this operation led to some extraordinary phenomena in London during 1890, and had much to do with our own investment markets during that and the three ensuring years. For although there was not a nation in the commercial world to which Great Britain's exports, during the four years ending with 1889, had not been heavily increased, its exports to no other nation increased as did its shipments to the United States.⁴ The consuming power of this country had grown enormously with the extension of its wealth and population. I have already noticed the increase of one hundred per cent. in annual use of iron; in 1889, consumption of cotton was reckoned larger by 2,600,000 bales than in any previous year of the nation's history,⁵ and these markets were typical. Nor were the increased

---

[1] *Annual Trade Statement of the United Kingdom*, 1891.
[2] London *Economist*, Commercial Review of 1889.   [3] *Ibid.*
[4] *Annual Trade Statement of the United Kingdom*, 1891.
[5] New York *Financial Chronicle*, September 14, 1889.

importations limited to any particular branch of foreign products. They embraced necessities and luxuries, finished manufactures and raw material of manufacture. In the four years prior to 1890, annual imports of iron increased $4,000,000 and imports of precious stones $4,000,000. There was a gain of $17,000,000 in foreign cordage-ware received, and of $10,000,000 in foreign silks. Along with a $15,000,000 increase in annual importations of woollen goods came increase of $9,000,000 in tobacco imports, nearly $2,000,000 in import of foreign wines, and no less than $1,800,000 in so small an item as foreign-made gloves.

These growing imports were doubtless evidence of increasing wealth. But nations as well as individuals will sometimes buy in excess of their means of ready payment; this being usually true of a speculative period, when hopes are high and money-lenders ready to make loans on easy terms and on all sorts of security. It is conspicuously true of such a period as that which we are reviewing, when foreign merchandise is taken and consumed in exchange for mere evidences of debt. Imports were equally heavy in the trade revival after 1879, but they were then for the most part Europe's method of settling its debt for our enormous grain exports. In none of the five years following 1885, on the contrary, did the annual breadstuffs-exports of the United States come within one hundred million dollars of the trade of 1880.[1] Out of the 498,000,000 bushels American wheat crop of 1880, 186,000,000 bushels

[1] *U. S. Bureau of Statistics*, Annual Report. 1892, p. 2.

were exported; out of the 491,000,000 bushels crop of 1889, foreign consumers took only 109,000,000. There had, in fact, been another immense expansion in the grain-fields of foreign competitors. Not only did Europe enjoy fair harvests on an extraordinary acreage, but India and the Argentine Republic, which had hardly been noticed in the grain export markets of ten years before, were now in 1888 exporting fifty million bushels of wheat per annum.

This was an immediate fruit of the British capital invested in the railways of those countries. The net result of this foreign competition was that the total outward trade of the United States decreased or held stationary at the moment when imports were increasing at the rate of twenty to forty millions annually. In 1888, for the first time since the specie-resumption law was passed, imports of merchandise exceeded exports; in 1889, the same phenomenon was repeated. Like other customers of England at the time, we settled our adverse balance by selling our own securities; but the sequel to this operation, with trade relations what they were, was in the main disastrous. For, let it be observed, although these heavy foreign purchases of American stocks and bonds contributed immense amounts of capital to our markets, the capital thus acquired was almost wholly based on debt. If these foreign investors were for any reason to take alarm over the outlook in this country, withdrawal of such capital, through sale of the railway securities on our markets, was an immediate possibility. Even a shock to confidence and credit in the home of this invested European capital would be reasonably sure to cause its abrupt withdrawal. This had happened once before, in the London panic of 1866, with consequent serious embarrassment to the United States. But the foreign capital invested here in 1866 was a trifle compared with the amount poured into American enterprises between 1886 and 1890.

This was, however, a problem of the future; existing conditions served very notably to strengthen the Treasury's position. Acting directly, the heavy home consumption added to the internal revenue; indirectly, it caused the increase in the customs. There seemed to be no check to the rise in revenue. In 1887, as I have already noticed, the public debt redeemable at par was extinguished, and the Government was forced to ask authority from Congress to enter the open market as a buyer of its own unmatured bonds at a premium. This, as the Secretary of the Treasury declared to Congress, was " a responsibility which ought not to be put upon any officer of the Government."[1] But there was absolutely no alternative. The few months during which the Treasury, while awaiting some authoritative action on the part of Congress, suspended bond redemptions, sent up the surplus money holdings of the Government nearly thirty millions. In August, 1888, it was literally true that the Treasury's cash surplus, wholly removed from the use of trade, was one fourth as large as the entire estimated sum in the country's outside circulation.

[1] Secretary Fairchild, *Annual Treas. Rep.*, 1887, p. xxviii.

It would have been larger even than this but for the use made, under pressure of necessity, of the depository banks. At the close of 1885, $12,901,432 of the Government's funds were thus deposited. On the last day of March, 1888, these deposits had increased to $61,231,647, and they had risen nearly twenty millions within four months. Now it is true enough that this method of putting a public surplus on deposit with the banks, where it may still continue to serve the purposes of trade, is legitimate, and in ordinary cases beneficial. No other temporary disposition of an excess revenue is ever thought of, for example, by the British Exchequer, whose funds go, as a matter of ordinary course, into the Bank of England. It is true, also, that these bank deposits of United States Government funds were abundantly secured, under the law, by pledge with the Treasury of Government bonds to a face value ten per cent. greater than the money thus entrusted.[1]

A careful effort was moreover made to distribute such deposits equitably; in 1888, they were shared by no less than two hundred and ninety separate institutions.[2] Nevertheless, this recourse was as unpopular with the community at large as it was in 1878, and it was, moreover, even more limited in scope and permanency. The Government's deposits were liable to immediate recall, and they were looked upon as temporary in any case. Yet to qualify for such deposits, a bank was obliged to obtain Govern-

[1] *Annual Treas. Rep.*, 1888, p. 453.
[2] *Ibid.*, p. 19.

ment bonds at prices forced to a maximum by the Treasury's own purchases.[1] From any point of view, therefore, the bank deposits were inexpedient. There was one very obvious recourse—reduction in the revenue,—and this the Administration urged on Congress. But Congress refused to act. The House of Representatives contained an Administration majority, and it had already, in 1887, passed the Tariff-Reduction Bill of Mr. Mills. But the Republicans then controlled the Senate, and all such legislation was accordingly blocked. As a last resort, therefore, in April, 1888, formal authority was wrung from Congress to devote the surplus to bond redemptions at a premium.

A very extraordinary chapter in American finance now opened. During 1888, the Government four per cents. ranged on the open market from 123 to 129[2]; yet at these high prices the Treasury bought, within seven months, upwards of $50,000,000.[3] The 4½'s, ruling, because of their near maturity, between 106 and 109, were redeemed, meantime, in the amount of $33,000,000. During 1888 and the two ensuing years, $45,000,000 was actually paid out in premiums; within four years, the enormous sum of $235,000,000 was expended for bond redemptions in excess of the annual sinking-fund requirement.[4]

To the world at large, this spectacle of public debt redemption, to the extent of nearly half a billion

---

[1] *Annual Treas. Rep.*, 1887, p. xxviii; 1888, p. 453.
[2] *Annual Treas. Rep.*, 1888, p. 457.
[3] *Ibid.*, p. 455.
[4] *Treas. Rep.*, 1887, pp. 58, 60; 1891, pp. 98, 100.

dollars in five years, was sufficiently astonishing. But admiration was at least tempered by contempt for the wild extravagance of the policy. That any such methods should continue long was inconceivable. If the people did not put a stop to them, outside conditions would themselves have forced the issue. By the middle of 1890, the total interest-bearing debt of the United States was reduced to $725,000,000. A few years more of wholesale redemptions, under the methods employed in 1888, and the entire debt would be extinguished. This result, except for the waste of public funds involved in the constantly advancing premium, would of itself have been no misfortune. But these very redemptions were extinguishing the bank-note currency, thus actually contracting circulation. After the debt's extinction, moreover, and the removal thus of the single outlet for excessive surplus revenues, what was to be the outlook? Apparently, this Treasury octopus would absorb the entire domestic circulation. No such situation has ever been presented, before or since, in the history of nations. It need hardly be a matter for surprise that the outside business community grew more and more uneasy. An excessive circulating medium is an undoubted evil; but a law which draws into the public vaults, and keeps in idleness, seven per cent. of the circulation every year is a source of possible mischief whose evil influence can scarcely be exaggerated. That something must be done to stop it, and must be done quickly, was agreed by all parties. Such was the situation at the close of 1889.

CHAPTER VI

THE TWO LAWS OF 1890

UNUSUAL as the problem of excessive public revenue was in the experience of modern governments, it was not wholly new to the United States. Almost exactly half a century before, a similar dilemma had arisen whose results, had they been kept in mind, might have given some useful warnings to the financiers of the later period. Between 1834 and 1836, the annual Federal revenue was doubled. In the first of those two years, as in the several years preceding them, there was a handsome Treasury surplus, which was applied to reduction of the public debt. Before 1836, however, this debt was wholly extinguished, and a sudden increase in the revenue left a surplus for the year of not quite twenty million dollars—something unprecedented in those days. This rise in public income resulted from an abnormally rapid growth of customs revenue and a great expansion of receipts from sales of public lands; both of these movements being stimulated, in 1836 as in 1888, by a season of interior development and speculation. The customs schedules might have been conservatively revised, but Congress refused to touch them. Instead, it voted to distribute $37,000,000 to the States, and then proceeded to increase public expenditure. The next year happened to be a season of trade disaster; customs receipts in 1837, and with them the total revenue, decreased one half from 1836, while expenses were enlarged by twenty per cent. The result was prompt and logical. The surplus revenue of twenty millions in 1836 was changed only one year afterward to a deficit of thirteen millions, the " deposits " with the States had to be suspended, and before the close of 1837 the Government was issuing bonds to ward off actual insolvency.

Whether the experience of 1837 was or was not a precedent worth regarding, there is no evidence that it was studied by the statesmen of 1888 and 1890. The question of the surplus did, however, become the focus of a vast deal of more or less intelligent popular controversy. This was a natural result of the fact that the perplexities of 1888 reached their acutest point on the eve of a' Presidential contest. Both political parties made the Treasury's situation the text of their campaign platforms, and both went into the campaign with a demand for reduction of the surplus. But the methods of reduction, as proposed by the two National Conventions, differed radically. At St. Louis, June 6, 1888, the Democratic party attacked the sytem of high import duties, to which it ascribed the excessive revenue. It accused the Republican party of endeavoring " to meet and exhaust by extravagant appropriations and expenses" the abnormal surplus, and pledged itself not only to "enforce frugality in public expense," but to "abolish unnecessary taxation" through reform of the tariff system.

It was plain enough, from this declaration, that the electoral contest would pivot, not on the main question of a properly adjusted budget of revenue, but on the familiar problem of protection. The Republicans accepted this gage of battle with a boldness and distinctness which left little obscurity to the issue. Conceding the needless excess in current revenue, they proposed, in their Chicago Convention of June 21st, "such revision of the tariff laws as will tend to check imports of such articles as are produced by our own people." This, of course, meant increase, not decrease, in the custom-house tax-rate. If this expedient should not suffice, the party declared for "the entire repeal of the internal taxes rather than the surrender of any part of our protective system." No reduction in public expenditure was recommended; on the contrary, the platform went on to say that "we demand appropriations for the early rebuilding of our navy, for the construction of coast fortifications, . . . for the payment of just pensions to our soldiers, for necessary works of national importance in the improvement of harbors and the channels of internal, coastwise, and foreign commerce, for the encouragement of the shipping interests." The pension legislation particularly, the Republican platform concluded, ought to be "enlarged and extended."

Now it is clear that either party's expedient,

greatly as the two plans differed in principle and method, could be made to reduce the surplus. The Republican plan of course offered the surer means of rapid and wholesale reduction, because, while the effect of mere alteration in schedules of taxation is more or less conjectural, the effect of increased expenditure is certain. However large a public revenue may become, it can at least be spent if appropriations are made sufficiently heavy. But it is hardly necessary to point out that the plan of using up a surplus revenue through extraordinary expenditure is hazardous. The revenue might change, as it had changed repeatedly in the history of our Government, through an unexpected accident of trade; but a budget of expenditure, once fixed, will not be easily reduced. When, therefore, it is proposed simultaneously to cut down the public income and enlarge the public outlay, the greatest possible legislative sagacity and discretion will be necessary to escape disaster. Exactly how far such qualities could be reckoned on, in reducing the surplus revenue of 1888, was presently to be tested. For although the Presidential contest of 1888 was close and for a long time doubtful, its result was a Republican victory. In the Electoral College Mr. Harrison received 233 votes out of 401, his majority of 65 being wholly obtained through the vote of New York State. On the total popular vote of the United States, however, Mr. Cleveland's plurality over Mr. Harrison was 100,476; which, curiously enough, was more than double the popular plurality of any successful candidate since 1872.

There was no good reason to doubt what general policy the Republican party would pursue. It is true that both parties, in their appeals to the people during the campaign of 1888, had more or less modified their platform declarations to suit the prejudices of particular sections or communities. Mr. Cleveland's letter of acceptance, for instance, declared against " abrupt and radical changes " where " reliance upon present revenue arrangements " had become an element in commercial plans. This assurance was addressed to the protectionist interests of the East. The Republicans were in a somewhat similar quandary as regarded the well-known anti-protectionist sentiment of the Northwest, and they accordingly hinted, during the crisis of the canvass, at changes in the import duties in the interest of consumers.[1] This policy of evasion is not at all unusual at such times, but in 1888 the Republican declarations in the West gave rise to some mistaken expectations. There was little ground for them. The national platform was perfectly distinct in its outline of policy. The letters of acceptance by the Republican candidates were quite as unmistakable. Mr. Harrison, while expressing his willingness to " modify rates " of import duties, frankly repudiated the idea of lower duties, while Mr. Morton, the Vice-Presidential nominee, went further still, asking whether, in case the existing tariff needed revision, it would not be " wiser and more patriotic to revise it with a careful regard to the interest of protection than with the purpose of lessening its protective features."

[1] Minnesota Republican Convention, September 7, 1888.

The successful party had, in short, pretty consistently advocated increase in import duties, whereby imports would be in a degree excluded, and it had promised increase in expenditure. It did not flinch from this second proposition after its success. Mr.. Harrison's inaugural address declared, it is true, that " wastefulness, profligacy, or favoritism in public expenditure is criminal." But this was a very general declaration. When he descended to particulars, in this address and in his first message to Congress, the President urged appropriations for river and harbor work, for coast defences, for " a more rapid increase in the number of serviceable ships," and for a pension to every veteran of the war unable to earn a living, whether his disability originated in the service or not.[1] Congress, he suggested, ought to adjust the revenue only after having estimated " these extraordinary demands " and " having added them to our ordinary expenditure."[2]

Mr. Harrison was undoubtedly sincere in his belief that he was outlining a judicious public policy. But never in the history of this Government was advice bestowed with more unfortunate results. Annual Government expenditure had already been increased some $49,000,000 since the heavy surplus revenue began in 1886, and half of this annual increase was in pensions, outlay for which was now three times as large as it was when General Garfield declared the reasonable maximum to have been reached. As for the river and harbor expenditure,

[1] Annual Message, Dec. 3, 1889.
[2] Inaugural Address, March 4, 1889.

Mr. Harrison might profitably have recalled the experience of President Arthur. That many of these expenditures were useful and necessary, no one doubted, but it was equally notorious that every committee and every President for ten years past had been driven to desperation to keep back jobbery and extravagance from such appropriations. No President before Mr. Harrison had dreamed of such a thing as urging river and harbor expenditure on Congress.

But it was hardly necessary to reason from the immediate past. Anybody who has studied the tendencies of legislative bodies, American and foreign, during the present generation, must admit that President Harrison's advice, on general principles, was exceedingly dangerous. A national legislature may be safely left to itself, if increased expenditure is desired, and nowhere is this principle more certain of application than in the United States. The immense variety of local interests represented in Congress; the pressure on each individual Congressman to obtain his district's good-will by procuring local expenditure of national funds; the virtual impossibility of getting a share in such appropriations without in turn favoring demands of other Congressmen—these are perhaps the most familiar incidents in legislation. They are, and always have been, emphasized by two serious vices in our legislative system: the haphazard construction of appropriation bills by separate committees not concerned in planning for the revenue,[1] and the

[1] J. G. Cannon, House of Representatives speech, *Congressional Record*, March 6, 1897.

unfortunate provision of the Constitution that the President may veto an appropriation bill only as a whole, and not in sections.[1] Finally there was added, in 1890, the powerful inducement of the so-called " Grand Army vote," which was believed to have carried some States in the 1888 election, and which, in the judgment of politicians, could be controlled by the largess of the Pension Bureau. All this ought to have been considered by a prudent Executive in his official advice.

It was at once apparent how little need there had been for any such stimulus to Congress. The revenue was first taken in hand. The Tariff Bill introduced on April 16, 1890, by Mr. McKinley for the House Ways and Means Committee, increased materially the rates on all competing products. The average rate imposed on dutiable imports in the year before the McKinley Act became a law was 44.41 per cent.; in the next year it was 48.71 per cent.[2] In the case of many classes of importations, this increase might foreshadow larger instead of smaller revenue. There was, however, one very important branch of customs revenue which was stricken off altogether. In 1889, the duty on imported sugar produced $55,976,228. The McKinley Law placed sugar on the free list, and in the twelve months ending with June, 1892, the customs revenue from that commodity was only $76,987.[3]

This particular source of public income—the

[1] President Arthur, veto of River and Harbor Bill, August 1, 1882.
[2] U. S. Bureau of Statistics. *Annual Report*, 1892, p. lx.
[3] *U. S. Statistical Abstract*, 1896, p. 16.

largest, with one exception, on the Government's accounts—was therefore removed completely and permanently. The question then remained, would the other articles left on the dutiable list yield more revenue than before, or less? If they continued to be imported in the same amount as previously, they would, of course yield more, and on this assumption the framers of the Act of 1890 estimated the outside reduction in the total annual revenue at forty-two to forty-three million dollars,[1] which was substantially the amount of reduction recommended by the President.[2] But President and Congress alike ignored two facts which ought not to have been omitted from the reckoning. The increased rates of duty might turn out to be so high as to exclude competing foreign products, which would, of course, curtail receipts at the custom-house. Or, without such artificial exclusion, the volume of importations, which was abnormally large in 1889 and 1890, might suddenly contract from natural causes. Previous tariff experiments had shown the possibility of either result, but the experience under the tariff law of 1890 was destined to be the most forcible illustration of all. As against the Congressional estimate of $43,000,000 revenue reduction, through the McKinley Tariff Act, the actual decrease in customs receipts, during the first fiscal year in which all the new schedules were in force, was $52,200,-000, and two years later,[3] with the revenue law un-

[1] N. W. Aldrich, Senate speech, September 30, 1890.
[2] Annual Message, December 3, 1889.
[3] *Treas. Rep.*, 1892, p. cxx.

changed, receipts had fallen $45,600,000 further.[1] Instead of forty-three millions maximum reduction, the ultimate decrease in annual customs revenue under the law of 1890 was close to one hundred millions.

The surplus revenue for the fiscal year before the Act of 1890 had been proposed was $105,053,443;[2] it will be readily seen, therefore, that the cut in revenue, even as estimated on the floor of Congress, left no great margin for increased expenditure. In case of a heavy decrease in dutiable importations, it left no margin whatever. Forty-three millions reduction from the revenue of 1889 would leave room for sixty-two millions increase in expenditure, in order to end the year without a deficit. But Congress put no such limitations on its drafts upon the public purse. Encouraged alike by the platform of the successful party and by the advice of the successful candidate, the first session of Congress under Mr. Harrison's Administration increased its annual appropriations $79,000,000 over those of the preceding session.[3] In the next year the budget of appropriations was increased $35,000,000 more, forty per cent. of the increase being for the account of pensions.[4] Every department estimate and every committee budget kept first in view the idea that an unlimited fund was at hand on which to draw, and that the public welfare would be subserved by drawing liberally on it. The jubilant pension commissioner who, on assuming office at President

---

[1] *Treas. Rep.*, 1894, p. cxxiv. [3] *Treas. Rep.*, 1890, p. cxi.
[2] *Treas. Rep.*, 1889, p. xxii. [4] *Treas. Rep.*, 1891, p. cxii.

Harrison's invitation, exclaimed "God help the surplus!" had very distinctly grasped the situation.

The surplus, indeed, was obviously doomed to speedy destruction. But it became evident, before the revenue and appropriation laws had been twelve months in operation, that something more than the dissipation of an accumulated surplus was threatened, and the Treasury officers soon took fright. If the expenditure of the ensuing fiscal year had been kept to the mark fixed by the permanent and annual appropriations of this spendthrift Congress, there would have been an immediate and heavy annual deficit in revenue. Only by the most strenuous exertions was such a deficit avoided. Fortunately for the Administration, not all the proposed drafts on the Treasury were compulsory. Some of the plans were hurriedly abandoned. The Government ceased buying bonds, except for the annual sinking-fund requirement, within seven months after the passage of the revenue law of 1890.[1] A year later, they abandoned any attempt to meet even the statutory requirement of "the purchase or payment of one per centum of the entire debt of the United States, to be made within each fiscal year."[2] Had this sufficiently distinct requirement been observed, public expenses in the twelve months ending with June, 1892, would have run some thirty-nine millions beyond the income of the year.[3] The pension expenditures in which the President had urged an in-

[1] *Treas. Rep.*, 1891, p. xxvi.
[2] *Treas. Rep.*, 1892, p. xxvii. ; *U. S. Revised Statutes*, sec. 3694.
[3] *Ibid.*, pp. xxi., xxii., xxviii.

crease grew to proportions so enormous that the President himself had to interfere, and rid himself of a commissioner who had been too literal in his interpretation of the Executive advice. By these and similar expedients, the emergency was staved off. There was a Treasury deficit in the fourth quarter of the fiscal year 1891, the first quarterly deficit in many years;[1] it was repeated in two of the quarterly periods of 1892;[2] but in each case a fortunate though temporary expansion of the revenue in other months helped the Treasury through the year. At last came a season when the trade from which the revenue was drawn contracted, with financial and political results as extraordinary as anything in our history.

The revenue and appropriation laws of 1890, then, had of themselves marked out a precarious future for the Treasury. But these laws were not the only or the most interesting achievements of the session. We have now to consider another law of 1890, of supreme and far-reaching importance—a law surpassed in its permanent influence on the national finances only by the Legal-Tender Act of 1862. I have noticed that the national party platforms of 1888 were so exclusively occupied with the revenue dispute that they quite ignored the lately urgent question of silver coinage. The Democratic Convention said not a word on the subject; the Republicans merely inserted the declaration that the party was "in favor of the use of both gold and silver as money"—a convenient platitude, familiar

[1] *Treas. Rep.*, 1891, p. 33.   [2] *Treas. Rep.*, 1892, p. 30.

in the platforms of both parties, which offended nobody and meant nothing, because it touched none of the questions of currency standards and mint restrictions on which alone the bimetallic controversy hinged. The campaign speakers and the candidates were as silent on the silver question as were the platforms. In his letter of acceptance, Mr. Harrison discussed the revenue, the immigration laws, the trust question, and the problem of civil-service reform, but he did not so much as mention the currency. He made no allusion whatever to the silver controversy in his inaugural address of March 4, 1889, although that address discussed the purposes of the new Administration on numerous points of public policy.

Clearly, then, there was no party issue at stake in the silver question, no party or personal pledge to be redeemed, and no reason to anticipate an early and radical move in that matter by the Administration. Yet in the two or three weeks before Congress assembled in the winter of 1889, there was prepared a plan for revolutionizing the United States currency, and to the exposition of this project the Secretary of the Treasury devoted nearly one third of his first annual report, urging the plan on Congress with all the argument and persuasion at his command, and ending by the formulation of a bill which he sent to Congress with a plea for early action.[1] So radical and unprecedented was this proposed legislation that some time was required before Congress or the people could under-

[1] *Treas. Rep.*, 1889, p. lxxiv. ; *Congressional Record*, January 28, 1890.

stand what it meant. So hurriedly was it contrived that the President himself, in his Annual Message submitted after the publication of the Treasury report, frankly declared that he had " been able to give only a hasty examination " to the plan, " owing to the press of other matters and to the fact that it has been so recently formulated." What was this sudden after-thought of a Presidential canvass, and why was a new system of currency forced upon the consideration of Congress by an Administration elected on wholly different issues?

President Harrison had chosen as his Secretary of the Treasury Mr. William Windom of Minnesota, who had already seen some service both in Congress and in the Cabinet. As Secretary of the Treasury under President Garfield, Mr. Windom had brought to a satisfactory close the Government bond-refunding operations of Secretary Sherman. His duty in this matter was only to carry out the plans of his predecessor, a task easily performed in the prosperous investment markets of 1881. Nevertheless, some of the glamor of a great fiscal operation successfully achieved remained with Mr. Windom, and Mr. Harrison's choice for his finance minister in 1889 was generally commended. The new Secretary, however, was not a great financier. He was not even a trained economist, and, as we shall presently see, his ideas on the problems of currency and circulation were singularly obscure and confused. But Mr. Windom was a skilful politician, and it was as a politician that he immediately applied himself to the silver question.

The situation, on the eve of the session of December, 1889, was peculiar. Although the Republicans had won a majority in the Electoral College of 1888, they had not, as we have seen, polled a popular majority. This failure had its natural influence on the Administration's support in Congress. In the House, its majority at the start was only eight, and included in the slender majority were Western Congressmen restive over the plan for a higher tariff. The Senate was still more of a stumbling-block. The Administration apparently controlled that chamber also by a majority of eight; but as an experienced member of the party has remarked, "the nine States west of the Missouri, commonly classified as silver or Western States, have eighteen senators"; a representation which gives the section "very decided advantage in tariff legislation."[1] How decided this advantage was may be judged from the fact that in 1889, seventeen out of the forty-seven Republicans in the Senate came from these very States, where their constituents were notoriously lukewarm if not hostile towards a high protective tariff. Without the greater part of these seventeen votes, the Administration stood in a minority in the Senate, and the tariff bill was the first measure on the programme.

Now it was pretty well known that the united support of these senators could be obtained in return for the passage of a free-silver coinage bill. Their support could be obtained, without such inducement, for party measures endorsed by their

[1] John Sherman, *Recollections*, ii., 1085.

constituents; but the high-tariff bill had not been thus endorsed. The Administration was properly unwilling to concede the question of free-coinage, and Mr. Windom undertook to frame a compromise. His plan as framed was a political concession, on the one hand, to the agrarian communities who demanded larger money circulation ; on the other hand, to the silver-producing States of the Rocky Mountains and the Sierras. The second of these concessions was the more important. The primary purpose of the bill, as frankly stated by its author, was to create an artificial market for silver; the question of increased money supplies being treated as a minor consideration.

In this regard, the measure was absolutely unique in legislation. All previous silver bills had contemplated restoration of the double standard—a plan at least economically intelligible—or at a pinch they had decreed compulsory additions to the currency supply through limited coinage of silver dollars. Mr. Windom's plan proposed that the Government should buy at the market price the entire annual silver output of the world, or as much of the output as silver-miners chose to offer; that it should store away this silver in bulk at Washington, paying for it, meantime, in notes of the United States.[1] All previous debates on the subject had urged remonetization, on the ground that prices of agricultural and other commodities would thereby be enhanced ; Mr. Windom concerned himself with no commodity but silver.

[1] *Treas. Rep.*, 1889, pp. lxxiv and lxxix.

Where other champions of the larger use of silver in the currency had pointed to the fall in wheat as the calamity which they were determined to avert, Mr. Windom discussed the fall in the price of the metal itself as the prime misfortune.[1] So firmly did the Secretary's mind seem to be fixed on this phase of the question that he recited as the chief advantage of his project the " utilization of silver " so that " a market would always be provided for the surplus product."[2] This notion of an artificial market was the only part of his Secretary's plan which the President grasped at once. Although waiving comment on the details of the scheme, Mr. Harrison called attention to the fact that he himself had " always been an advocate of the use of silver in our currency," because " we are large producers of that metal, and should not discredit it."[3]

This was not the only novel and curious feature of Mr. Windom's plan. The Treasury notes were to be issued " against deposits of silver bullion at the market price of silver when deposited "; but they were to be redeemable " on demand, in such quantities of silver bullion as will equal in value, at the date of presentation, the number of dollars expressed on the face of the notes at the market price of silver, or in gold at the option of the Government, or in silver dollars at the option of the holder."[4] The reader of this extraordinary para-

[1] *Treas. Rep.*, 1889, pp. lxii. and lxxiii.
[2] *Ibid.*, p. lxxvi.
[3] Annual Message, Dec. 3, 1889.
[4] *Treas. Rep.*, 1889, p. lxxiv.

graph will hardly wonder that the President declined, on short notice, to express his judgment of it. One inference was, however, readily to be drawn regarding its operation. An indefinite addition to the United States currency, either in paper or in silver, was proposed. The entire silver product of the world was to be made exchangeable at the Treasury for notes, and the notes, if not expressly legal tender, were at all events to be exchangeable again for legal-tender silver dollars. Mr. Windom himself predicted that not less than $37,000,000 worth of bullion, at the market price then ruling, would be exchanged each year for notes.[1] Even this purchase would involve yearly additions to the Government currency larger by fifty per cent. than those of the Silver-Coinage Law of 1878. If the annual silver product of the world were to be doubled, as had already happened since 1877, the issue of Treasury notes would double or quadruple along with it.

Plans for an unprecedentedly large increase in money circulation are usually based, like the Legal-Tender Act, on the necessities of Government, or, like the Silver-Coinage Act of 1878, on a theory that existing circulation is deficient. But the public revenue in 1889 was overflowing, while as to the circulation, Mr. Windom himself took pains to show that since 1878 the total increase in currency supplies had been seventy-four per cent., against only thirty-three per cent. increase in population.[2] These facts did not, he argued, " appear to justify a largely

[1] *Treas Rep.*, 1889, p. lxxxii.   [2] *Ibid..*, 1889, p. lxix.

increased coinage of silver dollars for the purpose of expanding the currency"¹; indeed, if the issues of such silver currency " should become so numerous as to endanger the free circulation of gold," " it would only be a question of time when the specie reserve in the Treasury would change from gold to silver to such an extent as to force the Secretary to pay out silver" for the public debt.² This was orthodox reasoning, but a singular argument to invoke in behalf of a plan for indefinite increase of notes redeemable in silver dollars, and the lack of any intelligent convictions in the Secretary's mind was equally shown by his argument, only a few pages further on, that the plan " would meet the wants of those who desire a larger volume of circulation."³ The report, in fact, is crowded with such strange contradictions. What, for instance, is to be thought of a financial document which begins by declaring that the silver dollars already outstanding can be maintained at par only " so long as their number is kept within safe and proper limits,"⁴ and ends by commending its own plan as a short road to conditions " where we can with safety open our mints to the free coinage of silver?"⁵

Mr. Windom could not fail to notice that even with his curious plan of redemption of the notes in silver bullion, a fall in the price of silver would in-

---

[1] *Treas. Rep.*, 1889, p. lxx.
[2] *Ibid.*, p. lxxi.
[3] *Ibid.*, p. lxxvi.
[4] *Ibid.*, p. lxvi.
[5] *Ibid.*, p. lxxvi.

flict enormous losses on the Treasury. A decline of ten per cent., for instance, would impair to precisely that extent the power of the deposited silver bullion to redeem outstanding notes. But Mr. Windom believed such a decline to be impossible. Silver, in his opinion, would advance to its old coinage parity, because the output of the mines of the United States would thereafter be held back from the export market.[1] This sounded reasonable, but it was based on the wholly erroneous presumption, already tested and disproved since 1878, that the annual silver product of the world would not be vastly increased by the new demand. The net annual export of silver from the United States, at the time of Mr. Windom's calculations, was a trifle over twelve million dollars,[2] or, roughly, thirteen million ounces. The increase in the annual silver product outside the United States, during the next four years, was thirty million ounces.[3] In other words, the entire silver output of the United States could have been spared by foreign consumers, and still their available supplies would have increased with exceptional rapidity. This increase in the foreign silver product came, as we shall presently see, in the face of a decline in silver. What the production would have been with a steady rise in silver's price can only be conjectured.

    Mr. Windom's extraordinary plan was not destined to be embodied in the statutes as its author framed

[1] *Treas. Rep.*, 1889, pp. lxxvi. and lxxvii.
[2] *Ibid.*, p. xxlxvi.
[3] *U. S. Mint Report*, 1893. pp. 22 and 57.

it. From its unlimited possibilities of currency inflation, every prudent statesman shrank. But all that conservative Congressmen accomplished was to bind in advance, so far as possible, this Frankenstein which the Administration had constructed. The House of Representatives began by limiting the issue of notes to $4,500,000 monthly; it made them legal tender and, like the older obligations of the Government, "redeemable, on demand, in coin." Thus modified, the measure passed the House on the day of its first consideration, June 5, 1890, by a majority of sixteen, the entire vote in its favor being Republican. It went next to the Senate, and that body promptly showed its opinion of Mr. Windom's compromise by substituting a flat free-silver coinage bill, which passed by a majority of seventeen votes, the majority vote including every Republican senator, with two exceptions, from the very trans-Missouri States which the Secretary was laboring to conciliate. The situation was sufficiently awkward, because the tariff bill was laid before the Senate on the very day when the Senate returned its free-coinage substitute measure to the House. With calm assurance in the strength of its position, the Senate turned down the tariff bill on its calendar and awaited developments.

It has sometimes been alleged that the preparation and enactment of the Silver-Purchase Bill[1] of 1890 were made necessary, not by senatorial obstruction to the tariff bill, but by fear that in default of a com-

---

[1] John Sherman, letter to J. H. Walker, July 8, 1893; *Recollections*, ii., 1070 and 1188.

promise, a free-coinage measure would be passed. Such an inference assumes that President Harrison would have signed a free-silver bill, which he could hardly have done, in spite of Mr. Sherman's insinuation to that effect, after declaring officially that the results of such a law " would be discreditable to our financial management and disastrous to all business interests."[1] But the theory also assumes the existence during 1890 of a free-coinage majority in the House of Representatives. If such a majority existed, the time for it to show itself was when the Senate's free-coinage substitute bill came back to the House for action. Mr. Bland at once proposed that the Senate substitute be adopted by the House, and his motion was promptly defeated by a vote of 152 to 135. The President's declaration and the vote of the House of Representatives prove, if they have any meaning, that the fear of a free-coinage bill was imaginary. Nor need such a conclusion be based only on general principles; there has been positive and authoritative testimony to the same effect. " On the day when the Sherman Bill passed," Senator Teller has since declared from the floor of Congress, " there was no more show of a free-coinage bill becoming a law than there was of the heavens falling."[2] There could certainly be no safer witness than this Colorado statesman, the leader of the silver Republicans in the Senate of 1890.

But the jeopardy, indeed, into which the tariff bill had fallen through the deadlock on the Silver-Pur-

[1] Annual Message, Dec. 3, 1889.
[2] Senate speech, April 29, 1896.

chase Act, was real, and an anxious week for its promoters followed. The silver bill, as usual in case of a disagreement between House and Senate, went to a conference committee. When it emerged, it was so altered than an entire new set of financial problems was called forth. The conference bill required the Treasury to purchase monthly, not $4,500,000 worth of silver bullion, but 4,500,000 ounces, or as much thereof as should be offered. Like the House bill, it directed the Treasury to pay for this silver in legal-tender notes. These notes were not to be redeemable in silver bullion, for a final quietus was now put on Mr. Windom's fantastic redemption plan. The Secretary of the Treasury, " under such regulations as he may prescribe," was directed to " redeem such notes in gold or silver coin, at his discretion." But as a limitation to this discretionary power, the following remarkable clause was added: " It being the established policy of the United States to maintain the two metals on a parity with each other upon the present legal ratio, or such ratio as may be provided by law."

This conference measure, with its famous " parity clause," was chiefly the work of Mr. Sherman, for which reason the law became subsequently known, somewhat unjustly, as the " Sherman Act." Those who have studied Mr. Sherman's handiwork in legislative compromise, notably in the Resumption Act of 1875, will recognize something familiar in this compromise of 1890. Like the Resumption Law, it conceded a thoroughly bad principle in order to avoid the enactment of that principle in a still more vicious form. Both laws were extremely obscure in their description of the duties imposed on the Treasury; each was susceptible of two diametrically opposite interpretations, according to the personal convictions of the Secretary who should administer it. Neither ventured to say in plain English what its author meant, and both were therefore destined to bring on their future administrators a storm of legislative protest and abuse.

There is, however, little doubt of the purpose of the Compromise Bill of 1890. The senator who, in the ensuing debate on the measure, described it as " a beckoning hand for interpreter,"[1] expressed fairly the general bewilderment. But other senators showed plainly enough the meaning attached to the measure by the silver faction. " This compromise," said one of the most determined silver advocates, " is an abandonment, a total abandonment of the double standard."[2] " In all these provisions," another silver senator declared, " the gold redemption is asserted and is made the essential and the unqualified and the operative and the valuable condition of the bill."[3] No one, during the whole debate, combatted this interpretation. The Eastern senators confined themselves to pointing out that, while the time would probably never come when the Treasury would be forced to make its choice of metals in redemption, the " parity clause " required, in case of such emergency, that the note-holder should re-

[1] John W. Daniel, Senate speech, July 9.
[2] Francis M. Cockrell, Senate speech, July 9.
[3] Wilkinson Call, Senate speech, July 10.

ceive whichever kind of coin he desired.' We shall
find this contemporary evidence highly important in
the discussion of a later episode.

The conference measure promptly passed both
House and Senate. It passed the Senate partly because senators from the silver-producing States, con-
vinced that the Treasury purchases would raise the
price of silver to the coinage parity, now took the
floor in favor of it.² But the true reason for its
prompt enactment was the heavy party pressure
now applied to recalcitrant Republicans. The final
vote of July 14, 1890, is remarkable from the fact
that in neither House of Congress did a single Republican member vote against the bill, or a single
Democrat in favor of it.

Thus did this extraordinary measure pass into
law. It was presently followed by the passage of
the revenue law for which, as we have now seen, the
silver-purchase legislation was the price. The situation at the close of 1890 was remarkable in many
ways. The Treasury's accumulated surplus was
about to be wholly dissipated. Prospect of making
both ends meet in Government finances was to be
subjected altogether to the chances of outside trade.
In the face of these impaired resources, outstanding
demand liabilities of the Treasury were to be increased by upwards of fifty million dollars annually,
and this forced addition to the country's paper circulation was to be made at the very moment when
the Treasury's hoards were thrown on the open

[1] John R. McPherson, Senate speech, July 9.
[2] John P. Jones, Senate speech, July 8.

money market and when contraction of bank-note circulation had ceased.

When Secretary Sherman was defending, in 1879 and 1880, his own plan of Government legal-tender issues, he was reminded of the possibility that a heavy revenue deficit might some time leave the Treasury with nothing but its gold reserve from which to meet expenses. To this he answered that it was not " to be presumed that Congress will omit to provide ample revenues."[1] He cited further the objection that the amount of notes " may be enlarged by Congress, and that this power is liable to abuse," but his reply was that under resumption of specie payments " there is no temptation for over-issue."[2] Fourteen years had passed, and Congress now had suddenly enacted one law destined to force a deficit on the Treasury, and another to increase without assignable limit the issues of legal-tender notes. That Mr. Sherman himself should have voted for both these measures and constructed one of them is another notable instance of the irony of history.

[1] *Treas. Rep.*, 1879, p. x.   [2] *Ibid.*, 1880, p xv.

CHAPTER VII

THE EXPULSION OF GOLD

SO far as the Silver-Purchase Act was designed to help the silver market—and this we have seen to be its almost single purpose—it was an early and complete failure. Mr. Windom's report and the subsequent Congressional moves were immediately reflected, it is true, by a violent advance in silver. The speculators promptly put their machinery in order, and by way of affording every possible facility to a speculative craze, the New York Stock Exchange arranged for the deposit of silver bullion and the issue, against such deposits, of negotiable certificates which could be bought, sold, and delivered on the Exchange like any other security. In 1889, the average price of silver in New York was 93½ cents per ounce.[1] By July, 1890, it had risen to $1.04, and the enactment of the Silver-Purchase Law carried the price with a wild rush to $1.21 on September 3d. But the speculative movement ended, as such movements usually do, as soon as the earlier and shrewder speculators began to take their profits, and the reaction was even more rapid than the ad-

[1] *Treas. Rep.*, 1889, p. lxxxvi.

vance had been. Silver fell below 98 cents an ounce before Congress assembled again in December, 1890, and the President regretfully confessed the failure of the effort " to give to the market for silver bullion such support as the law contemplated."[1] Mr. Windom's annual report, issued at the same time, insisted that in spite of the failure of the law to help the silver market, " its beneficial results will eventually commend it to general approval," since it had already been " the means of providing a healthy and much-needed addition to the circulating medium of the United States."[2] This, it will be observed, was a somewhat altered theory of the purpose of the law, but it was also adopted by the President, who declared that " the increased circulation secured by the act has exerted and is continuing to exert a most beneficial influence on business and on general values."

Now it should be remarked, first, that this is precisely such an argument as might have been employed in 1872, for instance, in behalf of the increase and perpetuation of the older legal tenders. It is the familiar inflation argument. But, furthermore, it will not be difficult to show that Mr. Harrison's view of cause and effect in the trade movement of 1890 was quite unwarranted. The volume of American trade in 1890 was doubtless larger than in 1889,[3] but profits were no greater,[4] and the average

---

[1] Annual Message, Dec. 1, 1890.   [2] *Treas. Rep.*, 1890, p. xlix.
[3] New York *Financial Chronicle*, January 10, 1891, p. 64.
[4] New York Chamber of Commerce, *Annual Rep.*, 1890, pp. 81, 89, 98.

of commercial prices not so high '—which sufficiently refutes the argument that the new legal-tender issues under the Act of 1890 were the cause. It is true that the rampant speculation which broke out for a time in the American market, especially in that for securities, was ascribed by many good authorities to the paper-money issues.² This would have been no illogical result, judged by the precedent of the inflation period. But even in this regard, the influence of the Silver-Purchase Act could have been only slight. About five million dollars monthly in the new currency were coming upon the market. But in the one month of September, 1890, the circulating medium outside the Treasury was expanded by no less a sum than sixty-two million dollars ³—the most rapid increase in the country's history, not excepting the period of legal-tender issues during the war. Clearly, this unparalleled expansion did not result from the Silver-Purchase Act. Its true cause is easy to discover. The appropriation laws of the Fifty-First Congress were then doing their most effective work, and in that single month fifty-five million dollars, or nearly one fourth of the Treasury's total surplus, were emptied into the money market.⁴

It is probable enough that this unexpected and violent enlargement of the bank reserves, though it had slight connection with the law to whose operation Mr. Harrison assigned it, did its part in fanning the flame of speculation. But the fundamental

---

[1] U. S. Senate, *Report of 1892 on Prices and Wages*, vol. i., p. 9.
[2] London *Economist*, December 20, 1890.
[3] *Treas. Rep.*, 1891, pp. 15 and 95.   [4] *Ibid.*, p. 84.

reasons for the summer advances of 1890 were quite independent of the American currency supplies. There were two such reasons. I have already described the feverish eagerness with which Great Britain had been engaged, since 1886, in developing the resources of young foreign communities, taking securities in payment. This movement reached its culmination in 1890. During the five months from February to August of that year, £100,000,000 in new securities were brought out on the London market. "Business," in the words of a contemporary London review, "was enormous, and the rise in all descriptions of prices was astonishing."[1]

Along with the powerful reflex influence on our markets of this foreign speculation had come visible evidence that the world's supplies of grain were running into one of their intermittent periods of shortage. In 1889, every important foreign wheat-producing state, with two exceptions, yielded a deficient supply; the United States, meantime, producing the largest crop since 1884.[2] These short foreign supplies of 1889, followed next season by another harvest only slightly larger for the entire producing world, gave an additional fillip to the upward rush of prices in the early autumn of 1890.

The Administration, then, was mistaken in ascribing the trade movement of 1890 to the Silver-Purchase Act. The truth was soon made manifest

---

[1] London *Economist*, February 21, 1891; Commercial Review of 1890.

[2] Liverpool *Corn-Trade News*, 1889; *Annual Rep.*, U. S. Department of Agriculture, 1889.

when the chief sustaining influence under the fabric of speculation was suddenly removed. Into no foreign state had English capital rushed with such reckless eagerness as into the Argentine Republic. The resources of that state were overestimated; its climate was precarious for production, its currency depreciated, and its government untrustworthy. Nevertheless, English investors had taken its securities in constantly increasing quantities, and the powerful London house of Baring Brothers had underwritten loan after loan in Buenos Ayres, even as late as the spring of 1890. In 1889 the wheat crop of Argentina, whose increasing annual volume had chiefly inspired this investment movement, turned out a failure.

This industrial disaster was followed, first by a bloody political revolution, and then, in September, 1889, by a financial panic in Buenos Ayres. Demand for Argentine securities in London slackened immediately, and a certain timidity over all foreign investments became perceptible. This caution seemed to disappear in the final upward movement of prices early in 1890—a curious but perfectly familiar phenomenon on the eve of every speculative collapse. But the reviving speculation failed to disentangle the bankers from their imprudent South American engagements. Rumors of trouble began to circulate in the autumn. At length, on November 20th, Baring Brothers, unable either to sell or borrow with their Argentine securities, defaulted on £21,000,000 home liabilities. Only through the united efforts of the Bank of England

and the London financial institutions generally, who guaranteed the doubtful Baring assets, did Great Britain escape a repetition of the Overend-Gurney panic of 1866. So serious did the strain become, during one critical week of November, 1890, that the Bank of England adopted the extreme precaution of borrowing £4,500,000 gold from the Bank of France and the Imperial Bank of Russia.

This London episode was of serious significance to the United States. In a previous chapter we found that our abnormal import of European merchandise, from 1886 to 1890, represented largely capital invested by Great Britain in negotiable American securities. It followed that in 1890, when London's foreign investment bubble had been pricked, recall of British capital thus invested must ensue. The "Baring panic" was reflected promptly, not only by collapse at Buenos Ayres, but by a disturbance in the American money market so severe as to force the New York banks to repeat their emergency operation of 1884 and 1873, and issue $15,000,000 Clearing-House loan certificates.[1] At one time, loaning rates on call in New York City rose as high as 186 per cent., and there were numerous banking failures. Recovery, however, was rather unusually prompt, because the season's heavy export of American agricultural products, and our active interior trade, offset for the time the movement of English liquidation. In December, notwithstanding the condition of Europe's money markets, the United States imported gold. But with the ending of the

[1] *Treas. Rep.*, 1891, p. 327.

harvest movement came a swift and ominous change in the situation.

Between July 1, 1890, and January 1, 1891, the money circulating in the United States outside the Treasury was increased, in all, one hundred million dollars.[1] The revenue and appropriation laws of 1890 prevented the recall of any portion of this sum into the Treasury. The Silver-Purchase Law guaranteed an increase in the circulation of something like fifty millions annually. Even contraction in the bank-note issues had been suddenly arrested; for, as early as April, 1891, the impending deficit in revenue had forced the Treasury to abandon all Government-bond redemptions at a premium,[2] and with the abandonment of this policy the retirement of the bank notes ceased.[3] During the active harvest trade of 1890, employment had been found for these enormous additions to the money supply. But with the close of the year the harvest trade was ended; the dull interior season began, and it is invariably such a season which tests, as it did even in 1880, the character of a currency. By January, 1891—to quote the words of the United States Treasurer—

"the people who had demanded this hundred million of ready cash had made their use of it, and were willing to part with it. But the Treasury, which had found the means of paying it out, was not in a position to call it back. Money began to find its way into the great commercial centres, foreign exchange began to rise, and gold bars began to be taken from the Treasury for shipment abroad. . . ."

[1] *Treas. Rep.*, 1891, p. 15. [2] *Ibid.*, p. xxvi.
[3] *Ibid.*, pp. 27 and 358.

By the end of June the exports of gold had reached the unexampled figures of $70,000,000 for the six months."¹

Unexampled such an outflow of gold might very properly be called; for in six months of 1891 the shipments had exceeded the total gold exports of any twelve months since the currency inflation of the war.² But in 1891, as usually happens when an inflated currency begins its work of mischief, any explanation of the gold expulsion was received except the most plain and obvious. The Government reports explained that the national banks of England, France, Germany, and Russia had reasons for wishing to increase their gold reserves; that these institutions were encouraging gold imports by payment of commissions; that American tourists had been spending more gold abroad than usual because of the Paris Exposition.³ When these particular influences disappeared, and still the heavy outflow of gold continued, it was further pointed out that the Austrian Government, then laying its plans for resumption of specie payments, had been making strenuous exertions to obtain gold for the purpose.⁴ Particular stress was laid on the fact that many export gold consignments, during 1891 and 1892, went out with sterling exchange a small fraction below the usual gold-shipping point.

Now the facts alleged were all correct; but they did not in the least explain the enormous shipments.

[1] Treasurer Nebeker, *Treas. Rep.*, 1891, p. 16.
[2] U. S. Bureau of Statistics, *Annual Rep.*, 1891, p. xxx.
[3] Director of the Mint, *Treas. Rep.*, 1891, p. 146.
[4] *Ibid.*, 1892, p. 154.

The inducements offered occasionally by the European banks were contrived simply to draw imported gold into their own reserves rather than into the open specie market; but they could not cause the import. If foreign exchange had declined at New York, not a dollar in American gold could have been obtained by any European importer. The European banks, especially the Bank of France, were making a similar strenuous effort to get gold during our own resumption operations of 1878 and 1879 [1]; nevertheless, as we saw in a preceding chapter, France itself was forced by the downward movement of American exchange to send $30,000,000 gold to New York, and our total gold import of the resumption year was eighty millions. The alarming phenomenon of 1891 and 1892 was the persistence of sterling rates so high as to force continuous gold exports from the United States. At a fixed rate of foreign exchange, gold must be shipped from any market in settlement of foreign liabilities. But the gold-exporters did not cause this high exchange. On the contrary, a gold-shipper must sell in New York his draft on London before he can obtain the gold, and therefore each successive shipment of the kind tends to depress exchange. What the foreign importers did was merely to avail themselves of gold already in motion from the United States [2]; and back of all the superficial reasoning of the day the

---

[1] London correspondence of the Treasury, *Specie Resumption*, pp. 129, 133, 358, 365, 369.

[2] G. Von Mauthner, manager Austrian syndicate, *Neue Freie Presse*, May, 1893.

unwelcome conclusion began to force itself forward that the gold expulsion was an index, as truly as the gold expulsion of 1862, to a disordered and inflated currency.[1]

The obvious danger from this heavy drain of gold was the possibility of a " run " on the Treasury gold reserve by holders of the redeemable legal-tender notes. The Treasury had been placed in the situation of a bank of issue which has dissipated its resources while increasing largely its demand liabilities. Nothing is more certain in banking than the fact that unless such an institution has the power of contracting its circulation, the first considerable export demand for specie will exhaust its coin reserves. The power of such contraction at its own discretion had been denied the Treasury by the Act of May, 1878, and the power of automatic contraction had been flung away by the revenue act of 1890. There was no immediate danger from that quarter, because this very dissipation of the Treasury's surplus had provided the banks with gold to meet the heavy export drain. Of the sixty-million outpour from the surplus during September, 1890, thirty-eight millions had been in the form of gold, and thirty millions more of Treasury gold had been paid out on balance before the close of the ensuing June.[2] At the New York Clearing-House, during this period, gold had been used for eighty per cent. of the payments made by the Treasury,[3] and the aggregate payments were the largest in the history of the Government. So long

[1] Treasurer Nebeker, *Treas. Rep.*, 1891, p. 13.
[2] *Ibid.*, p. 84.   [3] *Treas. Rep.*, 1896, p. 137.

as such a movement continued, there was obviously no occasion or inducement for the presentation of legal-tender notes for redemption.

But no such avalanche of specie could move out indefinitely. Already, in June, 1891, the gold reserve against the legal tenders had fallen below the low record of 1884, when Hugh McCulloch had warned Congress of a possible suspension of gold payments, and below even that of 1885, when Daniel Manning borrowed gold from the New York banks on the collateral of fractional silver. Fortune favored the Treasury, however, as it had often done before in the checkered financial history of the United States. An event was at hand, an accident of nature, which with the country's finances in a sound condition would have opened a chapter similar to that of the resumption period. We have seen that the short wheat crops of 1889 and 1890 had already drawn heavily on the world's supplies. In 1891, the stock of wheat in American and foreign storehouses was still extremely low, and on top of this came a total failure of the South Russian wheat crop, the second largest source of supply for the consumers of Europe, followed in France by the most serious harvest shortage since 1879.[1] In the face of this foreign catastrophe, the United States produced in 1891 the largest grain crop in its history, before or since. While Europe's total wheat yield decreased 156,000,000 bushels from that of 1889,[2] our own crops

[1] Beerbohm's London *Corn-Trade List*, August, 1891; *Bradstreet's*, August, 1891.
[2] Liverpool *Corn-Trade News*, 1891.

increased 255,000,000,[1] and exceeded by fully one hundred million bushels the largest American crop on record.[2] The market for this crop was as broad and eager as the market for the crop of twelve years before; the early demand especially was stimulated by the ukase prohibiting wheat exports from Russia and by the French decree removing the import duty. Export of breadstuffs from the United States, in the ensuing season, ran beyond the enormous outward trade of either 1879 or 1880.[3]

This remarkable freak of nature changed for six months the whole complexion of affairs. Beginning with September, there was imported from Europe, within six months, very nearly fifty million dollars worth of gold.[4] As in the autumn of 1880, so in the autumn of 1891, part of this gold went into the Treasury in exchange for silver and legal-tender notes, and the Government's gold reserves advanced again. But the movement ended as suddenly as it began. The season's export of grain was completed earlier than usual, because of the very urgent needs of foreign importers. For a few weeks during September and October, freight-room on out-bound grain ships was almost unobtainable, so great was the pressure of export supplies. But with this immediate demand satisfied, the harvest trade contracted, and the Western banks at once found their hands full of idle currency. In November this

[1] U. S. Department of Agriculture, *Annual Reports*.
[2] *Ibid.*, corrected by commercial estimates.
[3] U. S. Bureau of Statistics, *Annual Report* for 1892, p. 1.
[4] *Treas. Rep.*, 1892, p. 258.

currency began to move East in great quantities; it reached the city banks at the time when a movement of reaction was beginning on all the markets.

If prices and trade activity were dependent, as the fiat-money advocates contend, on the volume of money circulation, no such reaction would have been reasonable; for at the close of 1891 the circulating medium of this country, outside the idle Treasury holdings, was larger by $157,000,000 than it was when Congress passed the Silver-Purchase Bill.[1] But no theory has been more repeatedly disproved by ordinary experience. Wheat, for instance, had advanced some thirteen cents a bushel during the urgent foreign buying in August, but it declined again, after this demand subsided, simply because commercial experts discovered that the Agricultural Department had underestimated the season's American wheat crop by fully seventy million bushels. What concerned the East equally was the fall in security prices, under the heavy foreign liquidation. The recall of invested capital by London to meet its own necessities had long since ceased. But the shock of 1890 had discouraged new ventures in foreign fields, and the alarming condition of the United States Treasury and currency, which Europe perceived more clearly than the American people themselves,[2] had started a fresh movement to get rid of American investments. The strong-boxes of the English investors of 1887 and 1888 were one

[1] *Treas. Rep.*, 1892, p. 103.
[2] London *Economist*, December 20, 1890; December 26, 1891; February 20, and July 9, 1892.

after another unlocked; the true balance of international trade swung against us in the face of the heavy grain exports. In January, 1892, foreign exchange advanced sharply; in the six first months of 1892, $41,500,000 gold was shipped, and the shipments during July and August averaged two to seven millions weekly.

To the Treasury, the situation was now very different from what it had been a year before. The autumn imports of gold in 1891 had partly replenished the Government's reserve, but they did not make good the enormous gold disbursements of the previous twelve months. With the January interest-payments in 1892, there was another heavy loss of gold from the Treasury,[1] and by the close of May, 1892, the fund had fallen to $114,000,000.

Now the sum of one hundred millions gold had long been fixed as the minimum reserve to be maintained against outstanding legal tenders. Secretary Sherman had argued that at least the $95,500,000 gold received through sale of bonds under the Resumption Act " must, under the existing law, be maintained unimpaired for the purpose for which it was created."[2] This view was formally accepted by subsequent Treasury administrations,[3] but Congress took no action regarding the matter until 1882, when a law was passed suspending the issue of gold certifi-

[1] *Treas. Rep.*, 1892, p. 18.
[2] Letter to the President of the Senate, May 16, 1879.
[3] Secretary Folger, *Treas. Rep.*, 1881, p. x.; Secretary McCulloch, *Treas. Rep.*, 1894, p. xxxi.; Treasurer Jordan, *Treas. Rep.*, 1885, pp. 480 and 483; Secretary Foster, *Treas. Rep.*, 1892, p. xxix.

cates—the natural form in which the Treasury would pay out gold on balance—" whenever the amount of gold coin and gold bullion in the Treasury reserved for the redemption of United States notes falls below one hundred millions of dollars."[1] It was clearly declared and understood, in the progress of the debate in 1882, that the purpose of this proviso was to ensure a reserve against the legal tenders at least as large as the amount prescribed.[2] All subsequent Treasury administrations accordingly set that sum apart in their accounts; and in this very year 1892, when the question was referred by the House of Representatives to its judiciary committee, the majority report of this committee declared " that it was the intention of Congress to fix the minimum amount of this reserve fund at $100,000,000 gold and gold bullion, and that it should be maintained at that sum."[3]

The significance of this proviso, in view of the situation of the Treasury and of the foreign exchange market in 1892, is plain. During April and May, the Treasury's gold balance had been falling at the rate of five to six million dollars monthly. Three months more of such depletion would bring the fund below the hundred-million mark. Six months more, if the Treasury's monthly deficit in revenue continued, would bring the gold fund to a level where the bond-issue power of the Resumption Act would be the only recourse left, and a bond-issue, with a

[1] U. S. Statutes, 47th Congress, 1st Session, Ch. 290, Sec. 12.
[2] W. B. Allison, Senate speech, June 22, 1882.
[3] *Congressional Record*, July 6, 1892.

Presidential election at hand, would undoubtedly mean the political ruin of the Administration and its party.

What added to the embarrassment of the Treasury was the fact that less and less of its revenue was now received in gold. During the first half of 1890, ninety per cent. of the New York customs payments had been made in this form of money. Gold had in fact been used at that time in discharge of nearly all mutual balances between Eastern institutions. The obvious reason for these gold disbursements by the banks to the Government and to one another, prior to the Act of July 14, 1890, was that their legal-tender holdings had been rarely much in excess of the retail needs of customers. It is easy to see what had now altered this normal trade adjustment. After each succeeding harvest season, a larger volume of new paper currency moved from the interior to the East; the paper currency was increasing vastly more rapidly than the needs of trade. In the summer of 1890, the New York Associated Banks held in their reserves less than $31,000,000 legal tenders, which was near the average of the season in preceding years. In 1891 they reported fifty millions; in 1892, sixty millions,[1] and the bankers had to recognize, in providing for future needs of depositors, that under the Silver-Purchase Law there was no limit to this increase in legal-tender holdings, whereas the limit to the gold reserve in the vaults of city banks might possibly be reached in a single season.

[1] New York weekly bank statements, July 5, 1890; July 3, 1891; July 2, 1892.

The first result of this displacement of gold with paper money was the increasing use of notes in settlements between the banks. In the twelve months ending with September, 1890, only one per cent. of the New York Clearing-House balances were paid in legal tenders; in 1891, the legal-tender percentage had risen to thirty-five per cent; in 1892, it was fifty-seven and a half.[1] Under the conditions which we have noticed, it will hardly be contended that this change was abnormal. But if a decreased use of gold was logical in payments from bank to bank, it was equally logical in payments to the Government. In the first six months of 1890, as we have seen, nine tenths of the customs revenue at New York was received in gold; in the corresponding period of 1892, three fourths of it came in legal-tender notes.[2]

Exactly the same embarrassment was arising as had developed in 1880 and 1884, before the silver currency had been absorbed into circulation. But in 1892, there was this important difference; that the notes of 1890, redeemable in gold and available for all banking uses, were not excluded from settlements at the New York Clearing-House. When, therefore, Secretary Foster, who had succeeded to the Treasury on the death of Mr. Windom, found himself confronted on the one hand with a fall in the Government's gold reserve to the danger-point, and on the other with a rapid shrink-

---

[1] New York Clearing-House annual statements, October 1, 1890, 1891, 1892.
[2] *Treas. Rep.*, 1892, p. 46.

age of gold receipts in revenue, he quickly concluded that the Government's own disbursement of gold must cease. The legal-tender surplus of the Treasury, it is true, was also small; but all Government notes received on revenue could promptly be used again for payments, and so long as receipts and expenditures were equal, the gold fund would apparently be protected. Accordingly, in the summer of 1891 and the spring of 1892, a steadily decreasing amount of gold was paid out in the Government's New York accounts. After the first week of July, 1892, gold payments by the Treasury into the Clearing-House were practically abandoned.[1]

The circle of embarrassment was now complete. Gold was virtually hoarded, both by the banks and by the Government. The first step in the depreciation of the currency had been made; the others followed, some of them immediately, others only after a lapse of a year or more, but all in a sequence marked out by inexorable economic law. Neither the banks nor the Treasury were to blame. Both were victims of circumstances beyond their own control; both had taken the only action reasonably to be expected under the circumstances. We shall now, however, be able to understand the reason for the very remarkable and startling development which next arose.

We have seen that with the banks and the Treasury both guarding their gold reserves, payment of gold through the New York Clearing-House had practically ceased. Now the forty million gold

[1] *Treas. Rep.*, 1892, p. 49; 1893, p. 41.

exports, necessitated in the first six months of 1892 in settlement of European debit balances, had hitherto been provided through these Clearing-House gold payments. A sterling banker sold his bill of exchange on London, when rates were at the shipping point, to merchandise importers with foreign debts to pay. He took in settlement the checks of the importers, deposited the checks at his own bank, and asked for gold against them. This is the normal *modus operandi* of international exchange. Few banks, even then, carried an individual gold balance large enough to meet more than one or two large export orders; but with a normal currency, the matter was automatically adjusted. The checks of the merchandise importers went through the Clearing-House next day, the banks on which the checks were drawn settled their balances in gold, and the resultant credit balance passed into the gold-exporter's bank in that form of money. The sterling banker had in effect drawn on the aggregate gold reserve of the New York associated banks, and these banks, up to the middle of 1892, had provided all gold required for export.

But we have seen already how this situation had been altered through the Law of 1890. On June 30, 1892, with foreign exchange at the normal shipping point, $3,200,000 was ordered at New York for export.[1] The checks passed duly through the Clearing-House, but the credit balance thus created to the gold-exporter's bank was met in legal-tender

[1] U. S. Mint, *Annual Rep.*, 1892, p. 43.

notes. These notes could not be used by the sterling bankers to meet their drafts on London, and the two or three deposit banks with which they kept accounts were unable, out of their own reserves, to provide the necessary gold. What was to be done?

There were only two alternatives left to the sterling bankers: to bid an open premium for gold, or to present their legal-tender notes for redemption in gold at the Treasury. But the bid of a premium on gold, under such circumstances, would have been public witness to depreciation of the currency, and it was expressly to prevent such depreciation that the gold reserve in the Treasury had been established. The entire credit of the United States had been pledged, in the words of the Resumption Act, " to enable the Secretary of the Treasury to prepare and provide " against exactly such contingencies. There was no other object in the accumulation of a specified gold reserve in the Treasury. Therefore the bankers were not only not in duty bound to bid an open market premium for export gold, but such an act would have been a deliberate assault on the public credit. They made no such bid in July, 1892, but carried their notes to the Treasury to be redeemed in gold.

In the thirteen years from 1879 to 1891 inclusive, only $34,000,000 notes had been thus presented for redemption, and the largest redemptions of any year had been in 1879.[1] In fact, as we have seen in our review of previous autumn movements of currency, the tendency had been, not to present notes to the

[1] *Treas. Rep.*, 1893, p. 13.

Treasury for gold, but to offer gold in exchange for the Treasury's surplus legal tenders. The withdrawal of Treasury gold in quantity through presentation of legal tenders for redemption was therefore a decided and alarming novelty. But the reckoning for the wild performances of 1890 had now begun, and the spectacle soon became familiar enough. From June, 1892, throughout the whole series of troubled years which followed, almost every dollar of gold exported from the United States was obtained on note redemption from the Treasury.[1] In his annual report of 1892, the Secretary of the Treasury despondently confessed that a heavy deficit in revenue was impending, and that the whole redemption machinery of the Government was in peril.[2]

Extraordinary interest was lent to this complicated situation by the Presidential election of 1892. Ever since the enactment of the two laws of 1890, the Administration party had been unfortunate at the polls. In November, 1890, it had been overwhelmed by the most sweeping political reverse since 1882. As in the earlier year, so in 1890, not only the doubtful States but the Administration strongholds went over by heavy majorities to the opposition. Massachusetts had cast its vote for Mr. Harrison, in 1888, by a plurality of 32,037; in 1890 it elected William E. Russell, Democratic candidate for governor, by 9053. Robert E. Pattison and the opposition carried Pennsylvania by 16,554, against

[1] *Treas. Rep.*, p. 12; 1896, pp. 130 and 131.
[2] Secretary Foster, *Treas. Rep.*, 1892, p. xxix.

Mr. Harrison's 1888 plurality of 79,458. Nebraska went Democratic, for the first time in its history; Illinois and Michigan went over similarly to the opposition. The House of Representatives chosen in 1888 was Republican by twenty-one plurality; its successor contained the huge Democratic plurality of 149.

The influence of this electoral result, so far as concerned the legislation of the next two years, was of the slightest. The Senate was still Republican; no law of a radical or partisan character was therefore likely to pass both Houses. Mr. Sherman himself made a perfunctory move in the direction of revoking the worst part of the Silver-Purchase Act,[1] but his proposal was not taken seriously. Instead, both houses instantly set to work constructing free-coinage bills. The struggle over these measures in the new Democratic House of Representatives continued up to the eve of the Presidential campaign of 1892. Opponents of the bill were so fearful of results that they devoted all their energies to preventing a vote on the measure. Twice the House divided equally on the question of laying the bill upon the table, party lines on both occasions being absolutely broken. The Senate, meantime, taking the bit in its teeth, passed a free-coinage law on July 1, 1892, by a majority of four, both parties again disintegrating on the vote. What the result of this Senate vote would have been in the House of Representatives, under ordinary circumstances, is a matter of conjecture. But the season was very

[1] *Recollections*, ii., 1189.

late, the Presidential canvass had begun, and eventually the silver bill was left to die through the adjournment of Congress.

It might perhaps have been supposed that in view of the serious condition of the Treasury's finances, at least an effort would be made to readjust the revenue. But once more the mischievous entanglement of the revenue question with party prejudice obstructed any reasonable action. The House, with which, under the Constitution, revenue laws must originate, passed in the spring of 1892 by very large majorities a series of bills removing all import duties from wool and woollen goods, from cotton-bagging, and from binder-twine. This action was no doubt consistent with the platform of the House majority, and the plan of dealing with separate articles in separate bills was admirable. But for all this, the House measures did not in the least meet the real emergency. If enacted without supplementary legislation, they would merely have made a bad matter worse. Whether right or wrong in principle, the duties on these various commodities were raising revenue, and in 1892 no revenue could be spared. To cut off even these receipts in the Treasury's existing situation, without substituting some other source of income, would simply have been a piece of folly.

The bills failed in the protectionist Senate, and probably no other outcome was expected by their authors. One recourse remained—a recourse which had been promised repeatedly in party platforms. It was possible, while still leaving revenue unchanged, to save the Treasury from actual deficit by cutting down expenses. And in fact this Fifty-Second House of Representatives virtuously resolved at the very start, and by a vote of 164 to 95, that " in view of the present condition of the Treasury, . . . no money ought to be appropriated by Congress except such as is manifestly necessary to carry on the several departments, frugally, efficiently, and honestly administered."[1] But economy is an easier watchword in resolutions for public edification than in close committees, besieged by greedy Congressional applicants. A few appropriation committees made a resolute effort at retrenchment; other committees quite as resolutely unloosed the purse-strings, and the Senate, as usual, loaded down the bills with its own particular objects of extravagance.

The net result was curious and extremely mischievous. In its two sessions, this Fifty-Second Congress cut down naval appropriations nine million dollars; a proper enough reduction, if made as part of a consistent scheme of economy. But against this saving, it ran up river and harbor appropriations eight millions, raising them to the largest total by far in the Government's history. It saved three millions in the allowance for new fortifications, only to increase by the respectable sum of eighty millions the pension appropriations of its predecessors.[2] In short, the opprobrious title of " billion-dollar Congress," flung at the first Congress under Mr. Harrison because appropriations,

[1] *Congressional Record*, January 15, 1892.
[2] *Treas. Rep.*, 1893, p. cxvi.

annual and permanent, ran within thirteen millions of that handsome total, applied with literal truth to the Congress chosen in 1890, which had made economy its plea before the people.

With this rather complicated record, the two parties went to the people in the campaign of 1892, and the result was another sweeping Democratic victory. But it was not easy, when the campaign throughout the country was surveyed, to say exactly what the victory meant. High protection and tariff reform had locked horns again, and on these questions the verdict of 1892 was unequivocal. But as to where either party, and in particular the successful party, stood in the vital matter of the currency, no one could confidently assert. The Republican convention at Minneapolis on June 7th had neglected to say a word about the unlucky Silver-Purchase Act, and in view of the incidents already considered in this chapter, the omission was not surprising. But the attitude of the Democratic party, in its convention at Chicago two weeks later, was more singular. They " denounced " the Law of 1890, not as unsound finance, but as a " cowardly makeshift "—a phrase which certainly suggested deference to free-coinage sentiment. Nor did they even promise to repeal it. Strange as it may seem, all that the Democratic convention of 1892 distinctly did in this matter was to advise the Republicans to revoke the law. The possibility of danger in this " makeshift," so the Chicago platform calmly announced, " should make all of its supporters, as well as its author, anxious for it speedy repeal."

This declaration is a curiosity even among the oddities of American platform literature; it may almost be described as a political joke; for the final votes on the Silver-Purchase Bill in 1890 had disclosed on the affirmative side not one Democratic Congressman. But if this manifesto was ambiguous, the convention's general declaration on the coinage was a master-stroke at Delphic utterance. Every shade of conflicting economic and political opinion had its turn in the paragraph. The party believed in "the coinage of both gold and silver without discrimination." Yet it pledged "the equal power of every dollar at all times in the markets and in the payment of debts," which was, of course, entirely incompatible with the other declaration. The gold and silver dollars must, moreover, "be of equal intrinsic and exchangeable value," and this equality was to be attained, either "through international agreement," or "by such safeguards of legislation as shall insure the maintenance of parity of the two metals." As to what these legislative safeguards ought to be, the platform had nothing to say. The final declaration, "that all paper currency shall be kept at par with and redeemable in coin," was fortunately less ambiguous, and was useful for appeal in subsequent legislation. On the whole, it was safe to say that the interpretation of this currency plank depended wholly on the interpreter. The advocate of any policy could invoke some part of it in behalf of his own purposes, and the convention's choice of Mr. Cleveland as its candidate made conservative interpretation certain.

The business communities of the East, which gave Mr. Cleveland a good share of his support, were guided wholly by their confidence in the ex-President's conservatism, by their objection to the currency experiments of the Harrison Administration, and by their willingness to try a lower tariff. But the character of the canvass in the West and South was ominous. At least eight of the Democratic State conventions early in 1892—in Colorado, Florida, Georgia, Idaho, Kansas, Nevada, South Carolina, and Texas—had submitted flat and unqualified demands for a free-silver coinage law. Others in the more conservative Middle States, among them Illinois, Iowa, and Michigan, had framed somewhat more cautious declarations whose actual purport was the same. Three of them openly repudiated the coinage plank of the national platform. The South Carolina Democrats, on May 18th, within a month of the national convention, entered their " solemn protest against the nomination of Grover Cleveland " because of his well-known principles on the currency. After the nomination had been made, the Colorado Democrats, on September 13th, endorsed the national platform " with the exception of that part of it relating to silver and coinage," while the Nevada Democrats had already declared themselves " absolved from all obligation to support the nominees " of the party unless such nominees expressly declared themselves for free coinage.

These three States, it is true, were not fairly typical; for two of them were silver-producers, and in the third the Democratic party had surrendered to an agrarian movement based on currency inflation.

But the spirit animating these unusual party manifestoes broke out at intervals throughout the country. It focussed in the so-called People's Party, organized at Omaha on July 4, 1892, into whose ranks flocked the financial and social agitators of every sort, and whose members first applied to themselves the political term of Populists. This third party's platform described the maintenance of the gold standard as " a vast conspiracy against mankind, organized on two continents," and " rapidly taking possession of the world." The party proposed free and unlimited coinage of silver, and demanded that the circulating medium " be speedily increased to not less than fifty dollars per capita." Since the per capita circulation at the time, by the Treasury estimate, was less than twenty-five dollars, this was a distinct demand for the doubling of the Government's money issues. In addition to its currency plank, the Omaha convention declared for Government ownership of railroads, for a graduated income tax, and approved the application of the boycott in labor disputes.

Now there was little absolutely new in this Populist manifesto. With the exception of the boycott clause, each of its declarations had seen service in previous third-party platforms. But the third-party episode of 1892 is a matter of great importance, in view of the influence which its supporters were to exercise in the next Congressional session and in the Presidential canvass four years afterwards. The movement was remarkable even in 1892. The largest popular vote ever before obtained by a third-party candidate was cast in 1880, when General

Weaver of Iowa, running on a fiat-money platform, polled 308,578 votes, scattered all over the Union. In 1892, the same candidate, nominated by the Peoples Party, received the remarkable vote of 1,042,631, which was more than one fifth the poll of Mr. Harrison. Never since the election of 1860 had a third party carried a single State. In 1892 the People's Party carried Kansas, Colorado, Idaho, and Nevada, and cast twenty-two votes in the Electoral College. They sent to the Fifty-third Congress four senators and eleven representatives, and in view of the known sympathy of many professing Democrats with the principles of the Populist party, it was certain that their ideas would get a hearing.

It will readily be seen, therefore, that Mr. Cleveland's popular plurality of 379,000—the largest obtained by any Presidential candidate since 1872—meant less than appeared on its face. Nor did the Democratic House plurality of ninety-one, and the party's possession of a majority in both branches of Congress, for the first time since Buchanan's Administration, point to a harmonious Administration. Every experienced politician knew at the close of 1892 that a stormy session was ahead for Congress. But even the confused political situation was now overshadowed by the approaching catastrophe in the national finances.

CHAPTER VIII

THE PANIC OF 1893

WE left the Treasury, in our last chapter, confronted for the first time in its history with a heavy drain on its gold reserve to redeem outstanding notes. During the nine months after the beginning of this movement, Secretary Foster was engaged in a continuous struggle to save the redemption fund. The strain relaxed temporarily in the autumn of 1892, when interior trade was again very large. Practically no gold was imported, but, on the other hand, exports ceased almost entirely. Moreover, upwards of $25,000,000 legal tenders were drawn from the New York banks to the West and South,[1] and the Treasury obtained some gold from these institutions in exchange for notes delivered at interior points.[2] But when the Eastward flow of currency began again, at the end of the harvest season, gold exports were resumed and with them the presentation of legal tenders for redemp-

[1] New York weekly bank statements, July 30 and November 19, 1892.
[2] *Treas Rep.*, 1892, p. 13; N. Y. *Financial Chronicle*, July 9 and July 23, 1892.

tion. In December, 1892, and January, 1893, upwards of $25,000,000 gold was withdrawn by noteholders from the Treasury to provide for export needs.¹

By the close of January the Treasury's gold reserve had fallen to a figure barely eight millions over the legal minimum.² With February's early withdrawals even larger, Secretary Foster so far lost hope of warding off the crisis that he gave orders to prepare the engraved plates for a bond-issue under the Resumption Act.³ As a last resort, however, he bethought himself of Secretary Manning's gold-borrowing operation of 1885. In February Mr. Foster came in person to New York to urge the banks to give up gold voluntarily in exchange for the Treasury's legal-tender surplus.⁴

From a strict commercial point of view, there was good reason why the banks should not make any such exchange. But the plea that a panic must at all hazards be averted, combined with the argument of patriotic support of the Government, at length prevailed. The New York banks turned over to the Treasury, in exchange for notes, six to eight million dollars gold.⁵ This, with some small amounts still paid through the customs revenue, was enough to keep the Treasury afloat until March 4th, when the

¹ *Treas. Rep.*, 1893, p. 12.   ² *Ibid.*, p. 96.
³ Letter of instructions to chief of U. S. Bureau of Engraving and Printing, February 20, 1893.
⁴ New York *Financial Chronicle*, February 11 and February 18, 1893.
⁵ New York *Tribune*, February 9, 10, and 11, 1893; New York *Financial Chronicle*, February 11, 1893.

entire problem could be turned over to the new Executive. To his successor in the Treasury, Mr. Foster left exactly $100,982,410 in the gold reserve,[1] and barely $25,000,000 in other forms of money.[2]

Probably no financial administration in our history has entered office under such disheartening conditions. The condition of the national finances was almost as bad as when the Buchanan Administration relinquished office. The Treasury was empty and the public credit shaken. But even in 1861, the line of financial policy to be pursued in the emergency was clearly pointed out, whereas in 1893 the Cleveland Administration found it impossible to frame a policy. It was indeed open to the new Administration, as to its predecessor, to issue bonds under the Law of 1875. But such a move, at such a time, was likely to involve the political ruin of the Administration, and it would certainly destroy all possibility of gaining Congressional consent to the first and most urgent measure on the Administration's books— repeal of the Silver-Purchase Law. This was beyond doubt the reason why the President's inaugural address, on March 4, 1893, gave no intimation of his purposes regarding the gold reserve. Meantime the new Secretary of the Treasury merely adopted his predecessor's makeshift, appealing to the banks to give up gold in exchange for notes.[3] To this request, enthusiastically echoed in the press, and argued on the plea of patriotism, the banks again responded. In March and April, therefore, the

[1] *Treas. Rep.*, 1893, p. lxxii. [2] *Ibid.*, p. 96.
[3] *Ibid.*, 1893, p. lxxii.

astonishing spectacle was witnessed of some $25,-
000,000 legal tenders delivered to the Treasury for
export gold, offset by an almost equal sum of bank
gold turned over grudgingly for notes.

Such a situation could not continue long. The
very sight of this desperate struggle going on to
maintain the public credit was sufficient to alarm
both home and foreign interests, and this alarm was
now reflected everywhere. The feverish money
market, the disordered and uneasy market for
securities, and the renewed advance in foreign exchange, combined to bring matters to a head. On
April 15, Secretary Carlisle gave notice that issue of
Treasury gold certificates should be suspended.
This action was taken merely in conformity with
the Law of 1882, already cited. It was, however,
public announcement that, for the first time since
resumption of specie payments, the reserve against
the legal tenders had fallen below the statutory minimum. The news provoked immediate and uneasy
inquiry as to what the Treasury's next move would
be. No definite advices came from Washington,
but in the following week a very unexpected and
financially alarming rumor ran through the markets.
Out of the $25,000,000 legal tenders redeemed in
gold during March and April, 1893, nearly $11,000,-
000 had been Treasury notes of 1890.[1] Under one
clause of the Law of 1890, it will be remembered,
the Secretary was empowered to " redeem such
notes in gold or silver coin at his discretion." The
burden of the rumor of April 17th was that the

[1] *Treas. Rep.*, 1896, p. 130.

Treasury, now that its gold reserve had actually fallen below the legal limit, would refuse further redemption of these notes in gold, and would tender only silver coin.

During the two or three days in which this rumor circulated, general misgiving and uneasiness prevailed, the security markets fell into great disorder, foreign exchange again rose rapidly, and the money market ran up to the panicky rate of fifteen per cent. On April 20th, the Secretary of the Treasury gave out a public interview, declaring that in the exercise of his discretionary power he had "been paying gold for the coin Treasury notes issued for the purchase of silver bullion, and he will continue to do so as long as he has gold lawfully available for that purpose." But this official statement, instead of allaying panic, added fuel to it. What did the Secretary mean by "gold lawfully available for that purpose"? This was the very question at stake, and Mr. Carlisle's unfortunate, though probably unintentional, evasion had precisely the effect which such an utterance ought to have made impossible. The disturbance in the markets extended after the issue of this statement; it was not allayed until the President, on April 23d, took the matter into his own hands, announcing in a public interview with the Associated Press that despite the discretionary clause regarding redemption of the notes of 1890, "the declaration of the policy of the Government to maintain the parity between the two metals seems so clearly to regulate this discretion as to dictate their redemption in gold."

That the President was justified in this construction of the law, must be apparent from our examination, in a previous chapter, of the debate on the Silver-Purchase Bill. Even the free-coinage senators had declared in 1890, on the floor of Congress, that this was the actual meaning of the parity clause. It is, however, entirely probable that Mr. Carlisle wavered for a moment in the face of the emergency, and that moment's vacillation had done its mischief. The public mind was on the verge of panic. During a year or more, it had been continuously disturbed by the undermining of the Treasury, a process visible to all observers. The financial situation in itself was vulnerable. In all probability, the crash of 1893 would have come twelve months before, had it not been for the accident of 1891's great harvest, in the face of European famine.

But even this lucky accident served in the end to rouse again the spirit of speculation, extremely dangerous under existing conditions. Huge as this country's merchandise exports were, in the season after the harvest of 1891, the import trade increased with almost equal strides. A year later, the balance of foreign trade had actually turned, and in the nine months ending with March, 1893, imports exceeded exports by no less a sum than forty-seven millions—a record unprecedented since the days of irredeemable paper money.[1] Severe economy alone could have averted the approaching retribution, and instead of practicing economy the people, like the Government, were indulging

[1] U. S. Bureau of Statistics, *Report* for March, 1893.

in renewed extravagance. The bank returns were a striking witness to this tendency. Loans of the national banks had increased, during 1892, no less than $165,000,000—an increase greater even than that of 1880—and of this sudden expansion, nearly one hundred millions came in States west of the Ohio and south of the Tennessee line.[1]

The panic of 1893, in its outbreak and in its culmination, followed the several successive steps familiar to all such episodes. One or two powerful corporations, which had been leading in the general plunge into debt, gave the first signals of distress. On February 20th, the Philadelphia and Reading Railway Company, with a capital of forty millions and a debt of more than $125,000,000, went into bankruptcy; on the 5th of May, the National Cordage Company, with twenty millions capital and ten millions liabilities, followed suit. The management of both these enterprises had been marked by the rashest sort of speculation; both had been favorites on the speculative markets. The Cordage Company in particular had kept in the race for debt up to the moment of its ruin. In the very month of the Company's insolvency, its directors declared a heavy cash dividend; paid, as may be supposed, out of capital. As it turned out, the failure of this notorious undertaking was the blow that undermined the structure of speculative credit. In January, National Cordage stock had advanced twelve per cent. on the New York market, selling at 147. Sixteen weeks

[1] Comptroller of the Currency, statements of December 2, 1891, and December 9, 1892.

later, it fell below ten dollars per share, and with it, during the opening week of May, the whole stock market collapsed.

The bubble of inflated credit having been thus punctured, a general movement of liquidation started. This movement immediately developed very serious symptoms. Of these symptoms the most alarming was the rapid withdrawal of cash reserves from the city banks. There are two classes of deposits on the basis of which these larger banks conduct their business: deposits by individuals and deposits by other banking institutions. A country bank in the West or South, for instance, is required by law to hold in cash a sum fifteen per cent. as large as the sum of its deposits; but it may entrust to other banks at certain designated cities three fifths of this cash reserve.[1] Since demand for loans at these interior points is nominal except in the harvest season, and since the city banks are always willing to pay two per cent. for the use of such interior funds, it follows that the bulk of the country bank reserves is kept perpetually on deposit in the cities.

Opinions differ considerably as to the wisdom of this policy.[2] It is, however, practiced as regularly in Great Britain as in the United States, and its purpose is legitimate—to give the widest employment to the country's general money supply. The drain of currency from the cities to the interior in

[1] U. S. Revised Statutes, Sec. 5192.
[2] *Annual Rep.* Comptroller of the Currency, 1884, p. 57; 1893, p. 17; Comptroller Knox, *Treas. Rep.*, 1873, p. 95.

the harvest season, and its return after the crops are marketed—phenomena which we have frequently had occasion to notice—are managed through this very system of re-deposit of reserves. There are nevertheless some obvious dangers in the system in a time of panic, and it will readily be understood that a violent and arbitrary expansion of the Government's paper money must increase both the volume of such accounts and the incidental risk. During the two years after July, 1890, these deposits by interior banks in the city institutions had increased one third;[1] in New York they had actually doubled.[2] There had been no such ratio of increase since the establishment of the national banking system; not even during the resumption period. At the close of 1892, no less a sum than $204,000,000 stood in the city banks to the credit of such smaller institutions, every dollar of this amount being payable on demand. It was a "run" of depositors on these Western banks which in 1893 precipitated the urgent demand for return of deposited reserves from Eastern institutions.

Panic is in its nature unreasoning; therefore, although the financial fright of 1893 arose from fear of depreciation of the legal tenders, the first act of frightened bank depositors was to withdraw these very legal tenders from their banks. But the real motive lay back of any question between the various forms of currency. Experience had taught depositors that in a general collapse of credit the banks

[1] Comptroller Eckels, *Treas. Rep.*, 1893, p. 433.
[2] *Ibid.*, p. 431.

would probably be the first marks of disaster. Many of such depositors had lost their savings through bank failures in the panics of 1873 and 1884. Instinct led them, therefore, when the same financial weather-signs were visible in 1893, to get their money out of the banks and into their own possession with the least possible delay, and as a rule the legal tenders were the only form of money which they were in the habit of using. But when the depositors of interior banks demanded cash, and such banks had in immediate reserve a cash fund amounting to only six per cent. of their deposits,[1] it followed that the Eastern " reserve agents " would be drawn upon in enormous sums.

On the New York banks the strain was particularly violent. During the month of June, the cash reserves of banks in that city decreased nearly twenty millions; during July, they fell off twenty-one millions more.[2] The deposits entrusted to them by interior institutions had been loaned, according to the banking practice, in the Eastern market; their sudden recall in quantity forced the Eastern banks to contract their loans immediately. But in a market already struggling to sustain itself from wreck, such wholesale impairment of resources was a disastrous blow. In the closing days of June, the New York money rate on call advanced to seventy-four per cent., time loans being wholly unobtainable. The cash reserves of the New York

[1] Comptroller Eckels, *Annual Rep.*, 1893, p. 17.
[2] New York weekly bank statements, April 29, July 1, and August 5, 1893.

banks, that week, fell below the proportion to liabilities required by the National Banking Law. The banks resorted then to the emergency device adopted in 1873 and 1884. They appointed a committee to appraise such assets as any bank in the Clearing-House should offer, and issued against such assets certificates receivable for balances at the Clearing-House. Enabled thus to dispense in part with cash settlements, the banks managed, during the summer strain, to help out customers who were in serious straits.

But the strain was not relaxed. The use of loan certificates at New York, promptly imitated by the Clearing-House banks of Boston, Philadelphia, Baltimore, and Pittsburg, could not check the drain of cash from the East to the interior. Nor, in fact, did even this wholesale recall of deposits from the East avert the Western crisis. We have seen that the inflation of credit, during 1892, had been heaviest by far in the interior. The early withdrawals by depositors in the country banks were only a slight indication of what was to follow. In July, this Western panic had reached a stage which seemed to foreshadow general bankruptcy. Two classes of interior institutions went down immediately — the weaker savings banks, which in that section were largely joint-stock enterprises, and a series of private banks, distributed in various provincial towns, which had fostered speculation through the use of their combined deposits by the men who controlled them all. In not a few instances, country banks were forced to suspend at a moment when their own cash reserves were on their way to them from depository centres. Out of the total one hundred and fifty-eight national bank failures of the year, one hundred and fifty-three were in the West and South.[1] How widespread the destruction was among other interior banking institutions may be judged from the fact that the season's record of suspensions comprised 172 State banks, 177 private banks, 47 savings banks, 13 loan and trust companies, and 16 mortgage companies.[2] The ruin resulting in the seaboard cities from the panic of 1893 was undoubtedly less severe than that of twenty years before. But no such financial wreck had fallen upon the West since it became a factor in the financial world.

During the month of July, in the face of their own distress, the New York banks were shipping every week as much as $11,000,000 cash to these Western institutions.[3] Ordinarily, such an enormous drain would have found compensation in import of foreign gold, and, in fact, sterling exchange declined far below the normal gold-import point. But the blockade of credit was so complete that operations in exchange, even for the import of foreign specie, were impracticable. Banks with impaired reserves would not lend even on the collateral of drafts on London.

So large a part, indeed, of the Clearing-House debit balances were now discharged in loan certificates that a number of banks adopted the ex-

[1] Comptroller Eckels, *Annual Rep.*, 1893, p. 80.
[2] *Ibid.*, p. 14.
[3] New York *Financial Chronicle*, July 29, 1893, p. 164.

treme measure of refusing to pay cash for the checks
of their own depositors. Charged with such refusal
in the press and on the floor of the United States
Senate,[1] the banks simply intimated that they had
not the money to pay out. This was not far from
general insolvency. Long continued, a situation of
the kind must reduce a portion of the community
almost to a state of barter; and in fact a number of
large employers of labor actually made plans in 1893
to issue a currency of their own, redeemable when
the banks had resumed cash payments. On the
25th of July, the Erie Railroad failed, the powerful
Milwaukee Bank suspended, and the governors of
the New York Stock Exchange seriously discussed
a repetition of the radical move of November, 1873,
when the Exchange was closed. The very hope-
lessness of the situation brought its own remedy.

Relief came in two distinct and remarkable ways.
Large as the volume of outstanding loan certificates
already was, three New York banks combined to
take out three to four millions more, and this credit
fund was wholly used to facilitate gold imports. At
almost the same time, the number of city banks refusing to cash depositors' checks had grown so considerable that well-known money-brokers advertised
in the daily papers that they would pay in certified
bank checks a premium for currency. This singular
operation virtually meant the sale of bank checks
for cash at a discount. Checks on banks which refused cash payments were still good for the majority
of ordinary exchanges, but they were useless to

[1] *Congressional Record*, August 23, 1893.

depositors who had, for instance, to provide large sums of cash for the weekly pay-rolls of their employees. Being unavailable for such purposes, the certified checks were really depreciated—like paper money irredeemable in gold. Through the money-brokers, therefore, these depositors paid in checks the face value of such currency as was offered, plus an additional percentage.

This premium rose from one and a half to four per cent., and at the higher figures it attracted a mass of hoarded currency into the brokers' hands. The expedient was not entirely new; it had been tried under similar circumstances in the panic of 1873.[1] But in 1893 it was applied on an unusually large scale, and it had the good result of helping to keep the wheels of industry moving. Its bad result was that it caused suspension of cash payments in the majority of city banks; for, of course, when a premium of four per cent. was offered in Wall Street for any kind of currency, it was out of the question for the banks to respond unhesitatingly to demands for cash by speculative depositors. Most of the banks cashed freely the checks of depositors where it was shown that the cash was needed for personal or business uses; but other applications they refused.

As a permanent remedy, moreover, the currency premium was futile; for no sooner was the money thus obtained disbursed in wages than it was hoarded again for the anticipated profit. But occurring as it did at the moment when the banks had broken the

[1] Comptroller Knox, *Treas. Rep.*, 1873, p. 90; New York *Financial Chronicle*, October 4 and October 11, 1873.

deadlock of the foreign exchange market, the currency operation had an immediate and extraordinary influence. With gold imports at last made possible through the emergency credit system of the banks, and with four per cent. premium offered for gold on delivery at New York, the floodgates of the foreign exchange market were flung wide open. A gold importer is necessarily a buyer of exchange, but in a normal market he cannot afford to pay more than say $4.85 to the pound sterling. But with the New York premium offered for gold coin on delivery, as high a price as $4.87½ was paid in August, 1893, for drafts on London, and the drafts thus purchased were used at once to draw gold from the Bank of England and ship it to New York.[1]

There was much popular wonder at the time over the fact that the Wall Street premium was paid as readily for silver dollars or for Treasury notes of 1890 as for gold. But the need of the moment was simply for legal instruments of exchange, and of these the currency in small denominations was the kind that had most completely disappeared from sight. This fact was strikingly demonstrated when the imported gold arrived. The unusual sum of forty-one millions gold imported during August—the largest import of any single month in the Government's history—filled not only the depleted bank reserves but the channels of retail trade. People who had never before touched a gold piece found themselves making daily payments in eagles and double-eagles. With this relief, the acute spasm of 1893 ended.

[1] New York *Financial Chronicle*, August 19, 1893.

Congress was summoned in extra session at almost the darkest hour of distress. The President issued his call on June 30th, the date for the assembling of Congress was fixed at August 7th. It was probably unfortunate that the extra session was not opened earlier; but, as it happened, the financial situation indirectly favored the Administration's purposes. The session was expressly called to repeal the Silver-Purchase Law of 1890, and in the popular discussion of the day, entire responsibility was laid on this law for the existing distress. Congressmen from all business communities, and in fact from all the populous States, were made well aware of their constituents' wishes before they started for Washington. This was as true of the Republicans as of the Democrats; indeed, the Republicans were urged to sustain repeal not only by their constituents, but by their party leaders, among them Mr. Sherman, who then and afterwards declared regarding the forced issue of legal tenders: " From the date of the passage of that law to its final repeal, I was opposed to this compulsory clause."[1]

The result of this union of forces was interesting. In the House of Representatives the Repeal Bill was passed, within three weeks, by the large majority of 130. The free-silver Congressmen made an ineffectual struggle for a substitute, proposing successively bills for free coinage at the ratio of 16 to 1, of 17 to 1, of 18 to 1, of 19 to 1, and of 20 to 1. All these propositions were rejected, though a heavy Democratic vote supported each. A final substitute,

[1] *Recollections*, ii., 1189.

reviving the Silver-Coinage Act of 1878, was similarly defeated, with however more Democratic votes cast in favor of the substitute than were cast against it. In the end, although the Repeal Act was an Administration measure, one third of the Democratic representatives voted against it. On the other hand, although the Law of 1890 had been contrived, proposed, and for two subsequent years defended, by a Republican Administration, three fourths of the House Republicans of 1893 voted to revoke it.

As a matter of fact, this ample House majority, like many other similar majorities which we have had occasion to examine, was not partisan but sectional—the Eastern and Middle States voting solidly against the West and South. Such a division, of course, ensured majorities in the lower House, where representation was apportioned according to population. But we have already seen how different the situation was in the Senate. Not only did States such as Nevada, with its 45,700 population, have equal voice in the Senate with New York or Massachusetts, but the hasty conversion, during the four preceding years, of six frontier territories into States —Idaho, Montana, North Dakota, South Dakota, Washington, and Wyoming—had given to this thinly-settled agricultural constituency an actual numerical advantage in that body.

Party pressure had been powerfully applied to the Democratic silver senators, and enough of them had been won over or coerced to make a repeal majority possible. Perceiving this, the silver faction began to filibuster for delay, and five weeks were occupied with nothing but dilatory tactics. Advocates of repeal retorted by adopting the drastic expedient of a continuous session, without even a night's adjournment. But the physical endurance of the silver faction was equal to the test. Forty hours had to suffice; the silver senators kept the floor with a series of three-and four-hour speeches, and the attempt to force a vote was abandoned. Next came a series of efforts by the silver senators at compromise, chiefly based on a year's continuance of the Silver-Purchase Law, and the immediate coinage of the silver bullion. The President's assent was claimed to this provision, apparently under a real misunderstanding, for his prompt repudiation of the compromise called forth the angriest demonstration of the session from members of his own party. The plan of free-coinage substitute measures was then tried again, but the measures were defeated, sometimes by very close majorities. At last, on the 30th of October, the Repeal Bill passed by a majority of 11. In the Senate, as in the House, Republican votes were needed to carry it. Out of the 43 votes for this Administration measure of repeal, 23 were Republican and only 20 Democratic; one of the most anomalous incidents in the history of Congress.

The Law of 1890, then, was at length revoked. Nothing was left of it on the statutes except the provisions for coinage and redemption, and the clauses affecting notes already in circulation. Repeal was followed by only a moderate decline in silver bullion, the market for that metal having in fact taken its downward plunge in June of the panic year, when the price fell twenty-one cents per ounce within a fortnight, on the double news of the call of Congress and the suspension of free-silver coinage in India. On the other markets, the vote had little or no effect.

Its failure to cause immediate recovery is not at all surprising. Repeal of the Silver-Purchase Law stopped future mischief of inflation, but it could not change the mischief already done. It was hardly reasonable, therefore, to expect, as many people did in 1893, that the vote of Congress would restore prosperity. There had, it is true, been a sharp upward reaction in all the markets, when the worst midsummer strain was relaxed. Undoubtedly, the wholesale import of foreign gold had ended the period of acute distress; indeed, the mere news of the first gold engagement, immediately following the Stock Exchange's " Black Wednesday," July 26th, resulted in a violent recovery, affecting prices not only of securities, but of commercial products. The premium on currency declined, then disappeared, and presently, though not until after some hesitation, the hoarded legal tenders returned from their hiding-places. At length, with the opening of September, the six-months' drain of currency to the interior was ended. It returned to its accustomed channels as rapidly and suddenly as it had left them; in November, legal tenders were moving into New York at the weekly rate of eight to ten million dollars.[1]

[1] New York *Financial Chronicle*, November 18, November 25, and December 2, 1893.

Panic, in short, had ended, but not until the movement of liquidation had run its course. The record of business failures for the year gives some conception of the ruin involved in this forced liquidation. Commercial failures alone in 1893 were three times as numerous as those of 1873, and the aggregate liabilities involved were fully fifty per cent. greater.¹ It was computed that nine commercial houses out of every thousand doing business in the United States failed in 1873; in 1893, the similar reckoning showed thirteen failures in every thousand.² The after-effects of this wholesale destruction presently appeared. So long as prices in every security and commodity were forced abnormally low by the necessities of domestic holders, foreign capital came into the markets in great amounts in search of panic bargains. But with prices moderately advanced above the lowest, the bargain-hunters left off buying, some of them sold again to take profits, and domestic trade was left to the crippled American consumer.

· The consequent return of depression and industrial stagnation happened almost immediately after the final vote on the Repeal Bill; it was therefore alleged triumphantly by the silver party that the law which stopped the arbitrary issue of new legal-tender currency had stopped also the trade recovery. Their opponents had declared that repeal was needed to check the industrial disorder. Repeal had been agreed to, and the trade situation, instead of growing better, was growing daily worse.

¹ *Dun's Review*, January 13, 1894.   ² *Ibid*.

To people with a leaning towards currency inflation, this was a captivating *post-hoc* argument; it played its part in subsequent political campaigns. No argument, however, could have been more absurd as applied to the autumn trade stagnation of 1893. Trade, it is true, had been cramped and crippled by the almost complete disappearance of the circulating medium during the panic months. But in the four months beginning with July, 1893, the gold imports, the Government disbursements against its deficit, and the large issue of bank notes to supply the lack of currency,[1] had between them increased the actual stock of money by the huge sum of $125,000,000.[2] While hoarding of other currency was in progress, these new supplies merely filled the void in circulation. But we have already seen how, in the Autumn months, the hoarded currency poured back into the channels of trade. In the closing days of 1893, so far from true was the assumption that the currency supply had been contracted through repeal of the Act of 1890, that the increase in the available circulating medium was more rapid than at any previous period of our history.[3] We shall find this fact important in connection with the events of 1894.

It was the judgment of many experienced watchers of the national finances that the autumn of 1893 was the time to issue bonds for gold under the Resumption Act and restore the Treasury's impaired reserve. As a mere commercial question, there can

[1] *Treas. Rep.*, 1894, p. 13. [2] *Ibid.*, 1893, p. 18.
[3] *Ibid.*, 1894, p. 115.

be little doubt that this judgment was correct. The hoarded currency was returning to circulation, the gold supply in the banks was exceptionally large, and gold exports had not yet begun. Mr. Carlisle, however, made no move or inquiry in that direction, and we shall presently see what other arguments in his view outweighed this reasoning. During the financial convulsion of 1893, the Treasury itself had been passing through a curious experience. In July, the "currency famine" and the check to gold exports stopped the drain on the Treasury's gold reserve. The banks had not notes enough for their retail uses, much less had they any to spare for redemption, and if they had possessed such notes, there was no demand for gold to remit against foreign exchange.

The situation of midsummer therefore put an end to the gold withdrawals. The situation of the early autumn did more. The first use made of the imported foreign gold was in revenue payments to the Government. In August, forty-seven per cent. of the New York customs payments to the Treasury were made with gold coin; in September, fifty-eight per cent., and in the last six months of 1893, not less than $16,000,000 gold was received on revenue at the New York Custom House alone.[1] In other branches of the revenue, the Treasury must have received in revenue from fifty to sixty millions gold. If, then, the Government had used only legal tenders for its own disbursements—and at the time the notes would have been welcomed by the Treasury's

[1] *Treas. Rep.*, 1894, p. 121; 1893, p. 11.

creditors—its gold reserve would necessarily have risen, by the close of 1893, to at least $170,000,000. Instead of this, the $103,683,000 gold reserve of August 10th was actually the maximum of the season. " By October 19th," Mr. Carlisle remarked in his annual report, " it had been diminished by redemptions of currency and otherwise to $81,551,385, which is the lowest point it has ever reached."[1]

But the explanation of this seeming anomaly is simple. The loss of gold by the Treasury, in the face of its large receipts of specie, was not at all occasioned by presentation of legal tenders for redemption; Mr. Carlisle was entirely mistaken in his statement. During the four months after August, 1893, barely two million dollars in legal tenders were presented for redemption[2]—an altogether insignificant withdrawal. The truth is, that the Treasury had nothing left but the gold reserve with which to pay its ordinary bills. The Harrison Administration, as we saw at the beginning of this chapter, turned over in March to its successor only a meagre $25,000,000 available surplus outside the gold reserve. In the middle of 1893, when the country's commercial structure collapsed, sources of public revenue instantly dried up. Receipts had hardly met expenditures during the whole preceding year;[3] the sudden fall in revenue, therefore, left the Treasury with a heavy monthly deficit,[4] and an outflow of every kind of money in the Government's hands ensued. The customs revenue was the first to con-

[1] *Treas. Rep.*, 1893, p. lxxiii. [2] *Ibid.*, 1894, p. 10.
[3] *Ibid.*, 1893, p. 26. [4] *Ibid.*, 1894, p. 22.

tract; for with the blockade of credit and the paralysis of domestic trade, import of foreign merchandise necessarily fell to the narrowest proportions. It is hardly necessary to debate the familiar argument that the decrease in importations was caused entirely by expectation of a lower tariff.[1] Very possibly this expectation encouraged some hesitating merchants to hold off until the Administration's policy was defined; it would naturally have precisely that effect. But as compared with the deterrent influence exerted by the inability of importers to discount their notes for settlement of foreign purchases, and by the hopeless outlook for a domestic selling market, the influence of anticipated tariff changes was trivial.[2]

All branches of public income, in fact, fell off simultaneously in their yield, and the Treasury surplus continuously declined. The deficit was met from the legal-tender surplus as long as that surplus held out; when it was virtually exhausted, which happened very soon, there was nothing left to do but to stop payment on Government appropriations or to use the gold reserve. Mr. Sherman has denied the right of the Secretary to use this fund except in redemption of legal-tender notes,[3] and there is something to say for that contention. But the Acts of 1875 and 1882 were obscure on this vital question, and the alternative involved some disquieting possibilities. Mr. Carlisle, at all events, rejected the

[1] Sherman, *Recollections*, ii., 1206.
[2] New York Chamber of Commerce, *Annual Rep.* for 1893, Part II. pp. 86 and 87.
[3] "Deficiency in Revenue," *Forum* for April, 1896, p. 141.

expedient, and drew on the only surplus left in the Treasury. During the last six months of 1893 the sum of $79,000,000 in gold coin was paid by the Treasury to meet its debit balances at the New York Clearing-House.[1]

In the last month of 1893, then, there was presented the double situation of a heavy deficit in public revenue and a fall of the gold reserve twenty million dollars below the statutory limit. The monthly revenue statements showed a steady decrease in receipts, and a steady increase in the deficit. Not only was the gold reserve impaired, but the entire surplus in the Treasury, outside of fractional coin and unavailable bank notes, amounted to less than the proper minimum of that reserve alone.[2] Foreign exchange was rising rapidly, and a fresh outflow of gold, with consequent renewed pressure of legal tenders for redemption, was impending. It was plain that action of some sort by the Treasury must be taken, and very soon. In the face of this situation, Congress reassembled.

[1] *Treas. Rep.*, 1894, p. 119.   [2] *Ibid.*, p. 55.

CHAPTER IX

THE GOVERNMENT LOANS AND THE TARIFF OF 1894

SECRETARY CARLISLE was undoubtedly embarrassed by the relations of himself and his party to the Resumption Act. He had voted against the Law in 1875, and in so voting he had acted with every member of his party then in Congress. A bold and aggressive finance minister would probably, in the autumn of 1893, have ignored the past, employed such powers as could be asserted under existing laws, and grappled at once with the dilemma of the Treasury. But Mr. Carlisle's temperament was cautious; he had been the strictest of strict constructionists in his interpretation of executive powers; and, reasoning on that basis, he distrusted the powers, which were undoubtedly very vague, under the Act of 1875. He waited, therefore, until he could formally lay his case before his party's majority in Congress.

In his annual report of December 19, 1893, the Secretary pointed out the heavy deficit in current revenue, and the fact that, except for the depleted gold reserve, the Treasury's accumulated surplus was almost exhausted. He asked Congress to authorize a bond issue, proceeds of which the Treasury might draw upon to supply future deficiencies in revenue. As an alternative to a large issue, he proposed a plan modelled on the English system of exchequer bills; the proposition being to " execute from time to time, as may be necessary," Government obligations bearing three per cent. interest, redeemable one year from date, " and that he be permitted to sell them at not less than par, or use them, at not less than par, in payment of public expenses to such creditors as may be willing to receive them."[1] This was a rational proposition; it was vastly better than the general plan of a three per cent. five-year bond issue proposed in the last days of the preceding Congress.[2] The plan, in fact, embodied a principle adopted by almost every well-managed Government in a temporary revenue shortage, and it did not raise the vexed question of the gold reserve. This was the Secretary's first suggestion; it never received the slightest notice on the part of Congress.

Regarding the gold fund for the redemption of legal tenders, Mr. Carlisle's remarks were less judicious. They expressed distinctly his own misgiving over the Treasury's existing powers, which was not politic when a strong probability existed that he would be driven to use these very powers. What he asked of Congress was, " not only that he

[1] *Treas. Rep.*, 1893, p. lxxi.
[2] " Deficiency in Revenue," John Sherman, *Forum* for April, 1896.

should be clothed with full authority to procure and maintain an ample reserve in coin, but that the purpose for which such reserve is to be held and used should be made as comprehensive as the duty imposed on him by law," and he expressed his own belief that even a reserve of one hundred millions gold, in the existing status of the currency, was insufficient.[1]

Having thus made his formal appeal to Congress, the Secretary again, and necessarily, waited. Unfortunately, the financial situation could not wait. December and January are always months of heavy drain on the Treasury, even in normal years, and in January, 1894, the Government approached nearer to actual bankruptcy than at any time in the present generation. Outside of the gold reserve and unavailable funds such as bank notes under redemption and fractional silver coin, the Treasury held at the close of January barely twelve million dollars. As for the gold reserve itself, this fund had fallen, by the middle of the month, below $68,000,000.[2] As in the summer of 1893, it was now depleted, not by presentation of legal tenders for redemption—for little gold was going out as yet on export—but through its use for ordinary Government expenditures.[3] Beginning with October, the revenue deficit had exceeded seven million dollars monthly. A few months more of such deficiency would use up every dollar that was left in the Treasury, including the gold reserve.

[1] *Treas. Rep.*, 1893, p. lxxii. [2] *Ibid.*, 1894, p. lxviii.
[3] *Ibid.*, pp. 10, 119.

"Congress alone," Mr. Carlisle said in his report, "has the power to adopt such measures as will relieve the present situation and enable the Treasury to continue the punctual payment of all legitimate demands upon it."¹ Had this statement been strictly accurate, the outlook would have been dark indeed. For so indifferent was this extraordinary Congress to the Treasury's situation that the bills drawn up in accordance with the Secretary's views were repudiated by the very Congressmen who introduced them,² were not even granted the courtesy of a preliminary discussion, but were referred without debate to hostile committees, where they were buried. Nothing was ever heard of them again.³

When it was evident that the Congressional majority would not even discuss the needs of the situation, the Secretary's hand was forced. In the middle of January, Mr. Carlisle formally notified the chairman of the Senate Finance Committee that in default of action by the legislative body, the Administration would be compelled, in order to avert public insolvency, to assume the right asserted by its predecessors, and issue bonds to restore the gold reserve.⁴ Congress again did nothing; on January 17th, therefore, bids were invited for an issue of fifty million five per cent. bonds, redeemable ten years after date. Subscriptions, the circular continued,

---

¹ *Treas. Rep.*, 1893, p. lxxi.
² Remarks of D. W. Voorhees in U. S. Senate; *Congressional Record*, January 16, 1894,
³ Index to *Congressional Record*, 53d Congress, 2d Session, p. 118.
⁴ Letter to Senator Voorhees, January 13, 1894.

"must be paid in United States gold coin," and "no proposal will be considered at a lower price than 117.223, which is the equivalent of a three per cent. bond at par."

Several interesting incidents at once developed. The action of Congress, to begin with, showed again how completely Mr. Carlisle had misjudged that body in his appeal to it a month before. Bill after bill, and resolution after resolution, was introduced and angrily debated, denying the Secretary's right to issue bonds, declaring the proposed bond issue illegal, prohibiting interest payment on the bonds, and otherwise endeavoring to obstruct or cripple the whole operation.¹ It was now, indeed, that the Secretary's impolitic discussion of his powers, in his report of the previous December, had its logical result; the opposition rested its argument against the bond issue on Mr. Carlisle's own official language.²

During the progress of this debate, the obstructionists received some characteristic aid from an unexpected quarter. The leaders of the workingmen's Knights of Labor organization, which at that time was controlled by an unusually blatant group of agitators, applied to the courts for an injunction against the bond issue. But the result of this performance proved that the agitators had made a blunder. The injunction suit was promptly thrown out by the Federal District Court, first on the ground that the complainants had no standing in the case, but second, and of much more import-

¹ Index to *Congressional Record*, 53d Congress, 2d Session, p. 118.
² W. V. Allen, Senate speech, January 25, 1894.

ance as a precedent, on the ground that the Secretary had an undoubted right to issue bonds for redemption purposes, and to elect in his discretion that the bonds should be payable in gold.¹ The Knights of Labor had unintentionally done the Administration a considerable service; the courts of law had now publicly taken their stand beside the Treasury. Meantime, also, the Congressional opposition proved to be more vociferous than dangerous; the silent legislators took care that none of its measures reached a vote. Beyond this mild and equivocal support of the public credit, however, the conservative element in Congress did nothing.

With the bond issue formally announced, the Secretary's next concern was with the markets. The outlook in that quarter was hardly more encouraging than in Congress. Not the slightest eagerness was anywhere displayed by investors or institutions to subscribe for the new five per cents; nor is this reluctance difficult to understand. Along with all other domestic markets, the investment market had relapsed into stagnation and despondency. Prices for all securities were very low and capital very timid. There had been for weeks no demand for Government bonds on the open market; the outstanding four per cents, which had longer to run than the proposed new issue, were selling at $112\frac{1}{2}$, against the price of $117\frac{1}{4}$ asked for the new fives. So far as concerned the prospect of European bids, it should be noticed that the minimum price stipu-

[1] Decision of U. S. Judge Cox, District of Columbia, January 30, 1894.

lated for this ten-year bond was the equivalent of a three per-cent. bond at par,¹ whereas the French three per cents, a perpetual issue, were then selling at 97 in Paris, while the 2¾ per cent. British consols brought only 98¾. It is true the recent redemption of its own debt at a premium had greatly enhanced the credit of the United States. But against this advantage must be set the fact that Congress, at the very time when Europe was invited to bid for the bonds of 1894, was publicly discussing measures to repudiate the entire issue.

Judged by Executive precedent and tradition, there was need, in the face of this dubious situation, of prompt negotiation with the larger financial interests. That such solicitation is not only prudent business policy, but the legitimate office of a national finance minister, has been attested in nearly all issues of public loans, here and abroad, during the century. Mr. Carlisle was, however, very reluctant to give in any way the appearance of affiliation with the bankers. This reluctance would perhaps have been excusable, if anything was still to be gained or lost according as Congressional prejudice should be suited. But the time was past when Congress needed to be reckoned in with the Secretary's judgment of his duties; all that could possibly result now from neglect to meet the large investment interests face to face, was danger of losing the advantage in a bargain.

Only two weeks had been allowed between the issue of the circular and the closing of subscrip-

¹ Circular of January 17, 1894.

tions, and during three fourths of this period the
Secretary did nothing whatever. Four or five
days before the final date, it became evident, from
the slow receipt of bids, that as matters stood, the
loan would not be taken. This was too grave a
possibility to be lightly contemplated; the Secretary,
therefore, laying aside his scruples by virtue of necessity, came on in person to New York. He found
the situation really critical in this eleventh hour.
Most of the banks honestly did not wish to buy the
bonds; all of them looked on the investment as a
questionable business move. But the arguments
employed in 1893, when the banks were urged to
give up gold for legal-tender notes, were again in-
voked; the press again spurred on the reluctant
banking interests; above all, the plea that another
panic must at all hazards be averted was forced into
consideration. It might have been imagined, from
the extraordinary nature of the episode, that it was
Turkey or China which was standing hat in hand in
the money market. The outcome of this humiliating
incident was, however, that the fifty million bonds
were taken, eighty per cent. of them going to the
New York banks at the upset price.[1] If the " syndicate bid " from the New York banks were to be elim-
inated from the reckoning, the actual bids received
for the bond issue of February 1, 1894, would cover
less than ten millions out of the fifty millions offered.[2]

The lack of any thorough understanding with sub-

[1] Muhleman, *Monetary Systems of the World*, historical appendix, p. 221.
[2] Muhleman, appendix.

scribers had another very embarrassing result. The bonds, under the terms of the Resumption Act, were to be sold for " not less than par, in coin," and the circular to subscribers required payment in gold. Subscriptions were made in the form required, and $58,660,000 gold coin was duly delivered by subscribers to the Treasury. But before making these payments, subscribers first withdrew $24,000,000 gold from the Treasury through redemption of legal tenders, and then turned in this same gold again to pay for bonds. In effect, therefore, nearly half of the subscriptions were paid, not in gold, but merely in legal tenders.[1] That this was a proper move I do not believe. It was not, of course, illegal, because any holder of the notes had a statutory right to present them for redemption, and technically, the bond subscribers were as much entitled to such use of legal tenders as were the gold exporters. But there was this decided difference between the two operations: the gold-exporters had been forced by the Government to take the notes instead of standard money, and were therefore fully justified, in a trade emergency, in demanding gold redemption. The bond-subscribers, on the other hand, had consented to a contract under which they received a full consideration, while they knew the tacit consideration in the Government's behalf to be the adding of fifty-eight million dollars to its actual gold reserve. The use of coin obtained on note redemption was therefore an undoubted subterfuge. Its justification, if it can be justified at all, lies in the

[1] Muhleman, appendix.

fact that the New York banks were reluctant and unwilling subscribers, and that they chose this course as a means of saving the loan from failure, while protecting their own gold holdings which they were not willing to surrender. Whether this unfortunate result could have been avoided by early and definite negotiation with the banks is, of course, an open question. The fact remains, however, that no effort had been made by the Treasury in that direction.

If the bond subscriptions had all been paid in gold obtained from outside sources, the Treasury's gold reserve would have risen by the second week of February to something like $130,000,000. As it was, the highest point touched by the fund was $107,000,000, on the 6th of March, 1894. In other words, the margin over the traditional hundred-million limit, after the February bonds had been sold and paid for, was as narrow as it had been a year before, and it soon appeared that such a reserve was as inadequate as it had been in 1893. It is true, the presentation of legal tenders for redemption by subscribers to the bonds had increased considerably the Treasury's surplus in that form of money,[1] so that after January, 1894, the gold reserve was no longer drawn upon to meet the monthly deficit.[2] But we have seen that foreign exchange was by this time moving steadily against the United States, and we have also seen why the movement was commercially inevitable. The Treasury had indeed taken from outside domestic circulation, through its

[1] *Treas. Rep.*, 1894, p. 55.   [2] *Ibid.*, p. 119.

February loan, fifty-eight million dollars. But this withdrawal did not represent a sum one half as great as the additions to the circulating medium in the last six months of 1893, and the revenue deficit, moreover, was even now throwing back upon the money market four to nine millions monthly of the Treasury's increased surplus.[1] There was no employment for this money in the depressed interior trade. Even as compared with the similar period of 1893, the country's aggregate bank exchanges, in the first half of 1894, decreased no less than twenty-eight per cent.[2] In accordance with all precedent there could be but one result. Gold exports began in quantity during April; presentation of legal tenders for redemption followed; by August the gold reserve had fallen to a lower level than it reached even in January.

The movement of foreign exchange in 1894, with the heavy drain of gold, neither resulted from nor was attended by a balance of foreign merchandise trade against this country. It was, however, greatly emphasized by the recall of invested foreign capital. The total foreign investment fund in the United States had, to be sure, been substantially reduced by Europe's liquidation during the panic of 1893; the Treasury's estimate of the foreign capital then recalled was one hundred million dollars.[3] But at the opening of 1894, there still remained an immense

[1] *Treas. Rep.*, 1894, p. 22.
[2] New York *Financial Chronicle*, p. 3, July 7, 1894.
[3] W. C. Ford, U. S. Bureau of Statistics, *Annual Rep.*, 1893, p. xxiv.

investment fund subject to such withdrawal. One estimate, by an experienced dealer on international account, reckoned the aggregate of foreign investments in the United States as high as $2,400,000,000,[1] and the conjecture, though in all probability greatly exaggerated, gives some idea of the factors with which such a problem has to deal.

That liquidating sales for this account in 1894 were extremely large is a matter of public evidence;[2] nor, when the situation at the time is soberly reviewed, will it be found that the action of the foreign investors was unreasonable. A good share of this European capital had been placed, as we saw in our review of the period prior to 1890, in American railway shares and bonds. So great had been the strain of the panic on these largely over-capitalized enterprises, that within two years nearly one fourth of the total railway capitalization of the United States had passed through the bankruptcy courts.[3] Some of these failures had been of such a character as completely to shatter confidence in the methods of American corporations. Examination in one of the largest of these insolvencies proved that the company's officers, within two years, had sunk upwards of four million dollars in reckless speculation in the shares of other railways.[4] Deceptive balance-sheets

[1] "Why do We Export Gold?" A. S. Heidelbach, *Forum* for February, 1895; New York *Financial Chronicle*, vol. lx., pp. 542, 585, 630.

[2] New York *Financial Chronicle*, May 4, 1895.

[3] U. S. Inter-State Commerce Commission, *Annual Rep.*, 1894, p. 69.

[4] Report of the Philadelphia and Reading Railroad receivers, April, 1894.

were repeatedly shown up in the subsequent investigation, as with the Atchison, Topeka, and Santa Fé, whose $100,000,000 shares were distributed throughout Europe, and which, when its books were overhauled, was shown to have officially overstated income seven million dollars within three years.[1] Disclosures of this sort, a large number of which came to public knowledge during 1894, were certainly enough to start a movement of foreign liquidation. Nor was there any improvement during the year 1894 in the finances of the companies; all of them went from bad to worse.[2]

The prostrated transportation industry had perhaps the most immediate influence on the movement of foreign capital; but as reflecting the industrial situation, it was only an incidental symptom. Labor troubles inevitably follow financial collapse and industrial prostration; such demonstrations came on the heels of the panics of 1857, of 1873, and of 1884, as surely as they attended that of 1893. But in 1894 there were periods when industrial unrest seemed to assume the proportions of anarchy. In April began that extraordinary demonstration, of which it is hard to say whether the farcical or the tragic element predominated—the march of the so-called " Coxey's army "; a band of agitators and discouraged laborers, reinforced by such tramps as joined it on the way, which started eastward from the Mississippi, overrunning towns and seizing railway trains, with the avowed purpose of gathering

[1] Stephen Little, Report on the Atchison, Topeka, and Santa Fé Railroad accounts, August and November, 1894.
[2] N. Y. *Financial Chronicle*, Feb. 23, 1895.

the Eastern proletariat to its number and appearing by thousands before the Capitol at Washington to demand relief.

United States troops had to be summoned to disperse this rapidly increasing mob. Revolts of laborers against wage reductions followed in quick succession. Two hundred thousand coal-miners rose in the Middle States, and at the close of June the labor demonstration culminated in the Chicago Railway Union strike—an episode in many ways more serious even than the Pittsburg riots of 1877. In July of 1894 the labor organizations literally took possession of the railway system converging on Chicago. The Governor of Illinois refused to summon the State militia to protect the railways, and for ten days the country's interior trade seemed to be wholly at the mercy of two or three labor-union leaders, who opened formal headquarters in Chicago and issued proclamations with the assurance of military conquerors. Not until the Federal Government intervened with a body of regular infantry to protect the mails of the United States, and thus provided security for the moving trains, was it clear that anarchy could be averted.

Sometimes commercial and industrial distress, in a country of widely diversified resources, is mitigated by a fortunate harvest season. But 1894 was also a year of agricultural disaster. A considerable section of the United States gets its living from the annual corn harvest. So large is the aggregate market value of this crop, which has no competition of consequence elsewhere in the world, that even in the famous "wheat year," 1891, the total estimated value of the country's corn product was half as large again as the value of its wheat.¹ As late in 1894 as the middle of July, prospects for corn were notably favorable; the Department of Agriculture then estimated the condition of the growing crop as better than that of either 1892 or 1893.² A week or two later one of those scorching siroccos, which at intervals devastate the plains of the farming West, swept over the Missouri Valley. It was long-continued; when rain came at last, the corn crop of Iowa, Kansas, and Nebraska was ruined. In 1893 these three States had produced 548,000,000 bushels; in 1894, their combined yield was only 137,000,000.³

There still remained to the farmers their crop of wheat, and the wheat yield of 1894 was with three or four exceptions the largest in the country's history. But as if in a mockery of nature, the failure of the crop which commanded its own market was followed by a ruinous competitive market for the crop whose yield was ample. On top of the abundant supplies left over from the rich harvest of the year before, Europe increased its wheat production in 1894 by thirty million bushels. The whole world's product, outside of the United States, rose 160,000,000 bushels over even 1892.⁴ No crop approaching this in magnitude has been raised by the

---
¹ U. S. Department of Agriculture, *Annual Rep.*, 1891.
² *Bulletin* of July 10, 1894.
³ *Annual Reports*, U. S. Department of Agriculture, 1893 and 1894.
⁴ Beerbohm's *Corn-Trade List;* Liverpool *Corn-Trade News*, 1894.

agricultural world before or since. With such competition, and with a slow domestic market for any merchandise, wheat sold on the farm in 1894 at an average price only a trifle over forty-nine cents a bushel; by far the lowest figure ever touched, before or since.[1]

It was in the face of this series of industrial calamities, with trade prostrated, credit shaken, agriculture depressed, and labor in open revolt, that the Administration was called on to redeem its promise and reform the tariff. Action in this regard could not possibly be avoided; first, because the party and Administration were absolutely pledged to it, but second, because the existing revenue law had proved its inability, under prevailing trade conditions, to meet the expenses of Government. If Mr. Harrison had been elected in 1892, his Administration would equally have been forced to take the revenue laws in hand. Of this there cannot be the slightest reasonable doubt. Mr. Sherman, it is true, has gone so far as to declare, in a published review of the situation, not only that the Government's financial ills were primarily due to deficit in revenue, but that no such deficiency would have occurred " had not the President and both Houses of the Fifty-third Congress, then in political sympathy, united in passing a law reducing the revenue below expenditures for the first time since the close of the war."[2] But the reader is able now to judge the historical recklessness of this assertion. The tariff act of the new

[1] *Annual Reports*, U. S. Department of Agriculture.
[2] *Forum* for April, 1896.

Administration was not even introduced in Congress until December 19, 1893, whereas the revenue deficit had been continuous in every quarter since September, 1892, and had amounted in the five months ending with November, 1893, to nearly thirty million dollars.[1]

The further argument that revision of the import tariffs in 1894 ought to have been gradually and cautiously undertaken, so as to make absolutely sure of sufficient revenue while unsettling business plans as little as possible, is more honest and legitimate. I have already noticed the bad effects of the American practice of tariff reconstruction by wholesale, and there was probably never a year when such effects ought to have been more scrupulously avoided than in 1894. But politically speaking, revision of the taxes, conservatively and by piecemeal, was impracticable. General reduction of the import schedules was the solitary bond which still united the Administration party; with this removed, the Congressional majority would simply have resolved itself into its original elements. Furthermore, it was easily possible to procure an increased revenue through reduction of the duties. This must be manifest to any one who considers the nature of the two opposing tariff theories. Wholly aside from the general merits of the protective theory, its purpose is exclusion of competing foreign goods. So far, then, as it achieves its purpose, a law of this character necessarily removes a possible source of income.

[1] *Treas. Rep.*, 1893, p. lxix.

But to say that lower duties may be made a more remunerative source of revenue is not to say that any reduction will accomplish that result. Nothing had been more conclusively demonstrated, in the Government's recent history, than the danger to the public revenue if economic theories were alone allowed to govern the preparation of a law. The McKinley Act itself was an index to this danger, and there is little excuse for the absolute indifference of the Congress of 1894 to the warning. The truth appeared to be, however, that in 1894, as in 1890, an optimism which amounted to infatuation had seized on the public leaders of the majority. Mr. Carlisle remarked, it is true, in his report of December, 1893, that the extent to which "importations will be increased solely on account of reductions in the rates of duty, it is of course impossible to foresee."[1] This judgment ought to have foreshadowed cautious adjustment of the schedules. But the Secretary himself went on to say that conditions will be much more favorable hereafter for the collection of an adequate revenue"[2]— a prediction wholly unwarranted, either by the state of general industry, which was paralyzed, or by the movement of import trade, which was then decreasing twenty to thirty per cent. from the preceding year.

When this prediction was made by the Secretary, in December, 1893, it had at least the excuse of echoing the hopes of the financial markets. But Congress, before it passed its revenue law, had six

[1] *Treas. Rep.*, 1893, p. lxxxii.   [2] *Ibid.*, p. lxix.

months more in which to observe the growing trade demoralization, and in July it was no longer possible for a reasonable man to cherish the hopes which had been current in December. In fact, the legislators had already seen one of Mr. Carlisle's predictions, for the revenue of the first six months of 1894, turn out an overestimate by the enormous sum of forty million dollars.[1] Nevertheless, they constructed their own optimistic estimates on the basis of the trade of 1891 and 1892. But in truth, the estimates of revenue played as small a part in the season's tariff legislation as they had played in that of 1890. It was evident very soon, in the course of the debate, that the two Houses of Congress were guided by different and conflicting motives in their action on the Wilson Tariff Bill, and that neither House was giving any scientific attention to the question of sufficient revenue. The House majority was planning a law to remit taxation; those who held the balance of power in the Senate were secretly contriving to retain as much protection as they dared. Between the two, the urgent question of a deficit had little hearing.

The House not only struck off the import taxes on coal, iron ore, and wool, which were exclusively protective duties, and therefore logical subjects for revision, but it refused to restore the sugar duties, which were a revenue tax of the most productive character. The Senate replaced a duty of forty cents per ton on coal and iron, which was an utterly

[1] *Treas. Rep.*, 1893, p. lxix.; 1894, p. xxv.; Secretary Carlisle, letter to Senator Voorhees, January 13, 1894.

insignificant source of revenue, but it restored only such part of the sugar duties as should play directly into the hands of the refining companies. Considered merely as a law contrived to produce sufficient revenue, the Senate bill was undoubtedly superior to the House bill. The Senate sugar tariff, it is true, produced eventually hardly one half as much revenue as had been yielded by the sugar tariff of 1883,[1] but there was nevertheless collected from this source, in the first full year under the amended Wilson Act, the sum of $29,800,000, none of which revenue would have been obtained by the Government under the House bill's free-sugar provisions.[2] But the public refused for very obvious reasons to give the framers of the Senate amendments any credit for this achievement. On the eve of the passage of the Wilson Bill in the Upper House it was discovered that several senators, whose votes controlled action on the sugar duties, were speculating on Wall Street in the stock of the refining company chiefly interested. The angry public clamor over these disclosures was followed by an open letter from President Cleveland to his supporters in the House, declaring the senatorial changes to be " outrageous discriminations and violations of principle "[3]—an assertion which, in view of the platform of the majority, was certainly not unwarranted. From the floor of the Senate, the ringleaders of the protectionist compromise retorted publicly with

[1] *U. S. Statistical Abstract*, 1896, p. 285.   [2] *Ibid.*
[3] Letter to W. L. Wilson, July 2, 1894; *Congressional Record* July 19, 1894.

much show of indignation.[1] When, finally, after a long and stubborn struggle, the Senate tariff prevailed and passed both Houses, the President contemptuously refused to put his name to it, and left the emasculated bill to become a law without his signature.

The result of this haphazard reckoning on the revenue was a law which never produced a surplus. Even with its sugar import tax, the yield of the Senate bill, in the succeeding year, fell short of the estimate of its authors by no less a sum than eighty-seven million dollars.[2] It never brought the revenues to the low ebb of the fiscal year 1894, before the Wilson Bill was passed, but it produced a deficit of $42,805,223 in the fiscal year 1895, and of $25,203,245 in 1896.[3] For this exceedingly ill-timed miscalculation, the Forty-third Congress is properly held responsible. It is true that both Houses had added to the bill a tax of two per cent. on incomes over $4000, and in a comfortably indefinite way had reckoned that the product of this tax would make good whatever deficiencies might arise from other schedules. The income-tax provision did not stand the test of examination by the United States Supreme Court, and no public revenue was ever derived from it. " Representatives and direct taxes," provides the Federal Constitution, " shall be apportioned among the several States which may

[1] A. P. Gorman, Senate speech, July 23, 1894.
[2] Senate Finance Committee's *Report*, June 19, 1894; *Treas. Rep.*, 1895, p. xix.
[3] *Treas. Rep.*, 1896, p. 5.

be included within this Union, according to their respective numbers,"[1] and it further and still more explicitly declares that "no capitation or other direct tax shall be laid, unless in proportion to the census or enumeration hereinbefore directed to be taken."[2] The question then presented was, Is the income tax a direct tax within the meaning of the Constitution? If so, the fact that it was not apportioned by the Act of 1894 to the several States according to population, but was levied solely on citizens enjoying more than the stipulated $4000, and was levied, moreover, in proportion to their income, must be fatal to the law.

On April 8, 1895, the Court ruled that taxes on real estate, or on rents derived from real estate, were direct taxes, and it therefore annulled the law so far as incomes of this nature were affected.[3] At the same time, it pronounced unconstitutional the levy of Federal taxation on incomes derived from municipal securities, the Court's theory being that such a tax was a tax upon the borrowing power of a State or its instrumentality, and hence repugnant to the Constitution.[4] On the broader question whether the whole Act imposing an income tax was void for want of uniformity, the Court divided equally in April. It heard argument on the case again in May, 1895, and on the 20th of that month at length decided that a tax upon a citizen's whole income was a tax upon the property whence such income was derived; that, as a tax on property, it was a direct tax within

[1] Article 1, section 2.   [2] Article 1, section 9.
[3] 39 U. S. Supreme Court *Reports*, p. 759.   [4] *Ibid.*

the meaning of the Constitution, and was therefore void because of its unequal distribution.¹ This important ruling was sustained by five Supreme Court judges in a bench of nine, the majority vote including not only the Chief Justice, but the oldest and most experienced members of the Court—among them Justices Field and Gray. A change by one of the younger members, Justice Shiras, from a vote in favor of the law in April to an adverse vote in May was, however, the deciding influence in determining the Court's opinion.

The annulment of this income-tax provision, it was asserted then and afterwards, prevented the Act of 1894 from yielding a surplus revenue. The truth, however, is, that so incorrect were the forecasts of the legislators that a deficit would equally have occurred, even had the income tax remained in force. Congressional estimates of its yield were based on the supposition, unwarranted by all experience in taxation, that an income tax could be collected exactly as imposed. The delusive character of such expectations had been shown to the legislators long before they passed the Wilson Bill. The chief of the Government's statistical bureau had reported in April, as a result of careful investigation, that " the possible revenue under that income tax would range from $12,000,000 at the lowest rate to $39,000,000 at the highest," and the lower average was predicted for the early operation of the law.² Such a result

---

¹ 39 U. S. Supreme Court *Reports*, p. 1108.

² W. C. Ford, Chief of U. S. Bureau of Statistics ; letter to Senator Hill, April 3, 1894.

would have ensured a deficit only slightly less than those of 1895 and 1896.

In short, the Treasury had obtained little more real relief from its appeal for revenue legislation than from its appeal for authority to issue bonds. For a single month there was a surplus revenue, wholly due to payment of whiskey taxes in advance of the imposition of the increased internal schedules [1]; but by October, 1894, the monthly deficit had risen to thirteen million dollars, the largest of the year. Even when it had become evident that the new revenue act would not remove the deficit, Congress did nothing to help the Treasury. Its single proffer of relief, during the entire session, was a bill directing the Treasury to coin and use the fifty-five millions " seigniorage " theoretically acquired by the Government in buying silver at the market price and paying it out in over-valued silver dollars—a strange expedient in the face of a drain of gold forced by an already redundant circulation, and properly vetoed on that ground by the President.[2] This bill was urged on the usual ground that the country was suffering for lack of circulating medium, whereas the money supply, as we saw in the preceding chapter, had been increasing more rapidly than in any previous period of our history. Never had the American money supply approached the volume shown in the Treasury estimates of February, 1894. The absurdity of the complaint of an insufficient

[1] Classified Treasury statement of receipts and expenditures for August, 1894.
[2] President Cleveland, veto message of March 29, 1894.

currency was forcibly displayed in the autumn of 1894, when the Treasury deficit once more threw into the money markets twenty-five millions of the public surplus,[1] and when, as a consequence, the outward movement of gold again grew heavy. On August 7th redemption of legal-tender notes for export gold had reduced the Treasury's gold reserve to $52,189,500,[2] or less even than its minimum before the February loan.

Another appeal was made to the New York banks to exchange their gold for the legal tenders in the Treasury, and again the banks thus surrendered some fifteen millions gold.[3] But this was little help; it could not affect the gold-expulsion movement. Having borrowed on its surplus notes all of the gold obtainable, the Treasury again undertook in November to borrow on its bonds. The experience of January was repeated; a banking " syndicate " was hurriedly forced together. Half the subscription gold was again obtained from the Treasury through redemption of legal tenders—not immediately, for the large subscribers had tacitly agreed to obtain their gold from other sources, but afterwards, when subscribers who had quietly borrowed the necessary gold from other banks on thirty-day gold notes repaid such obligations at maturity through Treasury redemptions. In its original purpose, then, the loan was again a failure; the more immediately so in that the sight of a suddenly crumbling gold reserve, at a time when the Treasury

---

[1] *Treas. Rep.*, 1896, pp. 55, 125.
[2] *Ibid.*, 1894, p. lxix.   [3] *Ibid.*

was believed to be at last protected, awoke the wildest dismay in the home and foreign investment community. " We have," the President remarked to Congress on the completion of the loan, " an endless chain in operation, constantly depleting the Treasury's gold, and never near a final rest."[1]

The home and foreign markets were in fact forced to the belief, at the close of 1894, that preservation of the gold standard and of the public credit was no longer possible. It certainly had become impossible through the whipping into line of reluctant city banks. The first loan of 1894 had failed of its purpose within ten months; the second had failed within ten weeks, and, outside the loan market, no recourse was left to the Government. Such was the panicky rush of home and foreign capital to escape before the anticipated crash, that sterling rates advanced even above the normal specie-export point. In January, 1895, $25,900,000 gold went out on export, and the enormous sum of $45,000,000 was withdrawn from the Treasury in redemption of legal tenders.[2] The gold reserve had risen to $111,000,000 after the payments on the December loan of 1894; by February, 1895, it had fallen to $41,340,181, and it was falling at the rate of nearly two million dollars daily. In the first week of February, a telegram came to the Secretary from the Assistant Treasurer at New York, warning him that the New York office could hardly continue redemption of legal tenders more than one day

[1] Annual Message, December 3, 1894.
[2] *Treas. Rep.*, 1896, p. 131.

longer.¹ The crisis predicted in 1880 by Secretary Sherman and in 1884 by Secretary McCulloch, and foreshadowed with increasing distinctness ever since the enactment of the Law of 1890, was now so plainly imminent that the business community anticipated nothing else than suspension of gold payments.

Such was the situation in the closing week of January, 1895. Merchants and bankers now busied themselves putting their houses in order against the expected surrender of the Treasury. The falling markets during the first three days of that week, the half-suppressed excitement in business circles, and the discussion which began over the probable nature and immediate results of a lapse into depreciated currency, reflected the common feeling that a few days, and possibly a few hours, would settle the question finally. On Thursday, January 31st, a sudden change occurred. The markets rose rapidly, foreign exchange declined, gold-export engagements were cancelled, and the rumor ran through all business centres that the President had met the emergency.

¹ Assistant-Secretary Curtis, Associated Press interview of February 25, 1895.

CHAPTER X

THE BOND-SYNDICATE OPERATION

THE action taken by the Administration, in the Treasury crisis of 1895, involved one of the most remarkable experiments in the history of finance. It was the Treasury's double problem now to restore the gold reserve and to prevent the immediate withdrawal of the specie thus obtained, and this could not be done through another bond sale similar to that of December, 1894. It could not be done directly through the banks at all. There remained the large international banking houses which are commonly employed as agents for important Government operations in the money market, and which had been employed by Mr. Sherman in the resumption operations of 1878 and 1879.

What terms could have been made with these international interests, had they been approached in 1893 or 1894, is a matter of conjecture. Their terms as now submitted, in the crisis of January, 1895, were extremely harsh; they measured with little mercy the emergency of the Treasury. They unfolded what they believed to be a practicable plan for both restoring and maintaining the Treasury reserve, but they made the consideration for their services the allotment of a thirty-year four per cent. bond at a price equivalent to 104½, when the existing United States four per cents, with less than half as long to run, were bringing 111 on the market.[1] This was asking a heavy concession; no such demand has been made by any Government-bond syndicate during the present generation. On the other hand, the foreign bankers offered to bind themselves, under conditions which we shall presently examine, to guarantee the maintenance of the Treasury gold reserve, and they submitted one rather important counter-proposition. The four per cents, sold at the stipulated price of 104½, were equivalent to a 3¾ per cent. bond at par,[2] whereas the loans of 1894 had sold on a par basis of three per cent.; but the alternative proposition of the syndicate was that they would pay par for a three per cent. bond, provided payment should be expressly stipulated in gold. This was, on the whole, a safe proposition for the bankers to make, because express provision for gold payment could not be inserted without an act of Congress, and there was not the slightest likelihood that any such act could pass. A bill with that provision was in fact introduced in the House of Representatives in February, and was immediately defeated by a vote of 167 to 120. This vote was taken February 7th; on February 8th the Secretary of the Treasury

[1] Muhleman, *Monetary Systems*, appendix, pp. 224, 225; New York *Financial Chronicle*, February 9, 1895, p. 236.
[2] *Ibid.*

signed a contract on the syndicate's own terms with Messrs. J. P. Morgan & Co. and Messrs. August Belmont & Co., the second of these firms representing the powerful foreign house of Rothschild. The bonds thus sold amounted to $62,315,400, and they brought $65,116,244.

The wild clamor which instantly broke out at Washington seemed actually for the time to stun the Administration party. It was echoed in the opposition press; nor, indeed, did the Administration's supporters throughout the country show, as a rule, anything but bewilderment. In the storm of angry denunciation, perhaps the only unmoved figure was the President; who, having chosen his position, held to it with characteristic resolution. In his special message to Congress, February 8th, Mr. Cleveland wrote that in his judgment the transaction " promises better results than the efforts previously made in the direction of effectively adding to our gold reserve." Ten months later, in his Annual Message of December 2d, he declared that he had " never had the slightest misgiving concerning the wisdom or propriety of this arrangement," and that, individually, he was " quite willing to answer for his full share of its promotion." Let us now see what happened between the dates of these two declarations.

The two considerations in the contract with the syndicate, which had not appeared in any previous bond sale, were contained in the following provisions: " At least one half of all coin deliverable hereunder shall be obtained in and shipped from Europe," and " the parties of the second part, and their associates hereunder, . . . as far as lies in their power, will exert all financial influence and will make all legitimate efforts to protect the Treasury of the United States against the withdrawal of gold pending the complete performance of this contract." Since it was also stipulated that deliveries of gold from Europe " shall not be required to exceed 300,-000 ounces per month," and since 1,750,000 ounces in all were to be imported in order to fulfil the contract, it followed that this engagement in the Treasury's behalf would hold good during about six months.

Now there had been only two important sources of gold withdrawal from the Treasury: gold-exporters who were unable in any other way to meet their obligations on an advancing foreign exchange market, and subscribers to the bond-issues who converted their notes into coin to make their payments. There had been practically no withdrawal for simple hoarding purposes; in his intimation to this effect, in his report of 1894, Secretary Carlisle was mistaken.[1] The syndicate's engagement, then, was first a pledge to obtain all gold for their subscription elsewhere than at the Treasury, and second, it was a promise to stop, if humanly possible, the redemption of notes for export gold. The first of these pledges was simple enough; the second involved extraordinary difficulties.

We have seen in another chapter that withdrawal of Treasury gold for export purposes had become a measure of necessity, because the sterling bankers

[1] *Treas. Rep.*, 1894, pp. lxix., 10.

had in the ordinary course of business contracted foreign obligations which they were forced to meet through gold remittances, while they could get no gold for the purpose except at the Treasury's redemption office. If, then, the syndicate was to "protect the Treasury against the withdrawal of gold" for export purposes, it must do one of two things—provide in this country, at its own expense, the necessary gold for export, or provide a credit fund in Europe which should make gold remittances unnecessary. The first it certainly could not do; the comptroller's compilation of the previous December had shown that all the national banks in the country held only $146,000,000 gold, while the New York banks in February held only $82,000,000. No banker or combination of bankers had the power, in case of repetition of 1894's exchange-market conditions, to procure the $100,000,000 gold which had gone out that year on export.[1]

The second expedient was possible. A banker's draft on London, forwarded to a London creditor, must be redeemed in current English funds at a London institution. If the New York maker of the draft has shipped the necessary sum in gold, the draft will be honored on the arrival of the specie. But if the maker of the draft has borrowed the requisite sum in London on his individual credit, he possesses equally the means of foreign settlement. This was the principle on which the syndicate of 1895 undertook to act. They proposed to sell in New York whatever drafts on London should be needed by the

[1] U. S. Bureau of Statistics; foreign-trade statement for December, 1894.

banking and mercantile community, and to meet the drafts in London through the use of their own credit on the London money market.

The magnitude of this undertaking will readily be perceived. If the demand for such remittances, which had forced the hundred million dollars gold exports of 1894, were to be repeated, the failure of the experiment was inevitable. No banker or combination of bankers could borrow any such amount on its joint or individual credit. This well-known fact explains the reservation in the contract, whereby the syndicate pledged results only " so far as lies in their power." Both they and the Government, however, took the chance. With the double purpose of ensuring themselves against competitive sales of exchange and of ensuring the Treasury against export-gold withdrawals by competing bankers, the syndicate next took the unprecedented step of binding together in the undertaking every banking house and every bank in New York City with important European connections. All of these firms and institutions were admitted to the syndicate, part of the new four per cent. loan being distributed among them at profitable rates. In return for this allotment, they bound themselves, as the Belmont-Morgan syndicate had already bound itself, to draw no gold from the Treasury pending the execution of the contract. It was hoped by this means to set the Treasury on its feet.

The London critics instantly pronounced the undertaking impossible.[1] They pointed out, cor-

[1] London *Economist*, 1895, February 23, June 15, July 6, August 10.

rectly enough, that the syndicate proposed to dam up a natural commercial movement; from this they reasoned that eventually the dam must overflow, and that when this happened, the artificial obstructions erected by the New York bankers would be instantly swept away. We shall presently see how far this London judgment had a solid basis. The syndicate, however, was working on a different theory. Its members were aware, of course, that a withdrawal of foreign capital equal to that of 1894 or 1893, with the consequent excessive demand for drafts on London, would break down the whole experiment. But suppose this demand for remittances to Europe were not to be repeated. The mere fact that the Treasury and the currency were protected would remove one very important cause of the recent flight of European capital. If, in addition, such an agricultural year as 1879 or 1891 were again to be witnessed, it would be found that the syndicate operation had merely equalized the whole year's movement of exchange. In the spring they would sell their drafts on London, depositing at New York in current funds the proceeds of the sale. In the autumn the possession of this accumulated New York fund would enable them, when London needed remittances to New York, to draw on their New York deposits, sell the drafts to the European remitter, and with the proceeds pay off their London debt. It was, perhaps, a doubtful chance, but it was worth the trying.

On the basis of such contingent calculations, this remarkable experiment began. During many weeks, the moves of the syndicate were watched with scepticism in both London and New York. But the operation went on smoothly. Except for some insignificant West Indian consignments, there were no gold exports, and gold withdrawals from the Treasury fell to an unimportant minimum.[1] The foreign-exchange market continued very strong; in fact, the ruling rate was higher even than the average of 1894; but at these rates the syndicate supplied remitters with all necessary drafts on London, and the gold contracted for delivery from Europe duly arrived at the rate of five million dollars monthly. From the New York banks associated with the syndicate had been obtained, within a few weeks after the signing of the contract, most of the $37,500,000 domestic gold pledged for delivery to the Treasury. On February 9th, these banks reported specie holdings of $82,263,900; on April 6th, they held $64,471,200. They made no effort to recoup themselves through note redemption at the Treasury; a fact which at least suggests the possibility that skilful negotiation might have achieved the same result in 1894. On June 25th, the hundred-million Treasury reserve was again intact; on July 8th, it reached $107,571,230.

Long before July, the syndicate's expectations had apparently been fulfilled by a decidedly favorable turn in all the markets, and by a complete reversal of attitude by European investors. In these regards, the events of 1895 were among the most remarkable in our history. It must be remembered

[1] *Treas. Rep.*, 1895, p. 7.

that the industrial paralysis of 1894 had alike affected import trade and home production; both had fallen to the lowest level in many years. It resulted that surplus stocks of merchandise were abnormally small. A sudden demand would exhaust them very quickly, and such a demand began almost within a month of the February bond negotiation. The buying power doubtless came in some degree from actual consumers; but it was chiefly speculative, originating in the growing belief that with the Government's finances out of danger, healthy industrial conditions would return. During this season, the commercial markets presented for a time a spectacle almost equal to that of 1879. Hardly an article of domestic produce or manufacture failed to rise in response to this increased demand.

The iron market led the movement. From a weekly record of 157,000 tons in February, the country's iron production rose by November to 217,000 tons per week, the largest in the country's history, and in spite of this heavy increase in the output, the stock of iron on hand for sale had been decreased through urgent purchases nearly half a million tons.[1] The price of iron, meantime, had risen two to three dollars per ton. Along with this advance in iron came rapid recoveries in the grain markets; in cotton, provisions, oil; and notably in print cloths, the staple of the dry-goods market, whose price rose twenty-five per cent. between February and November. While these advances in commercial prices were in their beginning, during

[1] New York *Iron Age*, November 14, 1895.

the early spring, the market for securities moved up slowly and suspiciously, foreign scepticism over the bond operation still finding voice in speculative sales which offset the timid investment purchases at home. In May, however, came a sudden change. The month began with large purchases of new American securities by London banking houses. Bonds issued by several important railways, for improvement purposes, found a ready sale abroad, and brought unexpectedly good prices. This was apparently the only stimulus needed for real recovery of confidence. Almost simultaneously, a buying movement in "Americans" began on all the important European markets.

This sudden and enormously heavy foreign buying was in part explainable by the condition of the foreign investment markets. Since the Baring collapse of 1890, English capital had been timid and its investment and speculative ventures few. Against £189,436,000 new security issues taken by London investors during 1889, only £49,141,000 had been floated in 1893.[1] But now an important change was taking place. In 1885, gold had been discovered in the Kaffir country of South Africa; two years later, the gold production of that country had become considerable, and London capital began to seek investment in the Transvaal; by 1892, the annual output of the mines on the Witwatersrandt alone exceeded twenty million dollars.[2] Towards the middle of 1894, the incorporation of joint-stock

[1] London *Economist*, January 5. 1895.
[2] *U. S. Mint Report*, 1892, pp. 63, 65.

mining companies in London, enormously capitalized, was undertaken with unusual activity. The Rhodeses and Barnatos of the African domain began to cut an important figure on the London and Continental markets; with the opening of 1895, an old-fashioned popular craze of speculation broke forth throughout England.

It chanced, by one of those odd coincidences of which financial history is full, that this fever of speculation reached its height at the very moment when the United States Government-bond syndicate had apparently solved the problem of the Treasury. The sudden reversal in the American situation, and in particular the rise in prices on the commercial markets, offered at once a fresh field of activity for the excited London adventurers, and they started in suddenly to buy American securities. During two weeks of May, 1895, this foreign buying was so heavy on our own exchanges that every outbound European steamer carried a mass of American stocks and bonds consigned to European houses. Sterling exchange broke from the high level of $4.89, a figure which it had maintained ever since the February contract, and which would ordinarily compel gold exports, to $4.86⅝, or par, touched in the second week of May. The syndicate bankers were already selling in London drafts on their New York deposit fund, and paying off their London money-market obligations.

So far the experiment appeared to be assured of complete success. Whether, in the event of a particularly large and profitable merchandise-export market in the autumn, the syndicate could have achieved all of its purposes, is a matter of some uncertainty. But to those who looked below the surface, there were signs of danger in the very phenomena which were now inspiring the business community with new hopes. For one thing, the time was extremely unfortunate for hasty and extensive domestic speculation. The speculators ran far beyond the limit both of genuine trade demand and of available domestic capital. We have seen in previous chapters the bad results of such operations, even in the best days of the resumption year; we have also seen how far a similar movement paved the way in 1892 for the collapse of 1893. The commercial consequences of the speculation of 1895 were similar to those of preceding years. Prices were carried so high as to serve the purpose, doubly mischievous under existing conditions, of increasing merchandise imports and checking exports. During the first half of 1895, imports increased ten million dollars a month over the corresponding periods of the year before.

Nor were results any more fortunate in the export trade. The syndicate's hopes in this direction were utterly disappointed—partly, no doubt, because the corn-crop failure of the previous season had left little of that commodity to sell, but chiefly because of the wild domestic speculation for the rise in wheat. The early American wheat crop was damaged by frost; the later crop was very large; but the speculators, acting on the basis of the first reports, actually ran up the price, between February and June, thirty-three cents a bushel. As in the fall of 1879, this excessive movement brought the export trade to a halt. While speculation raged in Chicago, Russia was quietly supplying the needs of European consumers. In half a dozen staple markets, the course of events was similar. As against the heavy excess of merchandise exports during 1894, imports during the first nine months of 1895 actually exceeded exports by forty-three million dollars—decidedly the largest balance of merchandise trade against us since the climax of speculation in 1890.

What happened with wheat happened also with securities. Prices of stocks and bonds rose rapidly in May, in response to the foreign buying; but in the next two months American speculators for the rise carried prices so much higher that Europe, still more or less sceptical over the syndicate experiment, seized on the tempting opportunity to secure a profit, and sold back in quantity its holdings of American securities. Even the new four per cents, one half of which the syndicate had placed in London, taking all possible precautions to prevent their early return, were unloaded on the New York market almost as soon as they were released; the home speculators had forced up the price, within two months, from 119 to 124.

These various results followed the inexorable rule of commercial logic; but they doubled the strain upon the syndicate. Foreign exchange returned quickly to the normal gold-shipping point, after its sudden fall, and once more the bankers had to borrow heavily in London. Now, moreover, two radical defects in the syndicate's plan of operation began to betray themselves. The bankers had contracted to obtain one half the gold for the Treasury in Europe. Economically speaking, this was a mistake. It added precisely the sum of the gold importations to the syndicate's London debt, and it increased a domestic money supply already notoriously excessive.

The second defect in the syndicate plan was inevitable from the nature of the operation. By the coalition of all the international houses at New York, the bankers had in a certain sense cornered the foreign exchange market. They could not, to be sure, exact any very exorbitant price for drafts, because such a policy would have forced mercantile remitters to combine for mutual protection and ship gold on their own account. But the minimum selling price fixed for their drafts by the syndicate in midsummer was $4.90 to the pound sterling. A few months before, when drafts were "covered" in export gold, bankers had sold these sterling drafts freely at $4.88¼ or less. That is to say, a New York merchandise importer with a foreign-trade debt of £10,000 to settle, had to pay $49,000 for his draft in the middle of 1895, whereas the highest rates of 1894 had cost him only $48,850. The motive of the syndicate bankers in exacting this high rate was obvious enough. The success of the experiment was growing doubtful; their London borrowings had become very large. They might be forced to export gold, and they fixed their price for sterling drafts so high as to protect themselves from loss in such emergency.

But in so doing, they opened a wide inducement for competitive sales of exchange. Apparently the syndicate alliance of February had swept the market clear of competition. But the syndicate was destined to pass through the experience which awaits every manipulator of a market corner, whatever his purposes or motive. All commercial experience teaches that the most skilful possible preparation for a corner will, in nine cases out of ten, overlook some source of supply, able to fill current demand at lower prices, or that in the final strain upon the market some new source, hitherto unheard of, will be discovered. Exactly this happened in 1895. With a demand for millions of exchange drafts in the market, with no exchange house in New York selling below $4.90, and with a trade profit in selling exchange at $4.88½ and shipping gold to " cover," a New York coffee-importing house with powerful European connections entered the sterling market. It offered drafts one cent per pound below the minimum of the syndicate; the syndicate houses made no change in rates, and their new competitor therefore instantly had the market in its hands.

On July 20th, this house presented $1,000,000 legal tenders at the Treasury for redemption and shipped the gold to London against its sales of sterling in New York. During the next five months, $65,000,000 gold was shipped, all of the specie being obtained from the Treasury. From its summer maximum of $107,000,000, the gold reserve declined again to $63,000,000 on December 31st.[1] Recognizing that its undertaking to protect the Treasury had broken down, the syndicate did what it could to help out the Government through voluntary exchange of gold for notes. In August and September, it thus paid over some twenty millions gold, which was immediately engulfed in the specie exports; this being only the old and futile expedient of 1885, of 1893, and of 1894. In October the syndicate contract expired by limitation, and even the voluntary "reimbursement" ended. Apparently, the syndicate experiment had failed, and nothing was left for the United States but a repetition of the financial strain of 1894.

But the situation was not by any means as hopeless now as it had seemed to be a year before. The syndicate's partial mistakes of judgment and the plunge of domestic industry into speculation had done mischief, but they could not wholly offset the real recovery of trade during the interval of reassurance. There were other reasons why the outlook was less discouraging. The Fifty-third Congress, whose action or inaction on the question of the currency had alternately menaced the public credit, had gone to the people in November, 1894, and had been repudiated by an overwhelming vote. The Democratic House plurality of ninety-one under the elections of 1892 was turned by the vote of two years later into a Republican plurality of one hundred and forty. Little was expected in the way of constructive legislation, even with this radical change

[1] *Treas. Rep.*, 1895, p. 51.

of membership, and nothing was obtained. But it was at least anticipated, and correctly, that the Fifty-fourth Congress would take warning from the fate of its predecessor, and put a stop to the policy of financial agitation.

But more important than either of these two influences were two facts which bore directly on the currency dilemma in the closing months of 1895; first, that the country's actual commercial use of money was nearly eighteen per cent. greater than in 1894 and larger by twenty per cent. than in 1893[1]; and second, that the very process through which the Treasury's gold, accumulated through its successive loans, had been drawn out, had added to the Government's surplus of legal tenders no less a sum than $101,000,000.[2] This was one fifth of the entire amount of legal-tender currency in existence. Except through a revenue deficit, this Treasury legal-tender surplus was removed from the outside currency supply, and the revenue deficit, as a result of the merchandise import movement, had fallen to comparatively small proportions. At the close of December, 1895, even the New York banks held twenty-four millions less in legal tenders than they had held a year before, and twenty-seven millions less than at that date in 1893.[3]

These were important changes; but they had not

---

[1] New York *Financial Chronicle*, January 11, 1896, p. 62.
[2] Statements of January 31, 1894, and December 31, 1895 ; *Treas. Rep.*, 1896, p. 55.
[3] New York weekly bank statements, December 28, 1895 ; December 29, 1894 ; December 30, 1893.

yet undone the mischief. Trade at the close of 1895 was certainly no more active than at the close of 1891, and the outstanding supply of paper currency was as large or larger.¹ That the situation was still sufficiently precarious was shown not only by the gold withdrawals on the breaking of the deadlock in exchange, but by a sudden and violent outpour of gold in December, 1895, when the extraordinary Venezuela episode stirred the London investment community to its depths, and threw on the American market a load of liquidating foreign sales. But the nature of the problem was now much more plainly understood by both Government and people. The Administration acted promptly, and in a different way from any of its previous experiments. On January 6, 1896, the Treasury announced a new four per cent. loan for the very large sum of one hundred million dollars.

Subscriptions for this loan were again required in gold, and the use of gold obtained from the Treasury through note redemption was again as generally practised as in 1894. But we have seen that the floating supply of Government notes available for such purposes was now materially reduced. Gold or legal tenders subscribers must obtain to cover their subscriptions, and the demand for both these forms of money was increased by the fact that the loan was offered at popular subscription to the highest bidders, and that the number of intending subscribers was known to be extremely large. The result was curious. Some of these subscribers made

¹ *Treas. Rep.*, 1896, pp. 121, 122.

an open market bid for gold coin¹; some adopted the much more unusual expedient of bidding a fractional premium for legal tenders which might be used to get gold from the Treasury.² One or two bankers paid a premium for gold abroad, as the syndicate had done in 1895, and imported it for subscription purposes ; and this incoming gold actually passed on the ocean outbound gold consigned from the United States to Europe.³ All this situation was abnormal enough, but it arose from two really encouraging conditions—the existence of many competing bidders, which occasioned a demand for currency several times larger than the actual face value of the loan, and the fact that the dangerous over-supply of Government demand obligations on the market was already materially reduced and was about to be reduced much further. In effect, the Cleveland Administration was at last doing, by virtue of necessity, exactly what Hugh McCulloch had undertaken to do, thirty years before ; it was converting its floating debt into a funded loan. That it was not retiring permanently the notes thus redeemed from a redundant circulation, and replacing them by a conservatively constructed bank-note circulation, was not the Administration's fault. From his first report to his last, Secretary Carlisle had discussed and urged this

[1] New York *Financial Chronicle*, January 18, 1896.
[2] New York *Evening Post*, January 25, 1896 ; New York *Tribune*, January 26, 1896.
[3] New York *Financial Chronicle*, January 18 and February 8, 1896

solution of the problem; but Congress would not listen.

The loan of 1896 succeeded. It increased the Treasury's gold reserve to $128,291,327, touched on the 9th of April. The bonds moreover sold at good prices; the accepted bids ranging from 110⅜ to 120. It would undoubtedly have put in order the deranged public and private finances but for the panic which swept over the investment markets in the political crisis of the summer. But even with the disordered markets of this Presidential year, and with the gold exports stimulated as a consequence, the Treasury gold reserve never fell below the hundred-million mark. The pressure of an abnormally inflated paper currency had been stopped. In the autumn, for the first time since the harvest season of 1891, there was a heavy movement of gold from Europe to the United States, and, as in the days before the inflationist experiment of 1890, this gold flowed freely into the Treasury in exchange for notes.

With the successful loan operation of 1896 this history may properly close. The events which followed this reduction of the outstanding paper currency, through the Treasury's accumulations, to something like normal proportions, belong to another chapter in our history. The further facts that the closing months of the Cleveland Administration, and the early months under its successor, were marked by close economy in import of foreign merchandise, by steady liquidation of home and foreign debt, and finally by a grain crop as deficient abroad and as bountiful at home as the harvest of

1879, show that at least the opportunity for a new industrial epoch was opening. This period has its own problems to meet; if its public men are wise, they will meet them before a fresh emergency arises.

To the reader, I am content to leave this history without further note or comment. If it shall have succeeded in setting forth clearly the facts of our country's checkered financial history since the Civil War, and the relation of these facts to one another, it will have accomplished its purpose. The citizen who thoroughly understands the past may usually be trusted in his judgment of the future; but he must first make very sure that the facts have been correctly apprehended by him, and that his judgment of them is not colored by political or hereditary prejudice. The series of dangerous blunders in this country's financial legislation, during the past thirty years, have had their origin in every instance in imperfect knowledge or mistaken views of the events of our previous history. It has been the purpose of this book to contribute something to a better understanding of that history.

THE END

INDEX.

Agricultural Department of United States government, declares 1884 wheat prices unremunerative, 102; underestimates wheat crop in 1891, 165; early predictions of good corn crop in 1894, 221

Agriculture, extension in the United States after 1865, 3; in Europe, 4; its influence on politics, 5; depressed condition of, early in 1879, 52; foreign reverses in, 53-55; great prosperity in, for the United States, 56, 59, 60; influence on resumption, Sherman's opinion regarding, 67; foreign competition in, after 1881, 86, 114; depression in, during 1885, 117; severe depression in, during 1894, 221; recovery in, during 1896, 253

Aldrich, N. W., U. S. Senator, his over-estimate of revenue under McKinley Tariff act, 135

Allen, W. V., U. S. Senator, attacks bond-issue of 1894, 211

American Railway Union, strike of, in 1894, 220

Appropriations of Congress, vicious methods employed in, 133. *See also* Expenditures of U. S. government

Argentine Republic, increase in wheat exports from, after 1887, 122; investment of British capital in, 122; crop failure and financial panic in, during 1889, 157; English demand for its securities slackens, 157; foreign capital withdraws from, 158

Arthur, Chester A., president of the United States, urges reduction of import tariff, 88; vetoes River and Harbor Bill, 90; Republican approval of his veto, 91; his opinion regarding methods of appropriation, 134

Atchison, Topeka, and Santa Fé railway, escapes Gould's domination in 1880, 64; its deceptive reports of earnings, 219

Austria, railway extension in, prior to 1878, 4; crop failure of 1879 in, 55; accumulates gold for resumption purposes, 160

Baltimore, banks of, issue loan certificates in 1893, 192

Bank of England, high interest rate in Overend-Gurney panic, 15; opposes gold withdrawals for U. S. Treasury, 26; its relations with British Exchequer, 33, 124; its practice regarding

Bank of England—*Continued.*
note redemption, 48, 49; security for its note circulation, 109; action of, in panic of 1890, 158; increases its gold reserve in 1891, 160; gold withdrawn from in 1893, for New York, 196

Bank of France, lends gold in 1890 to Bank of England, 158; attracts gold in 1891, 160, 161

Bank of Russia, lends gold to Bank of England, 158; attracts gold in 1891, 160

Bank checks, tax on, repealed in 1883, 95; sold at a discount for cash in 1893 panic, 194

Bank deposits by U. S. Treasury, Secretary Sherman's methods in, 32, 33; reasons and authority for, 33; heavy increase in, during 1888, 124; difficulties in the way of, 125

Bank deposits, recall of, by interior institutions, 189; heavy withdrawal of, in 1893, 190, 191; suspension of cash payment on, 194

Bank notes, national, designed as permanent currency by authors of Legal Tender Act, 8; large circulation of, in 1884, 108; volume of, dependent on government bonds, 109; rapid retirement of, between 1883 and 1891, 109–111; contraction of, comes to a stop in 1891, 159; large issue of, during 1893 panic, 202

Banks of the United States (*see also* Banks of New York city), their policy regarding money holdings, 75; heavy retirement of their circulation, 109–112; government deposits with, in 1888, 124, 125; cash withdrawals from, in panic of 1893, 189; their re-deposit of reserves, 189, 190; run of interior depositors on, 190; recall of their Eastern deposits, 191; numerous failures among, in interior, 192, 193

Banks of New York City, reluctant to subscribe to the resumption bonds, 29; abolish gold deposits, 46; specie and legal-tender holdings of, in 1879, 48, 58; oppose payment of balances in silver, 76–80; pay gold for Treasury silver, 81–83; failures among, in 1884, 99, 100; issue loan certificates in panic of 1884, 100; lend five millions gold to the Treasury, 104; issue loan certificates in panic of 1890, 158; legal-tender holdings of, increase rapidly, 168; gold payments of, to one another, suspended, 169; to the Treasury, 169; provide export gold prior to 1892, 171; present legal tenders for redemption, 172, 173; ship legal tenders to interior, in 1892, 182; lend gold to the Treasury, 183–185; heavy increase in deposits of, by interior banks, 189, 190; recall of interior deposits from, in 1893, 191; heavy decrease in cash reserves of, 191–193; issue loan certificates, 192; draw gold from Europe, 194; suspension of cash payments among, 194; subscribe to loan of February, 1894, 214; draw out Treasury gold for subscription, 215; repeat the process in November, 231; lend gold to Treasury, 231; coöperate with Belmont-Morgan syndicate, 241

Baring Brothers, their Argentine operations, 157; their suspension in 1890, 157

Belmont, August, complains of Secretary Sherman's terms with bond-subscribers, 30

Belmont - Morgan syndicate of 1895, its contract with the

Belmont-Morgan—*Continued.*
Treasury, 235, 236; its arduous undertaking, 238; its apparent success, 242–244; its mistakes, 247; break-down of its undertaking, 248

Blaine, James G., candidate for presidential nomination in 1880, 70; nominated in 1884 and defeated, 102

Bland, Richard P., U. S. Congressman, introduces free-silver coinage bill, 1877, 37; threatens paper inflation, 38; proposes free-coinage substitute for Silver-Purchase Bill, 148

Bland Silver-coinage bill, debated in Congress, 35–38; sectional character of vote on, 40; modified by Senate compromise, 41; vetoed by President Hayes, 41; passed over veto, 41

Bonds of the U. S. government, power to issue for note redemption, granted in 1866, 10, 11; Democratic party declares for their payment in legal tenders, 16; power of issue, conferred by Resumption Act, 21, 23, 24, 29; sales of, by Secretary Sherman, 30, 31; the long term of the 4 per cents., 31; bill to revoke Treasury's power of issue, 35; payment in silver advised by Congress, 38; Sherman promises payment in gold, 29, 39; foreign investors in, 38, 39; sales of, by London, in 1879, 52; amount outstanding, in 1882, 88; purchases of, with the Treasury surplus, 88; their use as security for national bank circulation, 109; heavy redemption of, by the Treasury, 109, 111, 125, 126; high price of, in 1888, 125; redemption of, abandoned by Harrison Administration, 137, 159; issue of, contemplated by Harrison Administration, 183; Carlisle's reluctance to issue under act of 1875, 207, 209; issue of February, 1894, announced, 210; issue of, attacked by Congress, 211; sustained by the courts, 212; slow subscriptions to, on market, 212; taken by New York banks, 214; how paid for, 215; second issue of, in 1894, 231; its speedy failure, 232; issue of, to Belmont-Morgan syndicate, 236; foreign holdings of, re-sold to New York, 246; final issue of, in 1896, 251

Boston, its banks issue loan certificates in 1893, 192

Boutwell, George S., U. S. Congressman, opposes contraction of legal tenders, 12

Boycott, principle of, approved by Populist National Convention, 180

Bradley, Joseph P., Justice U. S. Supreme Court, believes the legal tenders to have been created as a temporary currency, 8

Bristow, Benjamin H., Secretary of the Treasury; his scepticism over obtaining foreign gold for resumption, 26

Butler, Benjamin F., elected Governor of Massachusetts in 1882, 92

California, its Congressmen vote solidly for Bland Silver Bill, 40; carried in 1882 by Democrats, 92

Call, Wilkinson, U. S. Senator; predicts gold redemption under Silver-Purchase Act, 150

Cannon, Joseph G., U. S. Congressman; his opinion on Congressional methods of appropriation, 133

Carlisle, John G., Congressman and Secretary of the Treasury, votes in 1877 for repeal

Carlisle, John G.—*Continued.*
of Resumption Act, 41; borrows gold in 1893 from New York banks, 184; suspends issue of gold certificates, 185; his interview regarding gold redemption, 186; his attitude in the emergency, 187; pays out the gold reserve for regular expenses, 204, 206; his embarrassing position, 207; proposes exchequer bills, 208; expresses doubt over Treasury's bond-issue powers, 208; asks Congress for plainer authority, 209; decides to issue bonds, 210; Congressional attacks on, 211; his policy with the bankers, 213; its unfortunate results, 214, 215; urges thorough reform of U. S. currency, 252

Cattell, A. G., U. S. Senator, blames McCulloch policy for hard times of 1866, 15

Cattle, large exports of, in 1879, 56

Chaplin, Henry, member British Parliament, opposes free right of entry to American grain, 55

Chase, Salmon P., Secretary U. S. Treasury, regards the legal-tenders as a temporary currency, 8

Chicago, Burlington, and Quincy railway, its large earnings in resumption period, 65; strike on, in 1888, 116

Chicago, railway strike at, 220

Chicago, Rock Island, and Pacific railway, doubles its stock in 1880, 64; its heavy earnings in resumption period, 65

China, its import of silver decreases, 78

Civil War, the, in U. S., its effect on industrial conditions, 2

Clearing-house, at New York, abolishes gold deposits, 46; admits Sub-Treasury to membership, 47; excludes silver from its balances, 76; denounced by Congress, 77; revokes its silver rule, 80; issues loan certificates in 1884 panic, 100; in 1890, 158; its use of gold in balances between banks, 162; legal tenders displace gold in payments of, during 1892, 169, 170; its function, in gold export operations, 171, 172; issues loan certificates in 1893 panic, 192, 194

Clearing-house, at Boston, abolishes gold deposits, 46

Cleveland, Grover, elected Governor of New York, 91, 92; elected President of the United States, 102; his unfavorable view of Treasury situation in 1885, 103; financial operations of his Administration, 104, 105, 106, 107, 110, 112; defeated by Harrison in 1888, 130; his popular plurality over Harrison, 130; his view as to manner of tariff revision, 131; renominated in 1892 by Democratic party, 178; sources of his support, 179; South Carolina Democrats protest against nomination of, 179; re-elected President, 181; his large popular plurality, 181; pledges gold redemption of legal tenders, 186; summons Congress in extra session, 197; repudiates compromise repeal of Silver-Purchase Act, 199; stops blockade of traffic in Railway Union strike, 220; denounces Senate Tariff Bill of 1894, 226; refuses to sign it, 228; vetoes seigniorage bill, 230; his remark on the "endless chain," 232; defends the bond contract of 1895, 236; his final and successful currency operation, 252

Cockrell, F. M., U. S. Senator, denounces foreign bond-investors, 39; declares Silver-Purchase Act an abandonment of bimetallism, 150

Coinage of silver dollars, *see* Silver

Colorado, carrried by Democrats in 1882, 92; its Senators vote against Silver-Purchase Bill, 147; its Democratic Convention of 1892 demands free coinage, 179; repudiates national convention's currency platform, 179; carried in 1892 by Populist party, 181

Commercial failures, *see* Failures in business

Congress of U. S., pledges in 1865 retirement of the legal-tenders, 11; passes contraction bill, 11; its debate on contraction, 12; revokes contraction power, 15; condemns Johnson's repudiation plan, 17; passes Public Credit Act of 1869, 17; scandals of, during inflation period, 18; passes Inflation Act of 1874, 20; Republicans lose control of, 20; passes Resumption Act, 21; undertakes to wreck the resumption plan, 34; House votes repeal of Resumption Act, 35; passes Free-Silver Coinage Bill of 1878, 35, 38; motives of, in 1878, 37; its attack on foreign bond-subscribers, 39; party chaos in, during 1878, 40; its sectional votes, 40; passes Silver Bill over Presidential veto, 41; adjourns, 42; influence of 1878 elections on, 44; votes for compulsory reissue of legal tenders, 49; denounces New York Clearing-House, 77; forces revocation of Clearing-House rule regarding silver, 77; its unwillingness in 1882 to reduce the tariff, 88; adopts policy of extravagant expenditure, 89; increases pension appropriations, 89; passes River and Harbor Bill over veto, 90; its policy rebuked in 1882 elections, 91; resists the tariff revision movement, 92; passes Tariff Act of 1883, 93; authorizes issue of small silver certificates, 108; defeats free-coinage bill of 1886, 117; House of Representatives passes Mills Tariff Bill, 125; authorizes bond redemptions at a premium, 125; its vicious methods of appropriation, 133; adopts McKinley Tariff Act, 134; its estimates of revenue reduction, 135, 136; its wild extravagance during 1890, 136; political situation of, in 1889, 141; tariff changes opposed in, 141; silver sentiment in, 141; action on Silver-Purchase Bill, 147, 148, 149; defeats free-coinage substitute, 148; asserts gold redemption under the Act, 150; fixes the hundred-million gold reserve in 1882, 166, 167; House divides equally in 1892 on Free-Coinage bill, 174; Senate passes bill, 174; tariff reduction bills of 1892, passed by House, 175; rejected by Senate, 175; promises economy, in 1892, 176; increased extravagance of, 176; Democrats obtain control of, 181; extra session of, in 1893, 197; struggle over repeal of Silver-Purchase Law, 197-199; sectional division in, 198; repeals the law, 199; refuses relief to the Treasury, 208, 210; attacks the bond-issue of 1894, 211; apathy of conservatives in, 212; its attitude towards tariff revision, 223; motives of the

Congress of U. S.—*Continued.*
House, 225; of the Senate, 225; action of the two houses on Wilson Bill, 225, 226; delusive hopes of, from income tax, 227; passes seigniorage bill, 230; refuses to authorize gold bond, 235; outcry of, against 1895 bond-issue, 236; Republicans regain control of, 249
Connecticut, goes Democratic in 1877 and Republican in 1878, 44; Democrats carry, in 1882, 92
Consols, British, low price of, in 1894, 213
Corn, large crop of, in 1879, 56; failure of crop in 1894, 221; influence of failure on syndicate operations, 245
Cornell, Alonzo B., elected Governor of New York in 1879, 68, 91
"Corners," in wheat, during 1879, 60; in wheat and coffee during 1887, 114; in wheat during 1888, 115
Cotton, depressed market for, after resumption, 51; revival of market for, in 1879, 57; speculation in, during 1882, 85; overproduction of, in 1882, 87; large American consumption of, in 1889. 120; rise in price of, during 1895, 242
"Coxey's Army," march of, in 1894, 219
Crossman, W. H., & Co., break through bond syndicate's plans in 1895 gold market, 248
Currency, of the United States (*see* also Bank notes, Gold, Legal tenders, and Silver), discussions on, affected by price of grain, 5; condition of, at close of the Civil War, 7, 9; contraction plan of 1866, 11, 12, 15; danger to, opinion of President Hayes, 72; movement of, in 1879, 75, 76; active interior demand for, in 1880, 81, 82; increase of, while trade demand decreased, 97; operations in, by the first Cleveland Administration, 105, 106, 107, 108; change in composition of, after 1885, 111, 112; heavily contracted in 1888, through Treasury surplus, 123, 126; party declarations on, in 1888, 138, 139; Secretary Windom's views regarding, 145; inflation of, under the laws of 1890, 151, 154, 155, 159, 162; effect of its redundancy, on foreign-exchange market, 162; volume of, not a necessary cause for high prices, 165; party declarations on, in 1892, 177, 178, 179; Populists demand that it be doubled, 180; hoarding of, during 1893 panic, 190, 194; premium on, in New York City, 194, 195; enormous increase in, during 1893, 202; reaches its largest volume in 1894, 230; syndicate operations increase supply of, 247; reduction of, through bond-issues, 250, 251, 252, 253
Customs revenue, requirement of payment in coin revoked, 47; large increase in, after resumption, 87; not materially affected by tariff act of 1883, 96; heavy expansion of, after 1886, 113; causes for rise in, 114, 115, 121, 123; decrease in, under McKinley Act, 134, 135; effect of 1893 panic on, 205; insufficient, under Act of 1894, 226, 227

Daniel, John W., U. S. Senator, his opinion of Silver-Purchase Act, 150
Darling, W. A., U. S. Congress-

Darling, W. A.—*Continued.*
man ; his opinion of the legal tenders, 13 ; of protective tariff, 13
Deficit of revenue in U. S. government finances, begins in 1891, 138 ; Congress of 1892 fails to remedy, 175, 176 ; met out of the gold reserve, 204 ; Sherman's theory regarding, 222 ; mistaken views of, in Congress, 224 ; amount of, under Tariff Act of 1894, 227 ; influence of income-tax annulment on, 229
Democratic party, adopts repudiation issue in 1868, 16 ; loses the Presidential election, 16 ; gains control of the House, 20 ; its Congressmen vote unanimously against Resumption Act, 21 ; threaten to repeal the act, 21 ; its opposition to resumption plans, 35, 37, 42 ; its division of opinion in 1878, 44 ; its pro-silver tendencies in 1879, 66 ; its defeat, 68 ; its currency plank in 1880, 69 ; defeated in the Presidential election, 71 ; electoral victories in 1882, 91 ; elects Cleveland President, 102 ; demands tariff reduction in 1888, 128 ; defeated in Presidential election, 130 ; attitude of, regarding silver in 1888, 139 ; its Congressmen vote unanimously against Silver-Purchase Bill, 151 ; victory in 1890 elections, 173, 174 ; its equivocal money platform of 1892, 177, 178 ; attitude of, in West and South, 179 ; wins the 1892 election, 181 ; breach in, during session of 1893, 198 ; majority of its Congressmen vote for free coinage, 198 ; attitude of, on bond-issue question, 207; tariff revision in Congress demanded by, 223 ; conflicting tariff views of, in House and Senate, 225

Dry-goods industry, depression at resumption of specie payments, 51 ; prosperity in, at close of 1879, 58 ; profitable trade in, during 1888 and 1889, 114 ; improvement of, in 1895, 242

Eckels, James H., U. S. Comptroller of the Currency, his opinion of interest payment on deposits of interior banks, 189
Economist, London, its view of agricultural conditions in 1879, 55 ; of the U. S. gold exports in 1891, 165; of the syndicate undertaking of 1895, 239
Edmunds, George F., U. S. Senator, draws up Specie Resumption Bill, 21
Elections, of 1868, 16 ; of 1874, 20 ; of 1876, 34 ; of 1878, 44 ; of 1879, 65, 68 ; of 1880, 71 ; of 1882, 91, 92 ; of 1884, 102 ; of 1888, 130 ; of 1890, 173 ; of 1892, 180, 181 ; of 1894, 249 ; of 1896, 253
England, relations to the American money market, 14, 15 ; crop failure of 1879 in, 53, 54, 55 ; ships gold to U. S., 58 ; increase in manufacturing trade of, after 1886, 119 ; export trade expanded, 119, 120 ; enormous investments of, in foreign securities, 120, 122 ; speculative markets of, early in 1890, 156; London panic in, 157 ; liquidation of security holdings by, after 1890, 158 ; heavy sales of American securities by, in 1891, 165 ; security issues in, after 1890, 243 ; gold-mining craze of 1895 in, 243 ; buys American securities, 244
Erie Railway, failure of, in 1893, 194

Europe, investments by, in United States, 3, 15; crop failure of 1879 in, 55; large sales of merchandise by, in 1883, 97; after 1886, 119; crop failure of 1891 in, 163, 164; its appreciation of the American currency dangers, 165; estimated volume of its investments in American securities, 217, 218; its heavy liquidation of such securities, in 1893, 217; in 1894, 218; large wheat harvest of 1894 in, 221; buys American securities in 1895, 241, 243; sells them back again, 246, 251; ships gold to the United States in 1896, 253

Ewing, Thomas, nominated by Democrats in 1879 for Governor of Ohio, 66; his overwhelming defeat, 68

Expenditure of U. S. Government, extravagance of, in 1882, 89; Republican Convention of 1888 recommends increase in, 129; President Harrison suggests increase in, 132; Congressional recklessness in, during 1890, 136; Congress of 1892 promises to reduce, 176; instead, it increases, 176

Export trade, in wheat, rise of, after the Civil War, 4; increase of, in all commodities, after the panic of 1873, 19; decrease early in 1879, 51; in wheat, heavy increase later in 1879, 56; in other commodities, increase of, 56; of 1879, checked by speculation, 60; of 1881, reduced by the crop failure, 84; decrease in, after 1885, 121; checked in 1895 by speculation, 245

Export of gold, *see* Gold; of Silver, *see* Silver

Failures in business in the United States, in 1877 and 1878, 34; in 1880, 65; in 1886 and 1888, 119; in 1893, 201

Fairchild, Charles S., Secretary U. S. Treasury, his operations with the Treasury surplus, 123-125; his opinion of bond-buying at a premium, 123

Felton, W. H., U. S. Senator, denounces foreign bond investors, 39

Fessenden, W. P., Secretary U. S. Treasury, regards the legal tenders as a temporary currency, 8

Field, Stephen J., Associate Justice U. S. Supreme Court, pronounces income tax of 1894 unconstitutional, 229

Florida, Democrats of, demand free coinage, 179

Folger, Charles J., Secretary U. S. Treasury, urges reduction of tariff duties, 88; warns Congress of dangers in silver coinage, 96

Ford, W. C., Chief U. S. Bureau of Statistics, his estimate of revenue under income tax, 229

Foreign exchange, high rates of, after resumption, 48, 52; fall in, during 1879, 57; relation to the currency, 78, 79; rise in, during 1881, 85; during 1891, 159, 161; nature of New York operations in, 161; rise in, during 1892, 166, 171; during 1893, 186; sharp decline in, during 1893 panic, 193; forced up by New York premium on currency, 196; renewed rise in, at close of 1893, 206; in 1894, 216-218; bond syndicate's operations in, 238-240; fall in, during 1895, 244; quick recovery in, 246; high rates for, 248

Foster, Charles, Secretary U. S. Treasury, stops gold disbursements by Treasury in 1892, 170; prepares for a bond-issue,

Foster, Charles—*Continued.*
183; borrows gold from New York banks, 183

France, accumulates gold during Sherman's preparations for resumption, 26; crop failures of 1879 in, 55; ships gold to U. S., 58; gold shipped to in 1891, from U. S., 160, 161; crop failure of 1891 in, 163

Franco-Prussian War, influence of, on the price of wheat, 4

Fuller, M. W., Chief Justice U. S. Supreme Court, pronounces income tax of 1894 unconstitutional, 229

Garfield, James A., nominated for President in 1880 by Republican party, 70; his electoral majorities, 71; effect of his death on the markets, 83; declares in 1872 that proper maximum of pension expenditure had been reached, 89

George, Henry, runs for Mayor of New York in 1886 on labor ticket, 117

Georgia, Democratic Convention of 1892 demands free coinage, 179

Germany, accumulates gold during this country's resumption operations, 26; adopts gold standard of currency, 36; sells its old silver coin, 36, 37; crop failure of 1879 in, 55; exports gold to U. S., 58

Gold, premium on, influence upon prices, 9; entire American product exported during inflation years, 14, 25; sales of by the Treasury, 14, 26; conspiracy in the market for, during 1869, 18; export of, checked, 19; stock of, in United States in 1877, 25; foreign banks unwilling to part with, 26; government bonds declared payable in, by Secretary Sherman, 29; hostile operations in 1878 market for, 30; adopted as currency standard by Germany, 36; Treasury's holdings of, at resumption, 45; special bank accounts in, abolished, 46; New York holdings of, at resumption, 48; exports of, in 1879, 53; heavy imports of, from Europe, 58; Treasury holdings of, increased, 58; used for regular government expenditure, 59; legal tenders recognized as redeemable in, 74; silver dollars not legally convertible into, 77; Treasury reserve of, decreases in 1882, 80; payments of, by banks, for Treasury silver, 82; exports of, in 1881, 85; heavy shipments during 1884, 97; use of, in revenue payments, decreases, 97; McCulloch's views regarding displacement of, by silver, 103; Treasury reserve of, declines, 104; five millions of, borrowed in 1885 by Treasury from banks, 104; redemption of notes of 1890 in, provided for, 149, 150; large amounts of, borrowed by Bank of England from France and Russia, 158; imports of, by U. S., in 1890, 158; heavy exports of, early in 1891, 159; popular explanations of exports of, 160; exports of, caused by redundant currency, 161, 162; Treasury's enormous disbursements of, in 1890 and 1891, 162; importation of, in 1891, 164; presented again to Treasury for legal tenders, 164; large exports of, in 1892, 166; fall in Treasury's reserve of, 166; amount of, reserved by law for redemption purposes, 167; decrease in payments of, in public revenue, 168; decreased use of, in settlements between

Gold—*Continued.*
banks, 168, 169; Treasury abandons use of, in its own payments, 170; provided by banks for export, prior to 1892, 171; Treasury's stock of, heavily drawn upon by legal tenders presented for redemption, 172; heavy withdrawals of, at close of 1892, 183; Treasury borrows six millions of, from New York banks, 183; amount of, left in Treasury by Harrison Administration, 184; twenty-five millions of, borrowed by Treasury in 1893 from banks, 185; issue of Treasury certificates for, suspended, 185; redemption of notes of 1890 in, rumor of its suspension, 185; use of, for note redemption, pledged by President Cleveland, 186; imports of, during panic of 1893, 194, 196; becomes almost the sole medium of exchange, 196; heavy payments of, in public revenue, 203; still larger use of, in Treasury's 1893 disbursements, 204–206; renewed fall in Treasury reserve of, 206, 209; amount of, needed for reserve, Carlisle's opinion on, 209; bond-issue to obtain, announced, 210, 211; issue of bonds for, declared legal by courts, 212; amount of, paid for loan of February, 1894, 215; withdrawals of, from Treasury, by bond-subscribers, 215; Treasury's use of, in regular disbursements, checked, 216; exports of, in 1894, begin again, 217; causes of, 218, 219; New York banks lend fifteen millions more to Treasury, 231; withdrawals of, for bond-issue of 1894, 231; contract for, with Belmont-Morgan Syndicate, 237; withdrawals of, stopped, 241; Treasury reserve of, restored, 241; discoveries of, in South Africa, 243; export of, resumed, 248; withdrawals of, for loan of 1896, 251; premium bid for, 252; imports and exports of, simultaneous, 252; exports of, early in 1896, 253; heavy imports of, 253

Gold reserve in United States Treasury, *see* Gold and Treasury

Gorman, Arthur P., United States Senator, defends the Senate's protectionist legislation of 1894, 227

Gould, Jay, his railway operations in 1880, 63; his methods, 63, 64; his great power, 64; his exhibit of his security holdings, 86

Government bonds, *see* Bonds of the United States

Grain trade, American (*see* also Agriculture, Corn, and Wheat), its expansion after the Civil War, 3; increase after 1873 panic, 19; great activity of, during 1879 and 1880, 56, 59; affected by foreign competition after 1885, 121; activity in, during 1891, 164; depression of 1894 in, 221; checked in 1895 by speculation, 245

Grant, Ulysses S., elected President of the United States in 1868, 16; his Administration and the scandals of inflation period, 18; vetoes inflation act, 20; candidate in 1880 for Republican nomination, 70

Grant & Ward, failure of, in panic of 1884, 100

Gray, Horace, Associate Justice U. S. Supreme Court, pronounces income tax of 1894 unconstitutional, 229

Hancock, Winfield S., nominated for President in 1880 by the Democrats, 71; defeated in the election, 71

Harrison, Benjamin, President of the United States, his electoral majority, 130; his views on tariff revision, 131; on public expenditure, 132, 133; on pensions, 132; interferes in the pension extravagance, 138; his curious remarks on Windom silver plan, 140; approves enlarged use of silver in currency, 143; disapproves free-coinage legislation, 148; defends Silver-Purchase Act, 154; his misjudgment of the trade situation, 154-156

Hayes, John L., made president of Tariff Commission of 1882, 92; his view of tariff-reduction policy, 93

Hayes, Rutherford B., President of the United States, favors maintaining silver as a precious metal, 7; elected Governor of Ohio, 27; elected President, 27; troubles of his Administration, 33; his disputed title, 34; vetoes Bland Silver Bill, 41; his negative influence on Congress, 41; refuses renomination for Presidency, 69; advises retirement of legal tenders, 72; his opinion as to results of compulsory coinage, 74

Heidelbach, A. S., his estimate of foreign investments in the United States, 218

Hill, Benjamin H., U. S. Senator, his view of the Matthews Resolution, 38

Hooper, Samuel, U. S. Congressman, regards legal tenders as a temporary currency, 8

House of Representatives, *see* Congress

Howe, T. O., U. S. Senator, opposes Hayes Administration's policy, 43

Idaho, Democrats of, demand free-coinage law, 179; choose Populist electors in 1892, 179

Illinois, its Congressmen vote solidly for Bland Silver Bill, 40; goes Democratic in 1890, 174; Democrats of, favor free coinage in 1892, 179

Immigration to the United States, after the Civil War, 3; increase in, after resumption, 61; reaches its maximum in 1882, 61; decrease of, in ensuing years, 115; increase in, during 1888, 115

Import trade of U. S., enormous increase of, during inflation period, 18, 19; stimulated in 1881 by home speculation, 84; effect on public revenue, 87; heavy increase in, after 1886, 113; reasons for increase in, 119-121; character of increase in, 121; sudden decrease in after 1893 panic, 205; violent enlargement of, in 1895, 245; contraction of, in 1896, 253

Income tax of 1894, Congressional ideas regarding, 227; Supreme Court discusses, 228, 229; pronounced unconstitutional, 229; its probable yield over-estimated, 229

India, deficient cotton crop of 1879 in, 57; silver imports of, decrease after 1877, 78; increase in wheat exports from, 122; effect of suspension of silver coinage in, 200

Indiana, its Congressmen vote solidly for Bland Silver Bill, 40; Democratic Convention of 1878 opposes resumption, 42; Republican Convention in, opposes financial agitation, 43

Ingalls, J. J., U. S. Senator, opposes Hayes Administration's policy, 43

Internal revenue, taxes reduced by Act of 1883, 93–96; increase in receipts from, after 1886, 113; enlarged in 1888 by active home consumption, 123; total abolition of, suggested by Republican Convention, 129

Iowa, its Congressmen vote solidly for Bland Silver Bill, 40; Democratic Convention in, during 1878, opposes resumption, 42; carried easily by Republicans in 1879, 68; Democrats of, favor free coinage in 1892, 179

Iron, depression in market for, after resumption, 51; violent advance in, during 1879, 57; speculation in, during 1880, 60, 61; overproduction of, in 1882, 87; large consumption of, after 1885, 115, 120; rise in price of, 115; active market for, in 1895, 242

Johnson, Andrew, President of the United States, proposes to repudiate interest on the government debt, 17; his proposition condemned by Congress, 17

Jones, John P., U. S. Senator, believes that Silver-Purchase Act would raise price of silver, 151

Jordan, C. N., U. S. Treasurer, his plans for circulating Treasury silver, 110

Kaffir gold mines, discovery of, 243; speculative craze in London over, 244

Kansas, its Congressmen vote solidly for Bland Silver Bill, 40; goes Democratic in 1882, 92; Democrats of, demand free coinage, 179; chooses Populist electors in 1892, 181

Kansas Pacific Railway, its dishonest amalgamation with the Union Pacific, 63, 64

Kelley, W. D., U. S. Congressman, his opinion on contraction of the legal tenders, 12; on protection, 13; opposes Hayes Administration's policy, 43

Knights of Labor, their strikes in 1886 and 1888, 116; apply for injunction against bond-issue of 1894, 211

Knox, John J., Comptroller U. S. Currency, approves government bond deposits, 33; disapproves interest payment on interior bank deposits, 189

Labor troubles (*see* also Strikes) in 1877, 34; in 1886, 116; their influence on the politics of 1886 and 1888, 117; in 1894, 219, 220

Legal tenders, amount of, outstanding at the close of Civil War, 7; purpose of their founders, 8; regarded as a temporary currency, 8; their effect on prices, 9; McCulloch proposes contraction of, 10; Congress promises contraction of, 11; contest over bill to contract, 11–13; contraction of, begun, 11; act of 1866 ineffectual, 13; contraction power revoked, 15; plan to pay part of government debt in, 16; redemption in coin promised by Congress, 17; increase in issues of, 17; effect of the inflation policy of, 18; Supreme Court declares them constitutional, 20; Congress votes new issues of, in 1874, 20; Grant vetoes bill, 20; act to resume specie payments on, passed, 21; made perpetually redeemable in

Index. 267

Legal tenders—*Continued.*
coin, 23; Sherman on question of reissue, 28, 50; Bland's threat regarding, 38; Western conventions demand their substitution for bank notes, 42; Sherman's opinion as to proper reserve against, 45; clearing-houses agree to accept equally with gold, 46; customs dues made payable in, 47; bank holdings of, in 1879, 48; amount in circulation fixed by Congress, 49; their reissue made compulsory, 50; presented at Treasury for redemption, in 1879, 53; gold paid to the Treasury for, 58; Hayes advises their retirement, 72; Sherman believes them a safe currency, 72; their ready circulation, 75; supply of, in New York banks, runs short, 81; dangers to Treasury reserve against, 103; absorption of, in small denominations, 105; Treasury substitutes silver certificates for, in outside circulation, 108; payments in, to the government, increase in 1886, 111; provisions of, applied to the notes of 1890, 147, 149; enormous increase of, in circulation, 155, 159; gold exchanged for, in 1891, 164; gold reserve against, legal authority for, 166, 167; displace gold in public revenue, 168; in New York bank reserves, 168; in clearing-house exchanges, 169; in payments by Treasury, 170; amount redeemed in gold up to 1891, 172; presented in 1892 for redemption in gold, 172, 182; in 1893, 183; used to obtain bank gold by Secretary Foster, 183; by Secretary Carlisle, 184, 185; rumors of silver redemption for, 185; Cleveland pledges redemption of, in gold, 186; hoarding of, in panic of 1893, 190, 196; premium on, 194; return of, to circulation, 200; use of, by bond-subscribers of 1894, to obtain gold, 215; exchanged by Treasury for gold, 231; premium on, for bond-subscription purposes, 252

Lincoln, Abraham, President of the United States, declares the legal tenders to be a temporary currency, 8

Louisville and Nashville Railway, its large earnings in the resumption period, 65

Maine, Democratic Conventions of, in 1879, declare for free coinage, 66; Republican majority in, increased, 68

Marine Bank, failure of, in 1884, 100

Massachusetts, carried by Democratic party in 1882, 92; in 1890, 174

Matthews, Stanley, U. S. Senator; his resolution declaring government bonds payable in silver, 38; his remark on foreign customers of the United States, 39; Sherman's peculiar letter to, 42

Matthews resolution, proposed, 38; curious debate on, 39; sustained by many Republicans, 40; has no effect on administrative action, 41

McClellan, George B., Democratic nominee for President in 1864, 16

McCulloch, Hugh, appointed Secretary of the Treasury by Lincoln, 10; his views on currency contraction, 10; declares the contraction law of 1866 ineffective, 12; his opinion as to the necessary conditions for resumption, 13, 28; his unfavorable view of con-

McCulloch, Hugh—*Continued*.
ditions in resumption year, 51;
reappointed Secretary of
Treasury by Arthur, 103; his
pessimistic view of the silver
question, 103
McKinley, William, U. S. Congressman, proposes tariff bill
of 1890, 134
McKinley Tariff Law, *see* Tariff.
McPherson, John R., U. S.
Senator, asserts gold redemption under Silver-Purchase Act,
151
Metropolitan Bank, embarrassment of, in 1884, 100
Michigan, Republican victory of
1879 in, 68; Republicans hold,
in 1881, 90; carried by Democrats in 1882, 92; in 1890,
174; Democrats of, favor free
coinage in 1892, 179
Mills Tariff Bill, *see* Tariff.
Milwaukee Bank, failure of, in
1893, 194
Mining market, of Nevada and
California, in 1874, 36; of
London, in 1895, 244
Minnesota, its Congressmen vote
solidly for Bland Silver Bill,
40; Republican Convention of
1888 in, hints at tariff reduction, 131
Missouri Pacific Railway,
Gould's influence on, 63; strike
on, in 1886, 116
Money market, of London,
high rates, in during 1866, 15;
during 1878, 30; of New York,
advance in, during 1879, 58;
excessively high rates, during
panic of 1884, 100; unsettled
in 1887 by interior land speculation, 115; excessive advance
in rates on, in 1890, 158; disturbances in, early in 1893,
185, 186; panic in, 191, 192
Morgan, J. P., & Co., contract
with U.S. Government in 1895,
236

Morton, Levi P., Vice-President
of the United States, his
opinion on tariff revision, 131
Morton, O. P., U. S. Senator,
blames McCulloch plan for
financial troubles of 1866, 15

Napoleonic wars, influence of,
on European industry, 2
National Banks, *see* Banks of
U. S.
National Cordage Company, failure of, in 1893, 188
Navy, U. S. appropriations for,
recommended by Republican
Convention, 129; urged by
President Harrison, 132; reduced by Congress of 1892;
176
Nebeker, E. H., U. S. Treasurer; his correct explanation of
the gold outflow after 1890,
159, 162
Nebraska, carried by Democrats
in 1890, 174; corn-crop failure
of 1894 in, 221
Nevada, rich silver discoveries
in, during 1873, 36; carried
by Populists in 1892, 181
New England, its Congressmen
vote solidly against the Bland
Silver Bill, 40
New Jersey, carried by Republicans in 1881, 90
New York City, protest of
merchants against gold accumulations in the national Treasury, 1866, 14; Sub-Treasury
at, admitted to clearing-house
membership, 46, 47; condition
of banks in, during resumption
year, 48, 58; its grain trade
checked by 1879 wheat corner,
60; financiering of its elevated
railways, 63; its clearinghouse excludes silver, 76–79;
exclusion rule rescinded, 80;
stock panic in, during 1884,
99, 100; during 1890, 158;
during 1893, 188

New York City banks, *see* Banks.
New York State, party conventions of, during 1878, favor resumption, 44 ; Republican victory in, 44 ; party conventions of, during 1879, approve resumption, 67 ; sweeping Republican victory in, 68 ; Republican Convention of 1882 in, approves veto of River and Harbor Bill, 91 ; Democrats elect governor in, during 1882, 91
Notes, United States, *see* Legal tenders.
Notes of national banks, *see* Bank notes

Ohio, elected Hayes Governor in 1875, 27 ; its Congressmen vote solidly for Bland Silver Bill, 40 ; Democratic Convention of 1878 denounces Resumption Act, 42; action of Republican Conventions in, 43; carried by the Republicans, 44 ; party conventions in, during 1879, 65, 66; carried by Republicans, 68; Republicans hold, in 1880 and 1881, 90 ; Democrats carry, in 1882, 91
Oil, brought to market by the pipe line, 57 ; large exports of, in 1879, 57 ; advance in price of, during 1895, 242
Overend, Gurney & Co., failure of, in 1866, 14

Panic, of 1866, in London, 14 ; its influence on the American markets, 15 ; of 1873 in New York, events which led up to, 18 ; good and bad results of, 18, 19 ; of 1884, in New York, its cause, 98 ; its character, 98 ; its peculiar incidents, 99 ; protective measures adopted in, 100; of 1890, in London, 157 ; how allayed, 158; its influence on New York, 158; of 1893, in the United States, outbreak of, 188; corporation failures in, 188; effect of, on interior institutions, 189, 190, 193 ; on the city banks, 190–194 ; on the currency, 195 ; on foreign exchange, 193, 196; on Congress, 197 ; on trade, 201 ; on the Treasury, 203
Paris Exposition of 1889, its alleged influence on American gold exports, 160
Pattison, Robert E., elected Governor of Pennsylvania in 1882, 92 ; in 1890, 173
Pennsylvania, Democratic Convention in, during 1879, its equivocal stand on the currency, 66 ; carried by the Democrats in 1882, 92 ; in 1890, 173
Pensions, Garfield declares in 1872 that maximum expenditure for, has been reached, 89 ; enormous increase in appropriations for, during 1882, 89 ; Republican Convention of 1888 advises increase in, 129 ; President Harrison suggests enlargement of, 132 ; political inducement for, 134 ; extravagant appropriations of 1890 for, 136 ; President Harrison alarmed at increase in, 138 ; heavy increase in appropriations for, by 52d Congress, 176
Philadelphia, its banks issue loan certificates in 1893, 192
Philadelphia and Reading Railway company, its failure in 1893, 188 ; its reckless financiering, 218
Pittsburg, railway riots at, in 1877, 34 ; its banks issue loan certificates in 1893, 192
Platforms, party, of Democrats in 1868, declares for repudiation, 16 ; of Republicans in 1876, ignores Resumption Law, 27 ; of Western Democrats in 1878, favor free coinage and

Platforms—*Continued*.
denounce Resumption Law, 42; of Western Republicans in 1878, oppose financial agitation, 43; of Democrats in 1879, declare for silver, 66; of Republicans, uphold specie payments, 67; of 1880, ignore silver, 69; of third party in 1888, based on labor question, 117; of 1886 and 1888, make an issue of trust question, 118; of Democrats in 1888, 128; of Republicans, 129, 139; of Republicans in 1892, 177; of Democrats, 178; of Western and Southern Democrats, favor free coinage, 179; of Populists, 180

Populist party, organized in 1892, 180; its radical platform, 180; its popular vote for President, 181; its showing in Congress and in the Electoral College, 181

Price, Hiram, U. S. Congressman, his skepticism over resumption, 12

Prices of commodities (*see* also Cotton, Dry-goods, Iron, Silver, Stock market, Wheat), high level of, during war inflation, 9, 10; obstacles presented by, to resumption, 13; fall in, after panic of 1873, 19; decline in, early in 1879, 51, 52; violent advance of, later in the year, 53, 56-60; continued strength in, during 1880, 61; high level of, in 1882, 85; reaction in, 86; renewed advances in, during 1887 and 1889, 115; during 1890, 154-56; decline in, during 1893, 200; recovery in, during 1895, 242

Protection, *see* Tariff

Public Credit Act of 1869, 17

Public lands, enormous sales of, in 1888, 115

Railways of the United States, their expansion after the Civil War, 2; shares in, sold by London in 1879, 52; speculation in securities of, during 1880, 61, 62; systems of, built up, 62, 63; reckless financiering of, in 1880, 62-64; enormous earnings of, 65; profits of, affected by 1881 crop failure, 84; construction of, in 1882, decreases, 87; financial embarrassment among, in 1884, 98; construction of, reaches its maximum in 1887, 115; labor troubles on, during 1886 and 1888, 116; presidents of, give their word of honor to maintain rates, 119; Populist Convention declares for government ownership of, 180; failures among, in 1893, 188, 194, 218; bad financiering of, 218, 219; decreased earnings of, in 1894, 219; labor uprising on, 220; their traffic blockaded by strikers at Chicago, 220

Railways, foreign, influence of their extension on world's wheat product, 4, 122; active construction of, before 1878, in Russia, 4; in Austria, 5; extension prior to 1888, in India, 122; in Argentine Republic, 122

Republican party, opposes repudiation issue in 1868, 16; wins the Presidential election, 16; defeated in the Congressional elections of 1874, 20; its condition after the panic, 20; unanimous vote of its Congressmen for Resumption Act, 21; ignores the Act in its platform of 1876, 27; its minority in the House of 1877, 34; its failure to support the Hayes Administration in Congress, 40; its platforms of 1878 favor the Administration, 43; its victory

Republican party—*Continued.*
in 1879, 68; its platform of 1880, 69; disputes over Presidential nominations, 70; elects Garfield President, 72; opposes tariff revision in 1882, 88; its Congressmen pass River and Harbor Bill over Arthur's veto, 90; defeated in the 1882 elections, 91, 92; in Presidential election of 1884, 102; its platform of 1888, 129; elects Harrison President, 130; its attitude on the tariff, 131; on silver, 138, 139; its division on high-tariff legislation in 1889, 141, 142, 148; its severe defeat in 1890 elections, 173, 174; ignores Silver-Purchase Act in its convention of 1892, 177; defeated in the Presidential election, 181; favors repeal of Silver-Purchase Law, 197; carries repeal in the Senate, 199; regains control of Congress, 249

Resumption of specie payments, planned by Hugh McCulloch, 10; pledged by Congress in 1865, 11; Sherman predicts that it will come automatically, 12; obstacles to, pointed out by McCulloch, 13; promised again by Congress, 17; the promise broken, 17, 18; Resumption Act passed, 1875, 21; its provisions, 21, 23, 24, 172; difficulties in the way of, 25, 26; trade conditions favorable to, 26; preparations for, 29-33; Congressional opposition to, 34, 35, 39; repeal of law proposed, 35; attack on, supported by many Republicans, 40; repeal act fails in Congress, 41; Administration's policy of, denounced by opposition State conventions, 42; endorsed by Eastern Republican conventions, 43; by Eastern Democratic conventions, 44; Sherman's final arrangements for, 44-46; gold held for purposes of, 45; specie payments resumed, 47; problem of maintaining, 48-51; limitations of the law for, 50; effect of, on the markets, 25; precarious outlook of, in 1879, 53; satisfactory outcome of, 56

Revenue, public, *see* Customs revenue, Internal revenue, and Surplus revenue

River and harbor expenditure, heavy increase in, during 1882, 89; bill for, vetoed by President Arthur, 90; passed over veto, 90; effect of, on 1882 elections, 91; Republican Convention of 1888 recommends, 129; President Harrison approves, 132; dangers of, 133; increase of, in 1892, 176

Rothschilds, expect gold exports from U. S. in 1879, 52; contract of, with Treasury in 1895, 236

Russell, William E., elected Governor of Massachusetts in 1890, 173

Russia, extension of its railway system, before 1878, 4; crop failure of 1879 in, 55; crops of 1891 in, failure of, 164; takes wheat market of 1895 away from U. S., 246

Seigniorage on silver coinage, bill of 1894 to coin, 230

Senate, U. S., *see* Congress

Seymour, Horatio, Democratic nominee for President in 1868, 16; rejects repudiation platform, 16

Sherman, John, Congressman and Secretary of the Treasury; his opposition to McCulloch contraction plan, 12; his belief in automatic resumption, 12; his judgment that money supply of

Sherman, John—*Continued*.
1866 was not excessive, 13; defers to public opinion on the legal tenders, 15; draws up Resumption Act, 21; defines powers of the Act, 24, 29; appointed Secretary of the Treasury, 27; his faults as legislator, 27, 28; his conflicting public utterances, 28; his good qualities as administrator, 29; declares government bonds payable in gold, 29, 39; his skill in negotiation, 29-31; his relations with the banks, 32, 33; assures bond-subscribers that bonds will be paid in gold, 39; his timid treatment of Bland Bill, 41, 42; his curious letter to Stanley Matthews, 42; does not approve veto of Bland Bill, 42; his view of proper amount of Treasury gold reserve, 45, 166; his final arrangement for resumption, 46, 47; his untenable theory regarding redeemed legal tenders, 50; his uneasiness over Treasury's situation in 1879, 53; orders use of gold in ordinary Treasury payments, 59; his remarks on the grain harvest and prosperity, 67; his candidacy for Presidential nomination, 70; reasons for its failure, 70; declares the legal tenders a safe currency, 72; his changing views on silver, 73, 74; his pessimism in 1880, 74; his expedient to circulate the silver dollars, 81, 82; his opinion regarding the silver Senators, 141; alleges that Silver-Purchase Act was necessary to prevent free coinage, 147, 148; frames compromise Silver-Purchase Bill, 149; his mistaken predictions regarding revenue and legal tenders, 152; introduces bill to repeal Silver-Purchase Act, 174; denies right of Treasury to use gold reserve for ordinary payments, 205; his unfounded assertion that deficit was wholly caused by Wilson Tariff, 222

Shiras, George, Associate Justice U. S. Supreme Court, his vote on the income-tax decision, 229

Silver, question of, prior to 1865, 6; increase in American production of, 7; President Hayes favors maintaining, as precious metal, 7; free coinage of, voted by House of Representatives in 1877, 35; its demonetization, 35; Bonanza discoveries of, in Nevada, 36, 37; debate on bill for free coinage of, 37, 38; government bonds declared payable in, by Congress, 38, 39; Western conventions demand free coinage of, 42; not favored in national conventions of 1880, 69; opinions of Hayes and Sherman on, 73; dollars not a popular form of money, 75; rejected by interior trade, 75; large use of, in payment of public revenue, 76; New York Clearing-House rejects, 76, 77; reasons for rejection of, 78, 79; increase in production of, 78; price of, rises in 1878, then falls, 78; decreased shipments to Orient, 78; used for interior remittances, 81; exchanged for certificates, 82; gold paid for, 82; trouble with, renewed, 96; Folger's opinion as to dangers of, 96; effect of compulsory coinage of, after 1881, 97; accumulates in Treasury, 97; revenue payments made in, 97; Acton suggests forced use of, in clearing-house payments, 98; effect of coinage of, on national finances, as regarded

Silver—*Continued.*
by McCulloch, 103; by Cleveland, 103; fractional coin, pledged with the banks in 1885 for gold, 104, 105; Cleveland Administration's plans to circulate, 105–107; certificates for, issued in small denominations, 108; takes the place of bank notes in circulation, 111; Treasury surplus of, decreases after 1886, 112; question of, not a political issue in 1888, 138, 139; advocates of, in Congress, 141; their power over legislation, 141, 147; Secretary Windom's plan for, 142–145; increased production of, after 1890, 146; legislation for, in 1890, 147–149; temporary advance in price of, 153; renewed decline in, 154; gold paid to Treasury for, in 1891, 164; free coinage of, voted in 1882 by Senate, 174; blockaded in House, 174; party declarations on, in 1892, 177–180; rumor of its intended use to redeem legal tenders, 185, 186; heavy decline in, on suspension of Indian free coinage, 200; Congress votes to coin "seigniorage" of, 230; President vetoes bill, 230

Silver-Purchase Law of 1890, proposed by Secretary Windom, 139; political origin of, 141, 148; confusion of ideas regarding, 142–145; modified by Congress, 147; altered in conference committee, 149; Congressional opinion on, 150; fails to keep up price of silver, 153, 154; President Harrison defends, 154; Secretary Windom defends, 154; its influence on currency in 1890, 155, 159; party declarations regarding, in 1892, 177, 178; Cleveland Administration proposes repeal of, 184, 197; its provisions tested, 185, 186; Republicans favor repeal of, 197; struggle over bill to repeal, 197–199; Congress repeals, 199; effect of repeal of, on markets, 199, 200

Sinking fund against U. S. public debt, annual requirement for, 125, 137; payments on, abandoned by Harrison Administration, 137

South Africa, *see* Transvaal

South Carolina, Democratic Convention of 1892 denounces Cleveland, 179; demands free coinage, 179

Spaulding, E. G., U.S. Congressman, regards the legal tenders as a temporary currency, 8

Specie payments, *see* Legal tenders and Resumption.

Stevens, Thaddeus, U. S. Congressman, his opinion on contraction of the legal tenders, 12

Stock Exchange, New York, arranges for silver speculation in 1890, 153; excitement on, during 1884, 100; closing of, during panic of 1893, discussed, 194

Stock market, of 1879, 61; of 1880, 61; used by Jay Gould, 63, 64; demoralization in, during 1884 at New York, 100; of 1890, at New York, speculation in silver, 153; influenced by the paper money inflation, 155; of 1890, at London, 156, 157

Strikes, of railway employees in 1886, 116; of laborers, for an eight-hour day, 116; their influence on politics in 1888, 117; of coal-miners and railway employees, in 1894, 220

Sugar, import duty on, its great productiveness, 134; removed by McKinley Tariff

Sugar—*Continued.*
  Act, 134; revenue from, in 1889, 134; in 1892, 134; in 1895, 226; partly restored by Senate's Tariff Bill of 1894, 225, 226
Sumner, Charles, U. S. Senator, regards the legal tenders as a temporary currency, 8
Supreme Court of the United States, declares the Legal-Tender Act constitutional, 20; declares rents and municipal bonds exempt from income-tax, 228; declares income-tax of 1894 unconstitutional, 229
Surplus revenue of U. S. Government, in 1882, cause of, 87; its political aspects, 88; continues large after tariff of 1883, 95; applied to bond redemptions, 109, 111, 112, 125, 126; heavy increase in, after 1886, 113; causes of increase in, 114; absorbs one fourth of the circulating medium, 123; deposited in 1888 with the banks, 124; becomes a menace to trade, 126; the precedent of 1836, 127; made a political issue in 1888, 128, 129; Democratic plan to reduce, 128; Republican plan, 129, 130, 132, 134, 135; disappearance of, in 1891, 137

Tanner, James A., Commissioner of Pensions, his remark about the surplus, 137; induced to resign office, 138
Tariff, import, suggested as a help to resumption, 13; Arthur Administration urges reduction in, 88; elections of 1882 declare for revision of, 92; plan for reduction in, 93; Congress opposes reduction of, 93; evils of wholesale changes in, 94; alterations in, have often preceded financial disturbance, 94; law of 1883, its character, 95; its effect on revenue, 95, 96; large receipts under, 113; bill of 1887, passed by House and killed by Senate, 125; reform of, demanded by Democratic party in 1888, 129; Republicans demand increase in rates of, 129; Republican policy regarding, 131, 132; McKinley Bill passed, 134; rates under, 134; reduction in yield of, 135; relations of, to silver legislation of 1890, 141, 142, 148, 151; bills to reduce, pass House of Representatives in 1892, 175; defeated in Senate, 175; contest over, in 1892 elections, 177; action on, by Congress of 1894, necessary, 222; mistakes in plans for, by Congress, 224, 225; erroneous estimates on, 225–227; conflict over, between House and Senate, 225, 226; President Cleveland refuses to sign bill, 227; failure of, to produce sufficient revenue, 227
Tariff commission of 1882, its protectionist membership, 92; recommends lower duties, 93; its plan altered by Congress, 93
Teller, Henry M., U. S. Senator, declares that free-coinage bill could not have passed in 1890, 148
Tilden, Samuel J., claim that he was elected President in 1876, 34; his plurality on the popular vote, 71
Trade, American, expansion after the Civil War, 2, 3; depression in 1877, 34; unfavorable outlook for, at resumption, 51; great recovery in, 57; its good condition during 1880, 60, 83; reaction in, after 1881, 84, 85, 96, 97; depression in, during 1884, 98; renewed activity of,

Trade, American—*Continued.*
after 1885, 114, 115; in 1890, 154, 158; stagnation of, after panic of 1893, 201
Trade, foreign, *see* Export trade and Import trade
Transvaal, gold discoveries in, 243
Treasury, U. S., granted power to contract the legal tenders, 9, 11; accumulation of gold in, opposed by business men, 14; contraction powers of, revoked, 15, 16; reissues retired legal tenders in 1873, 20; powers under Resumption Act, 23-26; its relation to the banks in 1878, 33; its gold fund at resumption, 45; its resumption arrangements with the banks, 45, 46; admitted to New York Clearing-House, 47; outlook for its reserve fund, 48; protective powers denied it, 49-51; gold withdrawn from, 53; rise in its gold reserve, 59; pays out gold on ordinary disbursements, 59; large silver payments made to, 76; increase of silver surplus of 77; its relations with the New York Clearing-House regarding silver, 76-78, 80; circulates its silver currency, 81-83; silver again accumulates in, 96, 97; begins to pay silver at New York Clearing-House, 103; borrows gold from New York banks in 1885, 104, 105; substitutes silver certificates for small legal tenders in the circulation, 105, 106; for national bank notes, 110, 111; buys bonds with its surplus, 111; circulates the silver certificates, 111, 112; trade conditions of 1888 favorable to, 123; enormous increase in its surplus, 123; deposits surplus with the banks, 124; its wholesale redemption of bonds at a premium, 125, 126; its experience in 1837, 128; effects of laws of 1890 on, 137; rapid fall in its surplus, 137; abandons purchases for the sinking-fund, 137; monthly deficits of, begin in 1891, 138; effect of Silver-Purchase Act on, 151; throws enormous sums of money into circulation, 155, 159; heavy gold disbursements by, in 1890 and 1891, 162; fall in its gold reserve, 163; receives gold in exchange for legal tenders, 164; its precarious situation in 1892, 166; its gold reserve, how established and prescribed, 166, 167; gold payments to, in revenue, decrease, 168, 169; ceases to use gold on its own disbursements, 170; legal tenders presented to, for redemption, 172, 173; dangerous condition of, in 1893, 182, 184; prepares for a bond-issue, 183; borrows gold from New York banks, 183-185; suspends issue of gold certificates, 185; rumors as to its redemption plans, 185, 186; effect of panic on, 203; large gold receipts by, 203; pays out its gold reserve on ordinary disbursements, 204; its right to do so questioned, 205; its general surplus impaired, 206, 207, 209: Carlisle's plans of relief for, 208, 209; bond-issues for, during 1894, 210-214; humiliating position of, 214; gold receipts by, for bonds, 215; gold withdrawn from, by bond-subscribers, 215; movement of its reserve, 216; temporary increase in revenues of, in 1894, 230; deficit begins again, 230; gold borrowed for, from banks, 231; second loan negotiated, 231;

Treasury, U. S.—*Continued.*
  collapse of its gold reserve, 232; syndicate of 1895 undertakes to protect, 236, 237; gold reserve of, restored, 241; renewed outflow of gold from, 248; final loan of, 250; increase of gold in, 253
Treasury, Secretaries of, Hugh McCulloch (1865–69, 1884–85), 10, 103; John Sherman (1877–81), 27; Charles J. Folger (1881–82), 88; Daniel Manning (1885–87), 110; Charles S. Fairchild (1887–89), 123; William Windom (1889–91), 140; Charles Foster (1891–93), 169; John G. Carlisle (1893–97), 185
Trusts, industrial, their sudden appearance in the United States, 118; magnitude of their operations, 118; denounced in the political platforms, 118; influenced by trade competition, 118, 119

Union Pacific Railway, Gould's influence on, 63; dishonest amalgamation of, with the Kansas Pacific, 63, 64

Vanderbilt, William H., his prediction of high prices in 1882, 86
Venezuela message of 1895, 251
Veto, of Inflation Bill, by President Grant, 20; of 3½ per cent. Refunding Bill, by President Hayes, 32; of Bland Silver-Coinage Bill, by President Hayes, 41; of River and Harbor Bill, by President Arthur, 90; of Seigniorage Bill, by President Cleveland, 230
Von Mauthner, manager Austrian bond syndicate of 1892, describes Austrian gold operations, 161
Voorhees, Daniel W., U. S. Senator, denounces foreign bond investors, 39; his indifference to Treasury's situation in 1894, 210; notified by Carlisle of bond-issue, 210

Wabash railway system, Jay Gould's influence on, 63
Wallace, W. A., U. S. Senator, opposes Hayes Administration's policy, 43
Warner, A. J., Cleveland's letter to, on silver, 103
Weaver, James B., third-party candidate for President in 1880 and 1892, 181; his vote in 1892, 181
Western Union Telegraph Company, Gould's operations with, in 1880, 63
Wheat, its high price in 1867, 3; increase in European production of, 4; world's crops in 1875 and 1878, 5; decline in price of, 5; failure of crop of 1879, in England, 54, 55; on the European continent, 55; large crop of, in U. S., 56; enormous exports of, from U. S. in 1879, 56; profitable harvest of, in 1880, 59; wild speculation in, 60; deficient crop of, in 1881, 84; high price of, 84; large foreign production of, in 1882, 86; fall in price of, 86; world's heavy crop of, in 1884, 101; low prices for, 102; corner in, during 1888, 115; great depression in, during 1885, 117; large exports of, from India and Argentina, 122; world's short supply of, in 1889 and 1890, 156; failure of Argentine crop of, 157; failure of European crop of, in 1891, 163, 164; enormous American crop of, 163; large exports of, 164; rise in price of, during 1891, 165; crop of, underestimated by U. S. Government,

Wheat—*Continued.*
165 ; world's enormous production of, in 1894, 221 ; extreme decline in price of, 222 ; speculation in, during 1895, 245 ; bad effect of speculation in, 246 ; large crop of, in 1897, 253

Wilson Tariff Act, *see* Tariff

Windom, William, Secretary of U. S. Treasury, under Garfield, 140 ; under Harrison, 140 ; his limitations as a financier, 140 ; proposes the Silver-Purchase Law, 142 ; his motives, 141, 142 ; nature of his plan, 142, 143 ; his confused views on currency questions, 144–145, 146 ; defends Silver-Purchase Law, 154

Wisconsin, its Congressmen vote solidly for Bland Silver Bill, 40 ; carried by Republicans in 1880 and 1881, 90

www.ingramcontent.com/pod-product-compliance
Lightning Source LLC
Chambersburg PA
CBHW031331230426
43670CB00006B/308